ANITA

ANITA

Anne Dunhill

QUARTET BOOKS

First published in 2012 by
Quartet Books Limited
A member of the Namara Group
27 Goodge Street, London WIT 2LD

A catalogue record for this book
is available from the British Library

ISBN   978 0 7043 7247 4

Typeset by Antony Gray
Printed and bound in Great Britain by
T J International Ltd, Padstow, Cornwall

PROLOGUE

30 November 2009

I've just come back from a meeting at the hospital where you died and I'm feeling absolutely furious. I basically had only one question – the name of the drug that killed you – and I didn't even get an answer to that. Oh yes they gave me a name – Midazolam – but that wasn't the name the night nurse gave me when she told me she had to ask permission to give you the injection and got me to hold your pathetically thin arm to stop you thrashing around while she did it. The only person I really wanted to talk to, to try and get to the bottom of the mystery, was the nurse who gave you the injection, and she wasn't there.

Today I was told that the effects of Midazolam are short term. In 'end of life care', it's regularly used to alleviate agitation, but all effects from it wear off after an hour or two. It also has the property of anterograde amnesia, useful for premedication before surgery to inhibit unpleasant memories. You had it when they performed the endoscopy on you in June and fitted the stent. I asked you afterwards how the procedure went, and you said you couldn't remember anything about it. This worried me. I knew you hadn't been unconscious, and I was afraid that you might have suffered, but had the memory of the suffering wiped. This isn't at all the same thing as not suffering. And what rubbish to say that whatever they gave you on your last night had only a short-term effect. You sank instantly into a heavy sleep and never woke again.

According to the notes, they gave you the injection at 11.30 pm and you died at 7.25 am on the morning you were due to come home. I lay in your room all night, sleeping and waking and listening to your breathing. You were on your right side with your hands clasped in front of you. During the night they got very cold and I covered you with an extra blanket and told you I loved you. I was allowed to spend the last three nights with you in the hospital and the night before had been very uncomfortable for you. I'd hardly slept, and hadn't been able to catch up during the day, so I was very tired by evening. Part of me wondered afterwards if you hadn't stayed alive through that last night out of consideration, in order that we could all get some sleep.

At 7.15 Tabitha came in and I went along to the bathroom to fling on my clothes. When I came back a few minutes later, the whole family – your siblings Ingo, Tabitha and Juliet and my ex-husband, your stepfather Anthony – were in the room. They'd all spent the night at the hospital in the patients' sitting room. As I entered, Tabitha told me in great distress that you'd stopped breathing. I went up to you, kissed you on the cheek and told you that I loved you. You took one last breath in, breathed out, and died. A pinkish liquid flowed out of your mouth and nostrils and Juliet gave a little moan of distress.

After being given the name Midazolam, I sat back quietly in the patients' sitting room and listened to Tabitha's questions. Present at the meeting were the Grief Counsellor of the Royal Marsden who'd set the whole thing up for us, a nurse and doctor, both female, who I recognised from your days on the palliative care ward, and a doctor neither of us had ever seen before and who'd never met you. She was blonde and pretty with delicate features and a pink, flowery shirt and in spite of the fact that she'd had nothing to do with your case, she'd been chosen as spokesperson. I soon saw why. She was elegant and articulate and spoke so fluently, with such intelligence and in such a reasonable tone, that it was evident she had been hand-picked to disarm even the most angry or grief-stricken of relatives. I hadn't been angry at all when I arrived, but listening to her dismiss all Tabitha's concerns with such fluency and eloquence, assuring us for example that you hadn't been given too much morphine when we knew for a fact that you had, made me want to kill her.

It also sent me back to the internet where I read that the toxicity of Benzodiazepine overdose and risk of death is increased when issued intravenously. Symptoms of Midazolam overdose can include coma and death. In an overdose an individual may cease breathing entirely and go into respiratory arrest, which is rapidly fatal. (You don't say!) No doubt Dr Flowery Shirt would say you'd been given the correct dose of that too, and that your death was just an unfortunate coincidence.

The reason I wasn't angry, only resigned, when I went in to the meeting was that you'd chosen to be treated by the NHS at the Royal Marsden and the NHS had told you from the beginning that the only treatment they could offer you was chemotherapy and that all chemotherapy could do was prolong your life by a few months. I tried not to admit it to myself, and I knew that you'd be absolutely furious if I said it, but I realised that by making that choice you had in fact elected to die. I don't know if you realised it as well, but after that our relationship was never as good again and I tried to remain as detached as possible from your treatment there, because I knew it was doomed to failure.

The Grief Counsellor was worried that Tabitha and I would be overcome by emotion at revisiting the palliative care ward, but we'd been back there anyway, the day after you died, to sign some forms preparatory to getting your death certificate, and that had felt far worse. After your death I found some comfort in visiting the places you'd visited, and being treated by some of the people who'd tried to help you – the healer Matthew Manning, the jin-shin jyutsu practitioner Carlysse Smith – anyone with whom I could release a few drops of the ocean of my grief, and perhaps be healed a little bit by their treatments in the knowledge that you were healed a little bit by them too. Visiting the ward where you died was actually a comfort, like rewinding time to be closer to you in a place where my only memories were of you, with nothing to distil their essence. And we had some happy times there too, didn't we?

When you were first admitted to the Marsden on a Thursday evening, I wasn't allowed to stay in your room with you, but we organised shifts so that someone from the family would be with you at all times during the visiting hours of 9 am to 10 pm. I happened to be there when you were moved up to Horder Ward on the following Monday. Horder Ward was the palliative care ward, but the words didn't strike me with dread as they did your friend Alice. Alice told me afterwards that to be moved to the palliative care ward was effectively a death sentence, as in fact it proved to be, but to me the word merely meant non-aggressive, soothing, comforting.

I packed up your few possessions – the Scrabble you'd been playing with Tabitha and her boyfriend John on the day you were admitted – you told me proudly that you'd well and truly thrashed Tabitha at the game – the black sweatpants she bought you on King's Road with the tie waistband so your poor, distended stomach wouldn't be so uncomfortable, and the smart maternity jeans Alice had splashed out on at the weekend with their elasticated front. You were so thrilled with them, but in the end they never even got taken out of their glossy carrier bag.

The atmosphere in Horder Ward was less efficient than in the surgical ward downstairs, even slightly chaotic. There was no bed in your room when we arrived and you were left on the trolley you'd been transported on. Casting round for something positive to say, I remarked on the lovely view of the church dome and squares of South Kensington, but you remarked, not complainingly but resigned, almost cheerful, that the position they'd put you in meant you couldn't see it. I unpacked your

Blackberry and the expensive moisturisers and night creams you'd asked me to bring in, although I don't believe you used any of them again.

I left you with Juliet at one and went to a free counselling session at Trinity Hospice. Extensive renovations had recently been carried out there and the reception area was light and clean with a view over the garden. I felt that you'd be far more comfortable there than at the Marsden, but the very word hospice filled you with dread. I remember first hearing about hospices in 1976 when you were a little girl of two and my Aunt Dorothy was dying of cancer. I think there was only one at that time, St Joseph's in Hackney, but I heard how inspirational it was and wished Dorothy could go there, and that I could go to one when my time came.

'But hospices are where you go to die!' you exclaimed in horror when one of the doctors at the Marsden mentioned the possibility to you. My poor, darling Anita, did you really not know? Or were you living on four different levels like me? Level one was knowing almost definitely that you were going to die. Level two was refusing to admit the knowledge to you because it upset you so. Level three was trying to convince myself you might get better in order to put on a better show in front of you. Level four was being unable to talk to your siblings about contingency plans in case a certain course of treatment you'd set your heart on didn't work, because if I tried to they'd round on me in fury and accuse me of being negative.

I went back to Horder Ward in the early evening for our first night together in the hospital. That was quite a happy occasion, wasn't it? Somehow, by manipulating the head of the bed to exactly the right position, and a judicious rearrangement of pillows, you actually had quite a good night. About six hours sleep, I reckon. I was also struck by the extraordinary sweetness of the night staff and, for the first time, felt almost glad you were there.

The next day continued on a positive note. A sweet-faced male nurse with a long pony-tail came and offered to give you a bed bath. You'd been so hooked up to drips and drains that you hadn't had a bath since you entered the hospital and you were thrilled. We took off your hospital gown and white thrombosis stockings and washed you all over. When the nurse left the room for a moment, you stood up, bent forward over the basin of water on the bed table and asked me to wash your hair. I was terrified. What if you fell and I couldn't hold you? But I knew I mustn't show it. I swept your beautiful, thick, dark blonde hair over your head, poured water over it with a jug dipped in the bowl and worked your expensive shampoo into it as best I could.

Looking back, I wonder how I could possibly have still hoped you would live if I was so frightened about you standing for a few minutes. Did I rationalise? Did I tell myself that once we got you home and off all the medication they were giving you that your strength would return and you'd be able to stand and walk again? I don't think so. It was the levels again. My brain knew you were dying but my heart couldn't accept it, while some kind of mediator between the two – my spirit perhaps? – told me not to be negative and not to accept defeat. Miracles did happen. Everyone had to die, but surely God would make an exception in my daughter's case.

When we'd finished and rubbed your hair dry and forced a comb through it – your lovely pre-Raphaelite hair that used to fall perfectly into shape after you shook it a few times – I remarked how beautiful you were. You denied it furiously and told me not to be ridiculous, but it was true. The ghastly pallor and black rings under your eyes that I'd noticed on the Sunday after they gave you too much morphine on Ellis Ward had disappeared in the exertion of the bath and you looked almost well again. Part of me wanted to bring a camera into the ward and take endless photos of you, but I knew how much you'd hate it, so didn't even suggest it.

The next night wasn't so good. Carlysse came to give you a treatment after your bath, so I drifted off home and went for a swim. I'd suspended my membership at Dolphin Square for the month of July when I thought we were going to China, but then you yourself had joined again – you used to belong when you lived here with me in 2001 before buying your flat. We went along together and talked to the very sympathetic Membership Secretary who said you could cancel or suspend your membership any time you liked. Your first act as a member was to buy ten guest passes for your sisters, and your first swim was a great success. You told me that while you were swimming your body felt normal again for the first time in ages. Your second swim, with Juliet, just four days later didn't go so well. You told me your legs had started to sink and when you went into the sauna a girl asked you if you were pregnant. You said, 'No, I have cancer,' and she and her friend were very sweet to you. They belonged to a prayer group and asked your permission to pray over you. You gave it, but never went there again.

After swimming I walked your dogs, who'd spent the night at Tabitha and John's. When you were first diagnosed, I tried to organise a dog-walking rota with your siblings. I felt it was something practical we could do for you to make your mind easier, and also alleviate the distress the dogs must be feeling at seeing you so ill. I don't know if they really were distressed, or if in fact they were happy to have you at home more, now you were relieved of your punishing work schedule. But if accidents on the carpet are any indication of a dog's state of mind, I'd say they were distressed.

In any case my suggestion was greeted with scorn and hostility, so of course I ended up doing it myself. To be fair, Tabitha lent me her car when she came to visit you in the evenings and I was able to drive to Battersea Park with the chihuahuas after five when parking was free and march down the peace mile, round the Pagoda and back – the regulation twenty minutes recommended by the breeder – and actually enjoy what was usually my only genuine pleasure of the day in watching them leap and cavort joyously at being in the fresh air and on grass.

As always they attracted a huge amount of attention and I was asked the same questions time and time again. What breed were they? Chihuahuas, of course. Were they puppies? No, indeed; respectable middle-aged ladies of seven and six. Were they related? Well, they were from the same breeder, so maybe. You bought Petal from Crufts, then, realising she needed company, travelled to Birmingham a year later to collect Snowy. Without realising what I was doing, I began to talk to strangers and smile in spite of myself at the dogs' antics. In looking after them, I was actually helping myself – not at all a side effect I'd anticipated, but one which I soon recognised.

I went back to the hospital about 6.30. The family was there, and you said you wanted some fruit, so Juliet and I went off to look for it. We'd been trying to give you nothing but organic food, but that had rather gone by the board since you'd been in hospital. By now we were actually quite grateful if you ate anything at all. You'd managed a yoghurt and half a piece of toast for breakfast, and I'd been immensely proud of you. Because I didn't really know the South Kensington shops very well, I went in one direction and sent Jules in another – left up the Fulham Road to the Sainsburys Local near the cinema that I'd known in so many different incarnations. What was it called now? The Cineworld. It had a maddening tendency to cancel performances or vary the programmes listed in the newspaper. I remember you and I going there about two years ago to see something I can't remember, only to find it wasn't on. We trailed home again and were just in time to watch the first episode of a new TV series called *The Tudors*, starring Jonathan Rhys Meyers as an improbably gorgeous Henry VIII. We both became utterly hooked, and I had to record subsequent episodes for you to make sure you stayed up to date. On the glorious day when you were allowed to bring Petal and Snowy back to England after their two years in Africa and subsequent six-month quarantine in Paris, I drove Tabitha's car through the Eurotunnel to Calais while you flew to Paris, collected the dogs from Bernard and Dominique, had them vaccinated and took the train to Calais to join me in the Holiday Inn. I arrived first and, fiddling with the TV, discovered it was possible to get BBC2. When you arrived in triumph with the dogs, we had room service, all together again, and watched that night's episode of *The Tudors*. Oh my darling, how very happy we were that night.

I went the other way to South Kensington. Jim Lee, a native of those parts, had told me of an organic supermarket near the station, but I couldn't find it. One of the late-night shops had some peaches, so I got them. I also got a surreptitious sandwich for myself and a quarter bottle of red wine. Juliet got back to the hospital before me. She'd found you some watermelon and you ate some pieces of that and one of my peaches. I slipped into the patients' sitting room to wolf down my sandwiches and wine. It upset you to see me eating and you reproached me bitterly on your first night in hospital when I, thinking I'd be allowed to spend the night with you, had asked Tabitha to get me an Indian takeaway for my supper.

I'm sure you know now how little I wanted to upset you. I'd try and eat discreetly when you were out of the room or talking to your visitors, and I took up cooking again to follow the macrobiotic recipes Simon Brown gave you. You did like some of the things I made at the beginning, didn't you, although you quickly got bored with the bland taste? My cupboards are still full of the expensive foods you ordered from the organic supermarket in Kensington High Street, and I still haven't felt able to sort through them and either use them or throw them away.

My greatest longing was for you to have enough fight in you to take charge of your own regime and follow it religiously, but it somehow didn't happen. You allowed your brother and sisters to work it out for you, and me or one of them to cook it and then, after all that, you barely even touched it. Gradually your slim, toned arms became thin and wasted and your stomach distended till it was bigger than Ingo's wife Victoria's who was eight months pregnant.

Early on in your illness we had some nice days when we were able to sit in the garden. As usual the family crowded round you, snatching time from work or after it, never telling me when they were going to pop in. During those sunny days in the garden I became aware of a young bird in difficulties hiding behind one of the urns. This had happened before. Our neighbours, John and Mario, great bird lovers, had warned me not to pick up the young fledgling or feed it because if I did so the parents would abandon it. On that occasion it had thankfully recovered and eventually flown away. I remembered this advice when I saw the second bird. It was difficult keeping the dogs away from it, but the parent birds were still very much involved and squawked fiercely at Petal and Snowy if they went anywhere near it. The urn was at the shady end of the garden and we mostly congregated in the sun, so I thought the best strategy was to pay the fledgling no attention so the parents would continue to feed it. This seemed to work for a day or two, but on the third morning I was shocked and distressed to come into the garden and find it dead.

The parallels with your situation seemed only too obvious – a young creature with loving parents surrounded by people who wished it well but who weren't able to save it.

'A bad omen,' I remarked gloomily to Ingo later in the day.

'If you choose to think so,' he replied.

The Tuesday night wasn't so good for you. I have something of a talent as a pillow arranger. Maybe this is because bed is one of my favourite places and always has been. As a pampered only child, my mother used to bring me breakfast in bed and then feel that gave her the right to stand over me and lecture while I ate it. Well, maybe it did. Certainly I shouldn't have allowed her to continue, knowing the price I was going to have to pay, but foolishly I always did.

The pleasures of eating in bed didn't pall till I was in my thirties and on my second marriage, when it began to dawn on me that it gave me indigestion and made crumbs in the bed. It was actually easier to get up and eat at table, then return to my cool, unsullied sheets with coffee and newspapers or whatever book I happened to be reading at the time. I wrote all my books in bed, and my university essays. At first I used to do the first draft of a translation in bed as well, but translations use a different part of the brain and I later found it more efficient to write them directly on the computer.

I bought something called the Wedge, a hard, triangular cushion like a piece of mouse trap cheese, which I arranged my pillows on to hold my back in the correct position while writing. I got it from one of those cheap catalogues that flutter irritatingly from one's Sunday newspaper. I haven't seen a wedge advertised for years, so I don't know what I'd do if anything happened to mine. Be totally lost, I imagine. Anyway, years of working in bed had made me something of an expert on pillows, even though I prefer not to sleep with my head on one at night. You used my wedge during the day for the first five weeks of your illness when you were at home, reclining on the sofa with Petal and Snowy and receiving streams of visitors, and sometimes at night I was able to relieve your pain by inserting a pillow vertically behind your back as you lay on your side. You also liked the hospital beds with their remote controls that enabled you to raise the head a fraction or lower the foot, but somehow that Tuesday we never managed to get it quite right, or if we did, the comfort didn't last for long. I also didn't always understand what you wanted me to do. All the drugs they were pumping into you had started to make you a bit incoherent – or was it just part of the dying process?

At one point when I had to ask you to repeat your instructions you said impatiently, 'Am I going crazy then?'

'No,' I replied too hastily. 'I'm probably just going deaf in my old age.' I think we were both very frightened.

By morning I was absolutely exhausted. You were taken down to X-ray at 9 am. You were also going to have a 'permanent drain' fitted so you could come home. We'd had a meeting with the doctor in charge of your ward the day before and she told me you'd expressed two wishes. The first was to see your two little dogs again and the second was to come home, but she warned me that you only had a few days to live.

I nodded politely with a brittle smile. We had a huge pile of cancer books at home. Someone would recommend a book and we'd order it on Amazon and then you'd barely even glance at it. I, on the other hand, was becoming quite an expert on the subject. The one I'd read most recently was by Jan de Vries. He was coming to London for a few days and seeing patients at John Bell and Croydon in Wigmore Street. You somehow managed to speak to him – you could still be very effective when you wanted – and he kindly agreed to come in half an hour early on his first day in order to see you. His book mentioned a young girl who'd been taken to Lourdes by her mother and given the waters. There was no sign of improvement and she was taken home and given the last rites, whereupon she'd miraculously recovered. I still had some Lourdes water in the fridge from my visit the year before. I hadn't thought of taking you there because you weren't a believer – or not exactly. One of your friends asked you in front of me if you believed in God and you replied, 'Yes, but not necessarily a Christian God.' I didn't think Lourdes was the place for you with its milling crowds and big screens with actors endlessly depicting the appearances of Our Lady to Bernadette, but Jan de Vries's analysis of the healing properties of Lourdes water was enough to make me start slipping it to you at every opportunity and keeping a small bottle in the fridge in the patients' sitting room.

So when the doctor told me you were going to die in a few

days, I still believed enough to think to myself, 'What do you know? We still have the Lourdes water up our sleeve.' She told me they were going to grant your wishes. Petal and Snowy were going to come in and visit you on Wednesday evening and you were going home on Thursday. You were being assigned a special hospital bed with an air mattress and Macmillan nurses round the clock. I was grateful and impressed. I never dreamed a hospital would allow dogs in, even such tiny ones as yours, and, as I've mentioned, you liked the hospital beds with their remote controls. The thought of the permanent drain made me shudder – what further mutilations and humiliations were going to be heaped on your young, beautiful, toned, body? – but again I brushed the thought aside. The drain was merely a means to an end. The important thing was that you were coming home.

You smiled bravely at me as you were wheeled down the corridor to X-ray on the Wednesday morning. Tabitha was due in to visit you shortly and I had a ten o'clock appointment with the Benefits Officer at Trinity Hospice, so caught a convenient bus from outside the Marsden to Clapham Common and spent an hour taking notes and filling out forms. Oh what enticing benefits were dangled in front of us – a disabled sticker for Tabitha's car so we could park outside the Marsden, one pound taxi rides to take you to appointments and a carer's allowance for me. I was told I probably wouldn't get that, but I had to make the application anyway. I'd already completed the nightmarish forms you needed for the Disability Living Allowance – £120 per week under what they called the Special Rule – for somebody not expected to live more than six months. I had to hide that section of the form from you when I got you to sign it. You'd been furious enough with me for even mentioning the allowance in front of one of your friends, but your attitude to benefits was different to mine. I was tremendously proud of having been able to persevere through the labyrinthine forms until I completed them.

I left Trinity at eleven with my notes and forms. Tabitha called me while I was standing at the bus stop near Clapham Common to say you hadn't yet come back from the operating theatre where you'd been taken immediately after X-ray, and no one seemed to know when you'd be back. We agreed I'd take her car from Sloane Square, drive home, walk the dogs, complete the forms and return to the hospital later.

Petal and Snowy gave me their usual lovely greeting when I got in. They'd spent the night at John's again. Tabitha had fallen asleep on the sofa in the sitting room and they'd jumped on top of her in the night. We used to joke about how they observed the pecking order. When I appeared, they'd shun Tabitha, but when you came back after one of your trips, even if they'd been staying with me for months, they'd go off with you without a backward glance. I often wonder if they're not still expecting you to come back.

I planned to walk them straight away, but suddenly found I was exhausted. I decided to take a short nap instead and got into bed with the dogs. You used to sleep with them in your bed, but I was too afraid of squashing them, although I allowed them to get in with me if I was just resting. A pension form had just arrived for me. I retired from Berlitz the day after you were diagnosed with cancer and elected to take my state pension, which I'd previously deferred. Two sums were involved – the basic pension and the extra amount I would receive for having waited two and a half years. I could take this either as a lump sum or as a weekly amount. I'd have to live another five years or so to end up in profit for having deferred, but since my mother and grandmother had lived to over ninety, I thought it was a gamble worth taking. You often said you were going to live to be very old too, but I wasn't going to think about that now.

To send myself to sleep, I completed the pension form. If I took the supplement as a weekly sum added to my basic pension,

I'd receive the princely total of £136 per week. It was actually more than I'd expected.

I was just dropping off to sleep when Tabitha called from the hospital. You'd come back from theatre about twelve and your breathing was erratic. She thought I should come in now.

Part of me was annoyed. Why did these crises always occur when I wasn't there – your admission last Thursday, the sudden lowering of your blood pressure after your stomach was drained last Saturday? Was Tabitha over-reacting or was it that my presence calmed you? You never had a crisis when I was there.

Even as I was thinking this, I was getting dressed again and lifting the dogs off the bed into their basket. Petal was exceptionally small, even for a chihuahua, and you'd been warned by the breeder that she could break a leg if she attempted to jump off the bed.

I ran into the street and hailed a taxi. No messing around with cars, I decided. I probably wasn't safe to drive anyway. The driver looked concerned when I told him my destination, but when I arrived in your room, a peaceful scene awaited me. You were sitting up in bed breathing normally. There was nothing to frighten me but the translucence of your skin and the hugeness of your dark-rimmed eyes, but you'd started to look like that at the weekend after they drained your stomach too rapidly, and even that look didn't shock me as much as it had before.

At two, Carlysse came to give you a treatment. It was Anthony who found Carlysse through his doctor in Denmark. We were lucky to find her available the week you were in hospital. It turned out that her husband had died exactly a year before and she'd kept the time free, thinking she'd be too sad to work. When the call came from Denmark asking if she'd visit you, she felt it was meant to be. She came in every day, reassuring us all with her healing presence and giving you strength, as you told us after your first treatment, and as I felt when she gave me a treatment after your death.

Carlysse told me afterwards that she felt you might slip away at any moment during your last treatment, but that you decided to stay by an act of will so we could all say goodbye to you. By now we were all at the hospital, summoned in by Tabitha, and at the end of the treatment we formed a circle by your bed. I was at your feet, I remember, and feeling rather self-conscious. It was all a little bit too American for my liking. But I knew reflexology was supposed to be a powerful way of combating cancer, so I held on to them and willed you to get better. The levels were still operating. The doctors had told us you had very little time left and you were looking increasingly fragile, but you were my daughter, my beautiful Anita, so of course a miracle was going to happen. There was no way any child of mine was going to predecease me.

CHAPTER ONE

22 March 2009

It's usually difficult to pinpoint the exact moment things start to go wrong, but in this case it couldn't be clearer. Ironically it was Mother's Day. Ingo and Victoria were in Brighton with Victoria's mother, whose birthday it happened to be, but my three daughters were going to come round in the evening and take me for a pizza. I was looking forward to it. Aside from a few minor niggles, life seemed to be going well for all of us, which, as I now realise, is probably a highly dangerous situation.

Ingo had been working for some years as a software developer. He and Victoria were happily married and had adorable Max, aged two, and another baby due in September. We all loved Victoria and felt she had civilised Ingo and brought him closer to his family.

Anita, having left her fiancé and her successful Pilates business in Sierra Leone two years before, had turned potential disaster into triumph by starting a new, even more successful business in London. After she died, one of her students wrote to me saying that Anita's pupils used to joke that if they worked hard enough, they'd end up looking like her. At just thirty-five, she was at her most beautiful. Tall – five foot eleven inches – slim (though less so than when Tabitha and I visited her in Freetown in 2006, when I found her thinness almost worrying), and exquisitely toned. She had stopped experimenting with her hair and now wore it shoulder length with blonde highlights and a fringe. She was currently single, though various admirers were hovering, and told me she wasn't in the least bit worried about it. She was sure she would still be able to have children. Hadn't my mother had me when she was thirty-eight, and her father Bobo's mother had him at the same age? She was certain she was going to live to a great age as her grandmothers had, and, looking at her in the full glow of her success and beauty, it was hard not to agree with her.

Tabitha and Juliet, my daughters by Anthony, were also tall and blonde. Tabitha was the same height as Anita, while Juliet was five foot eight like me – something of a relief, so I didn't feel too dwarfed in their collective company. Tabitha worked as a dietician and lived with her boyfriend John who she'd been going out with for ten years. They seemed very content and settled together and Tabitha, with her watery Pisces nature, was generally a competent and calming influence on the family.

Juliet was Anita's twin, but born six years later. Anita was induced and Juliet was born twelve days early, so it wasn't by my design that they shared a birthday. I think it really must have been intended. Anita blossomed after Juliet's birth. No longer the awkward middle child, she became Juliet's protector and defender. Juliet lived in Anita's flat while she was in Sierra Leone, went to her classes, and assisted her on her Pilates retreat in Spain in 2008.

It was a shock, therefore, when Juliet called me early that morning to say she and Anita'd had an awful row and she hoped it wouldn't affect our planned dinner.

Anita allowed herself one day off a week from her busy Pilates schedule and this weekend she was assisting a team of Canadian film makers on a documentary. She'd already helped them with research for a previous documentary and been paid handsomely, and this time she wanted to get Juliet involved.

For the past three years Juliet had been working in a series of jobs that sounded promising on paper but that she didn't really enjoy. She'd finally, the previous autumn, plucked up the courage to leave her current job and was determined not to accept another permanent one until she was absolutely sure it was right for her. In the meantime she was freelancing and going to interviews. Her boyfriend was supportive and they were planning to go travelling to the Far East at the end of the month.

I'm sure Anita's intention was to help Juliet, but she told me Anita had called her early that Sunday morning, woken her up, barked a series of instructions at her and got impatient when she asked for clarification. I have no idea which of them, if either, was in the wrong, but it upset me because they usually got on so well and this was the second quasi-serious quarrel they'd had this year. The previous one was at the end of January, in my presence, and I'd somehow got involved simply because I was there. To avoid a repeat performance, Juliet and I agreed that she and her boyfriend would come round early, about 6. Anita's work on the documentary wasn't due to finish till 7.30, so if things got awkward between Anita and Juliet, Juliet could just leave early.

Unfortunately our timing went wrong. Juliet came at the appointed hour followed by Tabitha half an hour later and Anita shortly after that. Her work had finished early. It was really quite awkward. The three girls sat on the sofa with Tabitha in the middle and Anita and Juliet didn't say a word to each other. Tabitha and Juliet had each brought me flowers and cards, but Anita was empty handed. I knew she'd been working all day, but did feel she could have managed something!

Annoyance changed to concern when Anita told me her father, the Venetian artist Roberto Ferruzzi, known to all his friends as Bobo, was dying. Hélène, her stepmother, had emailed her to say Bobo had cancer of the pancreas which had spread to his stomach, and she'd been told he only had months to live.

I was instantly stricken. Bobo was eighty-one and both his father and grandfather had died at that age. Anita was devoted to him and I knew she would feel his loss terribly. She'd told me on several occasions that I broke his heart when I left him, and even though he'd been happy with Hélène for well over thirty years, I felt guilty and afraid that on some level Anita would blame me for his illness.

Her phone rang and she got off the sofa and went out of the room to take the call. Tabitha and Juliet both knew Bobo. He'd even had them to stay in Venice. I knew they'd be deeply shocked, as I was, and hoped their sympathy would heal the temporary breach between Juliet and Anita.

When Anita came back she was smiling and excited. 'They want me to be in the documentary!' she exclaimed. After she died, Anthony was given the task of calling her friends to give them the terrible news. One of them was the documentary maker, who said how talented she was and how they'd hoped to use her as a presenter on future projects. She'd already appeared on the BBC's *This Morning* programme demonstrating Pilates, and I realised how good she would have been, but on that Mother's Day I was taken aback by her sudden change of mood and my jaw dropped. All our carefully prepared expressions of sympathy just didn't seem appropriate any longer.

We trooped across the road to Pizza Express where we took three tables for two pushed together for the five of us. I was in the middle. Juliet sat on my left with her boyfriend opposite her. Tabitha was next to him and opposite me, and Anita was on my right. Of course she had no one opposite her and was rather out on a limb, but she made little effort to join in the conversation. If I didn't talk directly to her, she spent the meal texting or even talking on her Blackberry. By the end I was feeling a certain exasperation. It was Mother's Day for goodness sake. It was supposed to be about *me*! Couldn't she have made a slight effort just for one evening?

When we finished, I asked Juliet if she and Anita would be travelling home together since they were near neighbours. I smiled as I said it, in what I thought was a conciliatory way, but Anita accused me of smirking. She started to talk about the quarrel she'd had with Juliet that morning, at which point Juliet and her boyfriend melted into the night together, leaving Anita, Tabitha and me standing outside the restaurant on the pavement.

A nasty scene ensued. I denied smirking and Anita called me a liar. I eventually walked off and left Tabitha to reason with her. By the time Tabitha came back, I'd had time to get into my pyjamas and have a long telephone conversation with Juliet. I believe Tabitha had some success in calming Anita down, but by now I was too tired to care.

Of course we know now that Anita was already terminally ill, but at that time she was displaying no physical symptoms. Since leaving Sierra Leone, she'd had trouble sleeping, she worked extremely long hours and was now grieving for Bobo, but even with all those factors to excuse her, I still worried that her behaviour was what my mother would have called beyond the pale.

Going to sleep I remembered Bobo and all we had been to each other.

*   *   *

I met Bobo in October 1969 when I was twenty-two. My marriage to Ken Sweet, documented with a fair degree of accuracy in my first novel, *A Darker Shade of Love*, had ended the month before. My aunt, Dorothy Arden, was taking a holiday 'in the footsteps of St Paul' with a group of friends and invited me to join her. Both she and my mother were keen to get me out of Ken's clutches, but though I wanted to get away too, I was so traumatised by the events of the previous months that I clung to my mother and home, unsure I could cope with spending two weeks in the company of strangers.

It was a chance meeting with an old boyfriend, the actor Guy Ross, that persuaded me to go. He knew Canon Francis Bartlett, the tour leader. Francis was the brother of Aunt Dorothy's friend, Josephine Paterson, who was also coming. Guy told me what good people they were and that they'd look after me and see I was all right, as indeed they did. The tour took us from Genoa to Venice via Naples, Athens, Istanbul, Izmir and Bari. Everyone in the group was much older than me and I became a sort of pet. They knew I was married but were too discreet to ask about my husband. This turned out to be the best therapy imaginable as the previous weeks had been spent rehashing the disaster endlessly with my mother and friends. Should I leave him? Should I stay with him? Not talking about it at all allowed the wound to heal.

When our ship arrived in Venice at the end of the tour, most of our group went home. Dorothy was friends with an American artist called Timothy Hennessy who owned a palazzo near San Basilio and rented out rooms to friends and acquaintances. We spent a week there before Dorothy had to go home. I was increasingly reluctant to go back to London. I was genuinely terrified of Ken, who had attacked me physically on several occasions and who I was afraid might murder me if I returned. Now that I'm in my sixties, I find it difficult to judge the fears of the twenty-two-year-old I was then. If I had been the same age as Ken instead of fifteen years younger, could I have stood up to him by using rational behaviour and calmed his rages before they tipped over into violence? My honest answer is no, I don't think I could. Was I right to be so frightened of him that I left my country and remained in exile for six years? I think I was.

After Dorothy left I was very lonely. Timothy had a friend called Iannis Kadamatis who was probably in his fifties at that time and who I felt instinctively was very wicked. He sometimes took me on walks around Venice. Once we went into a shop called *Roberta da Camerino*, now closed, but then, and for many years after, standing in a prime position next to the Piazza San Marco.

I was twenty-two, five foot eight and model thin, wearing one of the Ossie Clark mini-dresses my mother had bought me to cheer me up when I first ran away from Ken. Ianni, as he was known, was shorter than me, tanned and wrinkled and looked like the sort of man you'd approach if you wanted to buy some illegal substance in a Mediterranean port. He spoke to the manageress of *Roberta da Camerino* in Italian. I didn't speak it at the time, but I understood it quite well from having spent six months modelling in Milan in 1967. What Ianni said, in translation, was more or less: 'She's new to Venice, but if she comes in here and buys something, don't forget it was me who sent her. She's from some very rich English family, I can't remember the name . . . '

Here I spoilt the whole thing by showing I understood. I felt incensed and impotent at the same time.

'Dunhill,' I said angrily.

Ianni had the grace to look slightly embarrassed. We beat a hasty retreat and I never stepped inside the shop again. Their stuff was far too old for me anyway. It was 1969 and London was the centre of the fashion world. Later I came to adore and revere Italian fashion, but not till much later, long after I'd stopped living there.

It was on one of my walking expeditions with Ianni that I met Bobo. Actually all our expeditions were walking ones. I soon learnt that it was only tourists who took the vaporetto. The most a Venetian would do was take the Gritti traghetto – a gondola that went to and fro across the Grand Canal between the Palazzo Dario and the Gritti Hotel that saved one from having to cross the Accademia Bridge.

Before introducing me to Bobo, Ianni tried to fob me off on Bobo's older brother Ferruccio, known to everyone as Ucci (pronounced Ooo – chi). Ucci was Bobo's parents' eldest son. Both had been married before, and although Bobo's mother had been able to divorce her first husband through some legal loophole, his father had never managed it – a situation that would repeat itself with Bobo and me. Bobo's father, an antique dealer also named Ferruccio Ferruzzi, had seven or eight daughters by his first wife. They lived in Rome and I only ever met one of them. His grandfather was the artist, also named Roberto Ferruzzi, who painted the famous *Madonnina*, the most reproduced religious painting in the world, depicting a young girl in a yellow headscarf holding a baby. The original is lost, but I've seen reproductions everywhere, from Israel to Vietnam. Bobo's mother, the Contessa Emilia Balbi, who everyone called Balbina, had been known in her youth as *la Venere nera*, (the black Venus) and was still extraordinarily beautiful at the age of eighty when I met her. Her family was very grand. Once, when I asked her to speak to the manufacturers of my electric mixer which had broken down after a few months, she silenced them with the statement, 'But of course we know how to use an electric mixer. We have four doges in the family!' My favourite of her stories concerned the legendary writer, Gabriele d'Annuzio. He took Balbina to dinner then tried to seduce her on the way home by ordering his gondolier to stop in the middle of some deserted canal. Balbina, nothing daunted, jumped overboard and swam home to her own palazzo.

Ferruccio senior was extremely proud to have a boy at last after all those girls, and Balbina, who already had a son, but had lost a daughter at the age of ten months to an infection that would now be easily curable by antibiotics, was jealous of this bond and tried to come between them. When, two years later, she had twin boys, Bobo and his brother Emmanuele, known as Lillo, she told me she'd kicked their father out of her bed and slept with a twin on either side of her so she could feed them during the night without getting up. Ferruccio, spurned, found solace in the arms of a young widow, a dressmaker (Balbina said he'd met her in a brothel, but the rest of the family denied it).

After Ferruccio's death, shortly before I met Bobo, Ucci inherited the family palazzo on the Grand Canal at Ca'Rezzonico. He converted it into apartments, keeping the *piano nobile* with its magnificent balcony overlooking the canal for himself and housing his former wife Pupa and their son Barnaba in another. Ucci had inherited Balbina's striking looks, the dark, almost Egyptian features and startling green eyes, and had a shocking reputation with women.

Ianni took me to meet him on some pretext shortly after my arrival. He'd been telling me how beautiful Ucci was, so I was curious to see this combination of Adonis and Casanova, and don't even remember feeling embarrassed at Ianni's blatant attempts to matchmake. Presumably he'd invented some story to disguise his intentions.

The entrance to Ucci's palazzo was down a narrow street leading from Piazza San Barnaba (the square where Katherine Hepburn falls into the canal in the film *Summertime*) to the Grand Canal. Ianni rang the bell and we were buzzed in. Ucci came down the steps of his apartment into the dark hallway and we were introduced briefly. I remember thinking, 'Oh no!' I found his features too strong, too florid, too theatrical. He reminded me of a conjurer in a 1950s vaudeville. Later I was to revise my opinion completely but by then I was safely with Bobo.

Was it the next day, or certainly a very short time after, that Ianni and I went walking again and found ourselves by the Accademia? Ianni spotted a friend sitting outside the café on the bridge, who stood up to greet us.

'That's Ucci's brother, Bobo the artist,' Ianni muttered in my ear. 'He's not as beautiful as Ucci, but still . . . '

'No he's not beautiful,' I thought disloyally. Bobo had a studious look compounded by owl-like glasses. A thought entered my mind unbidden. 'But I bet he'd be kind to me if I went out with him.'

Bobo told us he'd bought a house on the Giudecca, and was refurbishing it. We made a date to visit it the following day and Bobo said he'd pick us up in his boat. Ianni, never one to miss out on an innuendo, told him he should paint me, preferably in the nude. Fortunately I didn't hear the last bit. Bobo told me himself later.

I've already told the story of my first date with Bobo in my novel *Web of Passion*. In the novel, I made Bobo an antique dealer. Why did I do this? It was really an attempt to muddy the waters in case Bobo read the book and objected, so I could say 'No, of course Giorgio's not you. He's an antique dealer, not an artist.' But in fact Bobo *was* an antique dealer too. His father and Ucci had built large fortunes on antique dealing and Bobo had an excellent eye. Once we were together I dragged him to London every winter for my birthday in December and kept him there as long as I possibly could. He would only paint occasionally in London. He preferred working outside – rising at five or six and going out in his boat to make endless loving depictions of the light and colour of Venice. London was too grey for him and too cold, but he kept himself busy making ceramics in a large kiln and going to sales at Christies and Sothebys where he met all his dealer friends and bought objects, singly or in partnership with them, which would find their way back to Italy and be sold for a large profit. Bobo was clever with money. I didn't realise then how lucky I was!

But it was unfair of me to portray him solely as a businessman in my novel. He *was* a good businessman, but his art was far more important to him. His art was the reason he couldn't really be happy in London, though he did his best and was always busy and made a point of being nice to my family and friends.

On my first visit to Bobo's house, he showed me a letter from his wife's solicitor requesting a divorce. His wife, Ruth, was a few years older than him. Half German and half Danish, she was bitterly ashamed of the German part after the war, and used her Danish mother's maiden name as her surname so people wouldn't know.

They met in the Louvre, which Bobo said was a bitter irony

since she wasn't really interested in art. Bobo was planning to emigrate to Chile and Ruth accompanied him there, then apparently spent their three years in Santiago trying to persuade him to come home. Back in Venice their relationship deteriorated. There were infidelities on both sides and Ruth eventually ran off to Paris with a Portuguese diplomat called José, taking their two children, Roby and Nora aged eleven and eight, with her.

I assumed Bobo was telling me all this to prove his intentions towards me were honourable. He looked genuinely sad when he told me Ruth had taken his children away from him and I felt a thrill of recognition because I was suffering from the beginnings of what turned out to be a year-long depression after having aborted Ken's child at three months because of his violence. In *A Darker Shade of Love*, I turn the abortion into a miscarriage – whitewashing myself again.

'I want children,' I said tentatively to Bobo, thinking that this was something I could do for him as well as for myself – give him back the children his wife had taken away.

I now realise that this was a key conversation in our lives, so I wish I could remember more details. I've kept a diary every day of my life from my eleventh birthday onwards, apart from the four years from 1966 to 1970. Those undocumented years encompass my six months modelling in Milan, where inevitably I picked up a lot of Italian, so that by the time I met Bobo my understanding was pretty good and I was also able to speak it, though on a fairly basic level. Bobo's English was probably about the same standard as my Italian. I'd have said it was better, but I remember he used to make some basic mistakes such as 'Have you cold?' instead of 'Are you cold?' on the way back from one of our boat trips, so although his confidence in speaking was greater than mine, I dare say he'd never had a grammar lesson in his life.

The fact that I had some knowledge of Italian when I met

Bobo saved me from being condemned to learn Venetian dialect like some of the other foreign wives. It was all Bobo ever spoke with his family and friends, which at first I found utterly bewildering and dismaying since it was a completely different language from Italian, but if I'd learnt it instead of Italian, I'd never have been able to get my two degrees in Italian or do my translation work.

The missing years in my diary also encompassed my marriage to Ken, my meeting with Bobo and, of course, this first conversation about children. I started my diary again three months later, on New Year's Day 1970, and have kept it up ever since. But if only I'd known the importance of that conversation with Bobo, I'd have run to the bathroom with a notebook and scribbled it down, or better still, tape recorded it.

My recollection of the conversation is that I told him I wanted children and he said he did too, 'in about two years'. But when, a year and nine months later, I discovered I was expecting Ingo, he insisted it was too soon. Naturally I pointed out that by the time the baby was born it would actually be two years and five months since our conversation, but this didn't seem good enough for him. And when, in 1973, I started telling him I wanted a second child, he insisted that our deal had been one child only. I could have pointed out that in colloquial English I was much more likely to have said 'I want children' than 'I want a child' when referring to a future event. If I'd said 'I want a child' it would have meant 'I want one now. Hurry up!' But unfortunately we had already got beyond rational argument.

I moved in with Bobo two weeks after our first date for all the wrong reasons. I could see from the expression in his eyes that he was in love with me, and I didn't think I was equally in love with him. The one thing I was sure about was that I didn't want to go back to England and Ken. I had vague ideas of finding work in Venice, and even though England wasn't yet in the Common Market and I would have had to get a work permit, I think with time I could have found something if I'd tried harder, or indeed tried at all. Bobo didn't want me to work. If I worked outside the home, other men would have access to me. He wanted me at home and he wanted me financially dependent on him, and instead of at least trying to get a job, I chose the path of least resistance and moved in with him.

I should also explain that living with Timothy and Ianni was making me feel uncomfortable. They wouldn't accept any rent from me and I felt I was building up an obligation to them that it was increasingly impossible for me to repay. I presume now that Ianni's plan was to set me up with a rich and powerful man who would pay him for the privilege and at the same time give him a permanent foothold in his camp. Ucci was his first choice but, as I later discovered, Ucci was travelling to Greece the following day with his soon to be ex-girlfriend. He told me six years later that they spent the entire flight talking about me, so I'm not really surprised she went off and married someone else shortly afterwards.

Bobo, not being the eldest son and not owning the family palazzo, didn't quite fit the bill in Ianni's eyes. He even said to me as I went off on my first date with Bobo, 'Have fun with him if you like, but don't marry him,' and when, amused and slightly startled, I asked him why, he replied with surprising intensity, 'Because I want you for a prince!'

My position with regard to money has always been slightly ambiguous. My grandfather, Alfred Dunhill, founded the tobacco company, and my father worked for it as a young man, but had long since left it and started his own company by the time I was born. My parents never talked about money when I was growing up. We lived in a two-bedroom rented flat in Marylebone and my father went to work every day, just as all my friends' fathers did. When I was about ten, he went to work for the American company Playtex, invited by his old friend Gordon Ogden. I remember once as a child being left in the street with Gordon briefly. He turned to me and said in his loud American voice, 'When people ask me who my girl is in London, I always tell them it's Anne Dunhill,' and a man nearby looked round at us and smiled. Gordon's first wife spent many years in a wheelchair. I think she may have had polio. She had a boy's name, Bobbie or Billie. I only saw her once, but I remember thinking what a romantic figure she was, pretty, delicate and tragic like the heroine of a Victorian novel.

My father was dead by the time Bobbie / Billie died, but my mother and I were electrified to read in one of the tabloids that Gordon had remarried, a former nun turned showgirl. I can't remember her name either, but she was dark and very pretty and friendly. I had dinner with them in New York when I was eighteen and had just split up from my first fiancé, Julian Moulton. Gordon looked me up in London the following summer and made a pass at me in his suite at the Dorchester. I wonder if my father took him to task for it when they met up in the afterlife.

Talking of Julian brings me back to the subject of money. As I say, I was never aware of any lack of it as a child. My mother always bought me beautiful clothes and generous presents for my birthdays and Christmas. As an only child, I didn't have to share them, and felt myself immensely rich. My maternal grand-mother lived in the flat next door to us, and after my father died, my mother said we might have to economise by all three sharing one flat. This upset me. I begged my mother not to give up my grandmother's flat, and the matter was never mentioned again.

My grandmother died two years after my father, when I was fourteen, and my mother inherited quite a lot of money from an old lady called Mrs Godding who we used to visit in Bedford. Much later, I learnt that my father had been married to Mrs Godding's daughter, Maisie, who died in 1951. My parents had been living together for about ten years by then, but couldn't marry until October 1951 when I was four.

Of course this situation must have made my mother feel very insecure. To have a child out of wedlock at that time was a terrible disgrace and both my mother and I would have been social outcasts if we'd been found out, but I never knew anything about it until I was twenty-one. My mother confessed all to me shortly before I married Ken Sweet. By then it was the Swinging Sixties and I thought how quaint and unnecessary it had been of my parents to keep the matter secret for so long. Who cared if my father had been married before?

But years later when I flew to Zurich to consult the astrologer and Jungian analyst Liz Greene, she told me that although I had been told nothing, I must have absorbed the atmosphere of insecurity and secrecy in my household when I was a child and suffered accordingly. Certainly I was a very frightened child. I was frightened of the dark and sleeping alone and cripplingly shy with strange adults. Certain books could reduce me to agonies of insomnia and terror, but whether these feelings were caused by my absorption of my mother's fear of social disgrace when I was in the womb or not, I simply can't say.

After we inherited Mrs Godding's money, which my mother told me had been settled on her by my father to revert to him after her death, we started to splash out a bit. We went to Venice on holiday, taking a glamorous flat on the Lido with my aunt and cousin Dicky for company. We took a beach hut in the front row of the Quattro Fontane beach and Dicky and I went to tea dances at the Excelsior Hotel. By the time I was seventeen all my friends seemed to be living south of Hyde Park, so I persuaded my mother we should move to a much bigger flat in Queen's Gate. This must have been a considerable wrench for her as we'd lived in Marylebone all my life, and she'd been there for many years before that. She was leaving behind all her memories of my father, of her parents, who had moved into our block of flats after their house in Kentish Town was bombed, and of my little cousin Rosalind, Dorothy's daughter and Dicky's sister who'd been crushed to death in the lift when she was six and I was two.

I believe Rosalind's death had a big effect on the way I was brought up. Dorothy was divorced from her husband, the actor Neal Arden, and had a job. On the morning Rozzy died, she came to my mother's door and asked if she and Dicky could come and play. My mother was busy and told her to come back at twelve o'clock, then reproached herself ever afterwards, because if she'd invited them in immediately Rozzy might never have died.

As it was, Rozzy called the lift at twelve o'clock. The Ardens lived on the fourth floor and my parents on the second with my grandmother next door. Dicky, who was then three, was teasing Rozzy and wouldn't get into the lift. She was standing waiting for him with the gate held open when someone else on another floor called the lift and, because Rozzy was so light, it moved anyway and she was trapped. I had no idea that Dicky remembered the accident. I always thought he'd decided to take the stairs and was safely in my mother's flat when it happened. We never talked about it till 1999, the year my mother died, when he told me he that he could still remember Rozzy's screams as she was crushed. My mother told me she'd held Rozzy's little hand as the porter tried vainly to free her and said she was sure my father would have saved her if only he'd been at home.

After that my mother spoilt me and gave me everything I wanted. She was absurdly indulgent with me and Dicky and suffocatingly over-protective. What Dorothy suffered and felt about the accident, I don't know. She never talked about it. She died of cancer when she was seventy, but that was nearly thirty years later.

When my father started working for Playtex, he sometimes had to go on business trips. My mother was always terribly worried about him and, since he'd had a heart attack in 1955, from which he'd supposedly completely recovered, perhaps she was right to be so. I decided to copy her, and imagined each time he went away that he might die and never come back. I thought that by imagining it I could prevent it from happening. The morning he set off on his last trip, 9 March 1959, I was twelve years old and in bed with 'flu. I remember him bending over my bed to kiss me goodbye. He was tall, six foot two inches, and had put on weight since giving up smoking after his heart attack. He'd been blond as a young man and still had a quantity of slightly thinning lightish hair worn in a side parting. I saw him through my mother's eyes as a prince and the handsomest man in the world.

The next day two policemen came to tell us he'd been killed in a car accident just outside Norwich. My mother was out when they arrived and my grandmother was looking after me. When I saw the policemen I knew instantly that one of my parents was dead, though I tried to persuade myself that perhaps it might be some more distant relation. My grandfather, Alfred, had died just two months before, so I knew it wasn't him. It was just a minor accident. My father was driving behind a lorry when two dogs ran into the road. The lorry braked sharply, my father's car ran into the back of it and their bumpers got entangled. My father got out and he and the lorry driver lifted his car clear, after which my father had a second heart attack and collapsed in the road. A retired nurse came out of her house and tended to him while they called an ambulance, but it was no good. He died in the ambulance on the way to hospital. Years later, on the advice of a counsellor, I looked up the records of the accident from the inquest. My father's last words were to the lorry driver. He apparently said, 'I saw the dogs. It wasn't your fault.' I found them very moving to read

Since visualising the worst was obviously ineffectual as a way of preventing it from happening, I decided to do the opposite when my children were born. If any worries or negative thoughts about them entered my head, I banished them instantly, literally hurling them out of my mind and refusing to let them re-enter.

Years later I was taught a meditation in which I had to imagine myself sitting within a circle of outward-facing mirrors. The idea was that any attempts to harm me or negative thoughts directed towards me would be reflected back on to their perpetrator, while I remained impregnable within my shield of glass. I was divorcing Anthony at the time and feeling particularly under attack, so I liked this meditation, which reminded me of the techniques I'd used when the children were small.

To finish with the money theme, the first and last time I got excited about it was when I was seventeen and met Julian Moulton in Paris where I'd gone to stay with a French family and study at *La Sorbonne* – my mother being of the generation that believed the only education a woman needed was to speak French and play the piano. Julian was twenty. On his twenty-first birthday in eight months time, he was due to inherit a fabulous, unknown sum from his father's estate. He was looking forward to this event with such excitement that I got excited too and imagined myself sharing in this adventure, dripping in diamonds and swishing along in mink coats – there were still six years to go before I became a vegetarian. Later we got engaged, and his mother, Geraldine, arranged a meeting with my mother, Marjorie, and explained to her that Julian and I would only be able to spend three months a year in England for tax reasons. Geraldine told my mother that she must buy Julian and me a house in London – why, if we were going to be so rich? – although actually you could pick up a pretty little house in Notting Hill for £8000 in those days, so I rather wish she had. My mother was also expected to give us an allowance to live on while we were in London. I can't remember where we had to spend the other nine months of the year, or who was going to support us during them, but I do remember feeling a sense of outrage and rebellion. What on earth was the point of being rich, I asked myself, if one couldn't go where one wanted and when one wanted?

Julian's money began to feel like a shackle rather than a ticket to freedom, and we broke the engagement off after a month. After that experience, I was never attracted to men with lots of money, nor they to me.

The press, with whom I'd become familiar during my debutante season in 1964, used to refer to me as 'Anne Dunhill of the tobacco family', which was true and acceptable even though after my father's death my mother, the most unpushy of people, had largely lost touch with my father's family. After the engagement to Julian, however, they suddenly and inexplicably started referring to me as the Tobacco Heiress, which was both irritating and inaccurate. I've no idea how much money you need in order to be officially declared an heiress, but I don't think the £30,000 or so that my mother inherited from Mrs Godding would have qualified us, even in those days. Whenever journalists called me, I would tell them I wasn't an heiress and the phrase would be omitted only to pop up again with distressing regularity.

Now, having decided I didn't want to marry a rich man, I faced the opposite extreme – of being targeted by fortune hunters who believed what they read in the newspapers. Because I had been able to earn a living from my looks, it required a certain mental shift for me to entertain the idea that anyone might want to marry me solely for my money but now, looking back, I think this was probably what Ken had in mind. His great friend was Dandy Kim Waterfield, notorious for marrying heiresses, and his (Ken's) first wife, who I never met, had apparently been very rich. Ken pursued me relentlessly, finding a mutual friend to introduce us and proposing marriage within a few weeks of our first meeting. After our marriage he turned on me with a terrifying hatred and hostility which I think can only have been a reaction to the hoops he'd had to jump through in order to ensnare me.

After Ken, me being rich or not didn't matter for the next twenty-six years because I was with Bobo, who was very generous and blissfully ignorant of the contents of the London social pages for six years, and then with Anthony for twenty. If any potential fortune hunters have appeared in the ten years since my second divorce, my antennae must have been acute enough to zap them automatically.

To go back to Bobo, my motives for moving in with him may have been the ignoble ones listed above, but I soon grew to love and respect him. He liked to get up very early, around 6am, and go out painting in his boat. I often slept till 11 and was woken by him coming home with five or six paintings already completed.

Later, after breakfast, I lay on the sofa reading while he drew me. In the first exhibition he had in Venice after meeting me, at the *Galleria Bevilacqua la Masa* in St Mark's Square, he hung two panels of drawings of me on the entrance wall and I got through the complete works of the Bröntes and George Eliot. This life suited me very well. I'm immensely lazy physically, but in this case I was able to tell myself that just by lying on a sofa all day, I was actually assisting in an important creative process.

Bobo was also keen that we should travel together. Our first trip, in December 1969, was to Copenhagen, where Bobo had an exhibition. We travelled there from Venice by train and ferry. To my amazement, Bobo had never flown. Although he had plenty of money, one of his idiosyncrasies was to travel as cheaply as possible. He liked to stay in scruffy, two-star hotels and, if he had to spend the night on a train, never bothered to reserve a sleeping car or even a couchette. I changed all that, but at the beginning of our relationship, when I was still only twenty-two, I rather enjoyed the adventurousness and informality of it all. Why pay for a sleeper when you could stretch out full length on the seat of the compartment – and during those first, winter journeys, you often could? Unfortunately, especially in France, sadistic guards would sometimes enter the compartment in the middle of the night, switch on all the lights and demand to see our documents. I didn't find this at all amusing, and soon persuaded Bobo into *Wagon Lits*.

Copenhagen in December 1969 was the coldest place I'd ever been to. I had a fur coat – there was still over a year to go before I became vegetarian – a wonderful red fox with horizontal pelts, but even that was entirely inadequate for the weather. Bobo spent his days at the gallery hanging his pictures, and as far as I remember, I just trailed along with him. There was a shopping centre we could walk through between the hotel and the gallery that kept us out of the cold at least part of the time. I'd set off with enthusiasm in my London clothes, survive as far as the shopping centre, but arrive at the gallery a shivering wreck.

It was at this exhibition that I began to understand Bobo's work a little. In Venice I'd found some of his paintings too bright, even garish, but in Copenhagen, against that cold, grey, northern light, I understood that he'd managed to capture the true colours of Venice. Looking at them hung was like looking through a series of windows at different Venetian scenes. The paintings were telling the truth. My admiration for him grew, which pleased him, since Venice was his great and abiding love, and to express this love was his life's work.

We both got ill in Copenhagen. I got gravel in my kidneys. I'd had this for the first time when I was nineteen. It hit in the middle of the night. I felt griping cramps in my lower back and started vomiting with the pain. My mother took me to Casualty at the old St George's Hospital, now the Lanesborough Hotel, where nothing was found. It was only after two more sessions of this torture that I was finally diagnosed. A kidney stone would have shown up on an X-ray, whereas gravel didn't. Apparently it was most unusual for someone of my age and the only cure was to drink lots of water and flush it out, which I eventually did.

For a year or so after that, I stuck to the water-drinking routine but when you're well, it's hard to remember what being ill is like, and I eventually slipped back into bad habits. Since living in

Italy – probably since embarking on the cruise at the beginning of September – I'd been drinking far more wine than usual, which had built up acidity.

So here I was on our second or third morning in Copenhagen in a two-star hotel with only a shower (lying in a hot bath can actually soothe kidney pain, though I'm not sure doctors recommend it) and feeling that horrible griping pain in my sides that I recognised so well from my previous attack. I can't remember the exact sequence of events, but I know Bobo had to go to the gallery and that I spent most of the morning squatting in the shower as I struggled to deliver the tiny bits of gravel that were causing me such extraordinary agony. Eventually a doctor came – Bobo must have summoned him before he left – and gave me an injection of morphine or something equally effective. The pain continued, but I didn't care about it so much.

Eventually, some time in the afternoon, the attack finished. Bobo and I went along to the nearest hospital where a urine analysis confirmed my self-diagnosis. As the attack was over, I was sent back to the hotel to rest.

Earlier that summer, Sharon Tate, Roman Polanski's wife, together with three companions, had been murdered at their Californian home. I hadn't met her, but I'd socialised quite frequently with Polanski the previous year when I was going out with an actor called Iain Quarrier who appeared in several of Roman's films. Their wedding reception had taken place at the London home of Tony Greenburgh, my doctor since I was eighteen. In fact it was Tony's locum, Peter Ryan, who sent Anita for the tests that resulted in her cancer diagnosis.

When the news of the murders broke, the newspapers were filled with lurid stories about the orgiastic, satanic lifestyle chez Polanski. These surprised me, since Roman had actually seemed rather straight to me during the period I went out with Iain. He never even so much as smoked a joint with us. But in a strange way, I found these stories comforting. If a victim has invited death by the recklessness of their lifestyle, it doesn't somehow seem quite as terrible as it would if the attack was completely random.

It was during our visit to Copenhagen that the story of the Manson family broke. Sharon Tate's father had played detective, mixing incognito in hippie circles where he'd heard rumours of the truth. These two facts – the loving and concerned father hunting his daughter's killer, and the random nature of the crime – the killers had apparently been told to go to the house and kill anyone they found there as an act of revenge against the house's previous owner – not only undemonised the beautiful Tate and turned her into an entirely innocent victim, but also made me believe for the first time in the existence of evil. Of course I must have known in my head that evil existed, but somehow I had never realised it in my heart before.

Looking back from a distance of forty years, I realise that I must also have been disturbed by the parallels between the Tate murders and my marriage to Ken. For years I felt that his violence and hatred towards me were somehow provoked by me – were in fact my fault. It was to be another six years before I chanced upon a translation of de Sade's *Juliette* amongst the very limited choice of English books in an Italian seaside resort where Bobo and I had rented a holiday flat. It was to be a profound influence on me. It made me realise that in my marriage to Ken I had been deliberately cast in the role of victim. In *Juliette*, a rich and powerful group of libertines send out each night for victims, pretty, innocent youths of both sexes, to be ravished, tortured and killed purely for the libertines' amusement. When they marry, it is to pretty, innocent youths with money, so they can take their pleasure and profit financially when they tire of them and kill them. Do I think Ken would have killed me? I certainly thought so at the time. It was the main reason I decided to stay on in Italy.

Back in Copenhagen in 1969, I didn't consciously consider the parallels between Sharon Tate and me except that we had moved in the same circles in London and she had been a nice girl with loving parents, so if it could happen to someone like her, it could also happen to someone like me. The night of my kidney ordeal I prayed silently in the bed of my hotel room in Copenhagen with Bobo sleeping beside me that if it were possible to relieve any of Tate and her friends' suffering posthumously by taking on some of their pain for them, I would be prepared to undergo another attack for their sake.

Be careful what you pray for. God, if indeed it was He, was kind enough to oblige, and I spent another eight or so hours the following day squatting in the shower under the merciful influence of morphine. After that my courage failed me, and I told God I was very sorry but I couldn't bear any more. Since then I haven't had any but the most minor kidney disturbances.

Strangely, when Anita told me on Mothers' Day 2009 that Bobo had cancer of the pancreas and stomach, she said that she had prayed to take on his pain. I wasn't particularly alarmed. She appeared to be in blooming health and at her most beautiful. It never occurred to me for a moment that Bobo would outlive her.

CHAPTER TWO

25 April 2009

My alarm went off at 5.30 and for a moment I struggled to remember that I was in Rome, on pilgrimage, sharing a room with my friend Josephine Siedlecka in a religious house, Santa Maria alle Fornaci, within sight of the dome of St Peter's Basilica. We'd been there for four days, and today the group was leaving by coach for Assisi. I was going to separate from them temporarily and make a pilgrimage of my own to Venice to say goodbye to Bobo. Ingo was staying with him, which was my excuse. 'I'm in Italy and I thought it would be nice to pop by and say hallo to you and Ingo' sort of thing.

Bobo didn't know he had cancer. He was told he had cysts on his pancreas, and I hoped it wouldn't occur to him that a four-and-a-half-hour train journey from Rome to Venice and a five-hour train journey from Venice to Assisi was rather a long way for me to go for a casual visit.

Jo kindly offered to go with me, but we agreed that it would be better if she stayed with the group and made sure my suitcase got to Assisi safely. Hélène was understandably very protective of Bobo, and it wasn't the moment to introduce a stranger into the household. The plan had already changed since I booked my train ticket on Thursday. I was originally invited to lunch, but since eating hurt Bobo and he liked to have an afternoon sleep, I was later told to arrive at four and have tea with him. This meant I'd only have about an hour and a half with him before I had to catch my train to Assisi. I was disappointed of course, but the main thing was to see him.

I managed to shower, dress and put on my make-up in the semi darkness and be out of the room at six. Jo woke to say goodbye and wish me luck. My packing was already done. I'd stayed up till midnight the night before after an excellent farewell dinner at *L'eau vive*, a restaurant run by a Belgian order of missionary nuns who danced and sang for us after our meal. Pilgrimages are far from the austere occasions that an outsider might imagine them to be.

The taxi I'd ordered the night before was waiting downstairs to take me to the station. I was sorry to be leaving Rome. Although I'd been there several times before, first modelling and later with Bobo and then Anthony, I felt that I'd seen and appreciated more on this visit than on all the others put together. Can it be true that the spiritual dimension, whatever that is, as Prince Charles might say, really does add some indefinable, intangible benefit to the experience of travel?

I think I always wanted to be a Catholic. I was christened in the Church of England and attended infrequent services at Marylebone church. I enjoyed going there, especially standing in the side chapel where Elizabeth Barrett and Robert Browning were secretly married, but it somehow didn't compare with the almost sensuous pleasure of slipping into the exquisite Catholic church of St James's, Spanish Place to look at their crib at Christmas time. To define the difference between Catholic and Anglican churches in one word, it would have to be warmth. Catholic churches invite one to linger, to light a candle, to kneel before a saint and to pray. Anglican churches are generally locked when one needs them, and all too often the services ooze coldness, sadness and emptiness. Charlotte Brönte put me off Catholicism for a while with her excoriating denunciation of it in *Villette*, but after the pilgrimage I went on with Aunt Dorothy in 1969, I saw what fun it was, repented my sins bitterly and longed to convert.

Bobo dissuaded me. His criticism of the Catholic church was

based on an occasion during World War Two when a bomb had dropped and some priests who were present had apparently panicked and pushed past the children into the shelter. I was far too ignorant at that time to argue that a couple of bad priests don't actually mean there's anything wrong with the religion they belong to. I felt myself vastly inferior to Bobo morally and thought it would be pretentious of me to become a Catholic when he was able to live such a decent life without the prop of religion. What I should have realised was that it was precisely because I felt myself to be so frail that I would have benefited from the strength and support of the Church, but I didn't. It was to take me another thirty-four years, but at least I made it in the end.

It took only twenty minutes to get to Rome station. There was time for a croissant and a strong, delicious cappuccino. Bobo always used to mock me for drinking cappuccino at all hours of the day, saying no Italian would dream of having one after 11am, but at this hour my right was unassailable. It strengthened me and made me start almost to enjoy myself, though I'd been feeling very nervous before leaving. The knowledge that Bobo was dying upset me terribly. Part of me wanted to go down on my knees to him and beg his pardon for betraying him with Anthony, but then fairness forced me to remember that he hadn't always been very nice to me either.

*   *   *

Back in Copenhagen, forty years earlier, Bobo was the next one to succumb to the cold. He had always been prone to nosebleeds, and a day or two after my second kidney attack he suffered a prolonged bleed that took us back to the hospital where he spent hours in a cubicle with a tampon up his nose.

The following day the performance repeated itself. It was decided his nose must be cauterised, but we elected to postpone the procedure till we got to London. Because we were both in such a delicate condition, we decided to fly. We were going to stay at my mother's flat and spend Christmas with her. I should have been happy and positive at the thought of seeing my mother and friends again and showing off my new lover, but on the morning of our departure to London, I woke with a terrible feeling of depression.

I've been told since that depression is inertia and nothingness. The inability to do anything but sit in an armchair staring out of the window, but that wasn't what I felt, so perhaps the clinical term for it wasn't depression at all. I'd felt it for the first time after my father died in 1959. He died on 10 March – a date I dreaded for years until it became, unexpectedly, Tabitha's birthday and could once again be celebrated – and for the first few months afterwards I was protected by the numb cocoon of shock. I remember the summer holidays being particularly bad. My mother was worried about money and we didn't go on holiday that year apart from a day trip to Seaford in Sussex. What I felt that summer was a painful combination of grief and fear. Grief for my father and fear of death in general and specifically that my mother would die too. I could hardly bear to let her out of my sight because I knew I wouldn't survive if anything happened to her. Looking back at my diary of the period, a five-year diary from 1958 to 1963, I find my inability to express my emotions in it quite heartbreaking. What on earth did I think a diary was for?

Admittedly it was so tiny that it only permitted me to write four lines per day. Thus the entry for the day of my father's death read, 'The worst day in my life. Two policemen came in the morning while Mummy was out and told me that Daddy had been killed in a car accident.' On what would have been his sixtieth birthday, six weeks after his death on 25 April (fifty years to the day before my visit to the dying Bobo), I didn't even mention him. I wrote, 'Went for the day to Flee. (Felicity Osborne, my best friend at Francis Holland, now mother of the more famous George.) In the morning we browsed in Woolworths. In the afternoon we rang up people for fun. Saw Gordon

Ogden.' What sort of calls were these, I wonder? Calling the zoo and asking for Mr Lion? Calling boys we fancied and flirting with them anonymously? Almost definitely not. At that age we didn't know any. And why did I see Gordon Ogden? Presumably he came round to offer my mother help and support. A typical entry for that terrible summer, when everything conspired to feed my terror of death and I would sometimes feel while walking along the street that I couldn't go any further and would just have to sink face down on the burning pavement and disintegrate into dust like the statue of Ozymandias, read, 'Saw Mummy off (to the hated morning job she'd been forced to take to make ends meet after my father died). Did shopping. Met Mummy. In the afternoon Mummy saw a solicitor. I waited in the rain for an hour. Bought a book.' Some things haven't changed. Reading, then as now, was my principal and often only solace.

During my second bout of depression in 1970, the year I resumed my diary after a four-year gap, I was equally reticent. My entries are bubbly, full of my love for Bobo and the fun times we were having visiting the sights of London, when I remember that every visit to a museum would trigger anguish because the people who had created and used the objects we were looking at were all dead, and the objects themselves were a constant reminder that we too would die. I used to feel that it was the most terrible thing in the world to fear death because for every other problem that might arise in life there was the possibility of escape through suicide, but if your problem was the fear of death, you were completely and utterly trapped.

Only once in my 1970 diary did I let the cheerful mask slip. On 23 February I was told by Bobo's doctor that a lump on my breast that I'd noticed the year before when married to Ken must be removed. I'd already shown it to Ken's doctor, a colourful character called Lew Newton, who said it was nothing and prescribed a cream to rub into it that he said would dissolve it. In all the turbulence of the marriage, I didn't bother to get the cream, but when Bobo's doctor said the lump must be removed, I was struck by the most abject terror. This, on top of the constant, dull terror of death I was already feeling, was enough to break through my reserve. I wrote, 'Since I was ill in Copenhagen, I've been horribly nervy and depressed. I haven't written about it because writing or even talking seems to make it more real to me, and it really had almost gone in these last weeks.' Who was I kidding, I now ask myself? I was ashamed of my feelings. I felt depression was a stigma and was too inhibited to express it. I was lying to myself in my own diary, just as I did when I was twelve and never mentioned my father again after his death.

To be fair to me, I was also adhering to the 'stiff upper lip' tradition of the time, when an outpouring of grief would have been looked on with distaste and regarded as rather vulgar, but I had a marvellous secret weapon with which to express myself – the blank, white page of my diary which nobody but me would ever see unless I wanted them to. How terribly sad that I never took advantage of it.

My other secret weapon was, of course, Bobo, who was unfailingly tender and supportive during that period. He once told me he fell in love with me because of the sad expression in my eyes, but the way he pampered me when we were first together went a good way towards eradicating it. A girlfriend he had when his marriage was breaking up, who'd been kept discreetly hidden from even his closest friends, expressed amazement at the way he took me everywhere. I suppose there was a certain amount of PR involved. If everyone knows your wife has left you for another man, it's not displeasing to be able to display a younger model to the world, especially one whose Italian isn't good enough to grasp all the undercurrents of the situation. For my part, all the hesitation I'd felt before moving in with him disappeared. I was so grateful to him for his kindness that I fell deeply in love with him and became convinced we would spend the rest of our lives together.

So what went wrong exactly between me and Bobo? I'm afraid it was having children. Before that we were so carefree. Bobo worked hard, but didn't appear to work at all. He'd paint early in the morning while I slept and if he had work appointments to do with his antique business, we'd incorporate them with some treat like buying me a dress or going to the cinema.

In London he'd make ceramics or go to auctions at Christies and Sothebys. We'd see my friends, all of whom liked him, and eat in Italian restaurants or visit galleries and stately homes where he'd marvel at how many Italian old masters the crafty English had managed to get their hands on. We were always together, and he always made me feel loved, valued and protected.

For the first year I allowed Bobo to lull my conscience into accepting the life of a kept woman. He told me he needed me to model exclusively for him, that I was his inspiration, his muse, and indeed for a while I appeared to be. A typical diary entry of 1970 read, 'Woke early and Bobo drew me all morning. I really enjoy it, sitting there naked reading and feeling I'm doing something helpful, whereas really it's much easier than getting dressed and bathed and made up and all the boring things I usually do.'

By 1971, however, my conscience was starting to reawaken, and in January of that year I started voluntary work at SHAC (Shelter Housing Aid Centre) a Roman Catholic organisation working to house homeless people. It was there I met one of my dearest friends, Suzanne Heckert, now living between Palm Beach and Los Angeles and married to the divine Ralph. Five years younger than me and still impossibly glamorous, I wrote of her that first day that I was working 'in company with their stunning blonde secretary who had sensational eye make-up. I'd dressed myself to look dead straight, but I shan't bother tomorrow.'

Suzanne had a boyfriend, Stewart, who made belts, and Bobo, who was easily old enough to be both of their fathers, struck up a friendship with him and painted some wonderful designs on velvet for Stewart to make up. This was typical of Bobo. All my friends liked him and liked us as a couple, and for the early years of our relationship I felt strongly that our nineteen-year age difference didn't matter at all. He seemed to have much more energy than me and I often felt he was younger than I was. He attempted to teach me how to print fabrics. I tried, but didn't really enjoy it. Even then I knew that writing was my thing, and my diary was my first attempt at it. Later he would teach Hélène how to print, which enabled her and Bobo's daughter Nora to set up their highly successful business Norelene, selling beautiful velvet clothes and furnishings, that ran for many years.

The voluntary work at SHAC, which I did every morning for the six weeks we remained in London, was the start of trying to do something for myself. Leaving London again in 1971 was a terrible wrench. I loved Bobo, but I also loved London, my mother and all my friends. Venice was beautiful and Bobo's family couldn't have been more warm or welcoming to me, but ultimately I had nothing to do there. I was just an appendage to Bobo. Sometimes I felt like a well-groomed and much indulged pet dog – paraded through the streets, bought treats and trinkets or ensconced at home on a velvet cushion sleeping in the sun.

We travelled by train and spent two weeks in Paris so Bobo could spend time with Roby and Nora. Soon after our arrival, my doubts and misgivings manifested themselves as a hideous pain in the back of my head that continued for several days and inspired me to open up for once in my diary: '24 February 1971: I think the time has come to write some of my thoughts in this diary as I'm certainly not as placid and easily pleased as I make myself appear in it, though I distrust emotional outpourings and am also very inhibited by the thought of rereading them during future periods of calm. I'm still going through the period of depression which started in December 1969 in Copenhagen. I think it's getting better, but it continually breaks out – like every time I hear of some fatal or agonising illness, I immediately start producing symptoms common to it. I'm also very conscious of being twenty-four and not having done anything with my abilities i.e. a good brain and a social conscience and of not being able to start an interesting career in Venice or of having any hope of starting one in a life where we're constantly travelling round. I so enjoyed my month at SHAC and it was very frustrating to leave and made me ask myself where I'm going, what I'm doing. Do I really love Bobo enough to be an Italian wife? Do I like the Italians? My last two answers were in the negative. I like and respect Bobo, perhaps love him, but in lots of things we are far apart. I'm not interested in antiques and not much in art, his friends are mostly too old and square for me. He doesn't share my love of books and we can't discuss literature or history much because of our different –

PAUSE

Bobo just came in with the children. He was sweet and loving and we went to lunch. It is more than liking I feel for him. He's helped me enormously and I really don't know what would have become of me if I hadn't met him. I would probably have drifted back to Ken out of loneliness, and would now be undergoing my nineteenth nervous breakdown, though even with Bobo's help I haven't done so well. I seem calm on the surface and don't do stupid hysterical things any more, but I have a nasty feeling that the cauldron is on the boil and could bubble over one of these days. The point is that I can't do without Bobo now, but feel that I may be able to do without him in the future. Sometimes I admit this to myself and sometimes not, and I don't like myself for it. I say to myself, "if only he was English", then it wouldn't matter if we weren't twin souls, we could get on with doing our own things in our own way and have quiet, friendly evenings together, but I wonder if the solution's in me, whether I'm not really the marrying kind, whether – but these are whole new depths I can't go into now.

This way of writing is in no way a relief to me. It's difficult and unnatural. I seem totally liberated – sexually etc. – but perhaps I find it easier to liberate myself sexually than to begin the painful struggle of spiritual liberation. Underneath I feel as great a bore as the occasional drunks who weep on one's shoulder in foreign restaurants, knowing that they will never see one again.

So tonight I lie in my bed with pains in the back of my head, hearing the sea roaring in my ears and comparing myself to the schizophrenic Zelda Fitzgerald (I'd just been reading her biography by Nancy Milford).

Should I go to a psychiatrist, or does this happen to everybody?'

In spite of my misgivings about opening up and revealing my dark side in my diary, the little that I managed must have helped because the headache disappeared as suddenly as it had come. It had been so bad that for several days I remained conscious of and took physical pleasure in its absence. What particularly saddens me, looking back, is that the answer to my problems is now so blatantly obvious to me. I should have started writing and, in fact, when we got back to Venice I did just that. I began the first draft of *A Darker Shade of Love* on 14 March, writing on a portable Olivetti typewriter with English keys that Bobo had kindly presented me with and finishing in a manic burst of energy on 10 April, less than four weeks after I started. I've never managed to work at that pace before or since. Having children seriously diluted my creativity while at the same time imposing on me the mental stability I was so lacking in before and the self-discipline I needed to bring my projects to completion.

Shortly after starting the book, I decided to stay at home and write rather than accompany Bobo on an antique buying trip to Padua. I 'paid for my independence by staying awake all night worrying about the disasters that might befall me left alone in Venice i.e. burglars, petrol tankers exploding nearby etc.' I was also suffering from painful mood swings perhaps partly caused by the terror of unleashing the creative process and by the black memories of my marriage to Ken that it stirred up. On 20 March

I wrote, 'Had one of those awful nights. Lay awake till four thinking I was suffocating and finally woke Bobo and told him how unhappy I was and how I hate Italy. Stupid really. I am and I do, but I haven't the guts to go back to London alone so there's really no point in mentioning it.' On 5 April I wrote, 'I honestly don't know if what I'm writing is any good, it's certainly very painful at times, but I do know that if it wasn't for being with Bobo and living in Venice I would probably never have got round to writing anything ever, so whatever happens to me, please don't think I'm ungrateful.'

I think the truth is that I loved Italy but just didn't want to live there. Although I started to write there, I was at the age, twenty-four, when I probably would have started to write anyway. Certainly my subsequent books were all written in London or at our houses in Suffolk and France. The joy of being a writer is that you can write anywhere, and while I used to think it was necessary for me to be in a stable relationship in order to write, I now see that it all boils down to what Virginia Woolf realised nearly a hundred years ago – a private income and a room of one's own.

It was in this uneasy atmosphere of misplaced gratitude and equally misplaced hostility that I discovered I was pregnant. When I first embarked on my relationship with Bobo, I had an IUD inserted. They were still comparatively new, and some experts maintained they were unsuitable for women who hadn't had children. I suffered several unpleasant side effects, including pain and excessive bleeding. We talked about it to Bobo's doctor, who hadn't even heard of the IUD but thought it sounded like '*una cosa malsana*', and agreed that I'd have it removed when we next went to London in December 1970 and rely on the rhythm method which had always worked for me in the past.

It worked for six months. In May 1971 we made a trip back to London. Bobo was planning to produce a documentary film about the damage to Venice caused by the industrialisation at the port of Marghera with our friend the photographer and film director Jim Lee, and I wanted to show my novel to an American literary agent I'd met in Venice the year before with her politician husband. She'd been tremendously encouraging when I told her I was writing a book, but when I called her to say we were in London she promised to get back to me and never did. I was too feeble to contact any other agents, and thus the publication of *A Darker Shade of Love* was delayed for twenty years! On a happier note, I was also able to visit Felicity Osborne who had just given birth to her first son, later to become George, of whom I wrote, 'he really is adorable, not puddingy at all like most babies but full of character with adorable long hands which he clasped demurely in front of him.'

On almost our last night in London we had dinner with friends in Primrose Hill and I was conscious of feeling acutely nauseous. The next day was spent packing, then we travelled to Venice by train, not stopping in Paris as Roby and Nora were on holiday. We arrived in Venice on 7 July. By now the nausea was accompanied by a splitting, throbbing headache and in the afternoon I went to see Bobo's doctor, Franco Franco, who immediately suggested a pregnancy test.

Of course I'd begun to wonder if I could be pregnant, but since I'd been getting my periods, though admittedly somewhat irregularly since the removal of my IUD, and not put on any weight, I couldn't really believe it. My friend Suzanne from SHAC had come to Venice for the summer to stay with Ucci and speak English to his son Barnaba. They all came round to see us after my visit to Dr Franco, but I was feeling so ghastly by then that I could hardly talk.

The following day the pregnancy was confirmed. Bobo picked up the results from the lab and came home with them at lunch time – basically the scene I recounted in *Web of Passion*, only worse.

The next four days were a sort of nightmare in which Bobo,

who never smoked and only drank in moderation, lay on the sofa chain smoking and drinking whisky and repeating endlessly the words, 'I didn't think it would be so soon' about the pregnancy and 'You said you knew what to do' about the rhythm method that had suddenly failed.

I felt that he was being horribly unfair. In my nauseous state, his smoking made me very ill and I couldn't see a great difference between one year and nine months and 'about two years'. Yes, I had said I knew what to do to avoid pregnancy and I'd been wrong, but repeating the accusation as he did, efficacious though it was as a form of torture, was ultimately pointless. If he was so against having a child, then he should have taken responsibility for contraception himself.

I felt very strongly that my feelings of hurt and betrayal at what I considered to be his unreasonable attitude were damaging the baby, tiny as it was, and in the end, four days after the test result, I flew to London. Bobo accompanied me to the airport. There was an hour to wait before the flight and we sat there arguing. Basically I was asking him to choose between me and the baby or neither of us. If he insisted on me having an abortion, I'd go to London and oblige him, but I wouldn't come back as there was no point us staying together if he didn't want children with me.

He wouldn't commit himself until after the flight was called, and it seemed too late for me to travel. Then he suddenly said, 'OK, go.' But those were the days before endless queues and security checks and I was able to rush to the desk, buy a ticket and depart instantly, much to Bobo's astonishment. One of the lingering symptoms of my depression was a fear of flying, but on this occasion I felt nothing. Already the fact of having a child to protect was giving me strength.

When I got home, my mother was horrified but sympathetic and as always my room was there waiting for me, no questions asked. I proceeded to spend a cosy week in London, looked after by my mother, seeing a few close friends and family and negotiating with Bobo – me and the baby or no baby and no me – on the phone. This was much better than being with him in person, nauseated by cigarette smoke and terrified by the new hostility he was manifesting towards me. I saw my doctor, Tony Greenburgh, who reckoned I was about ten weeks pregnant, and even started to knit some 1970s-style baby clothes – a bright purple cardigan and sweater. Knitting was another outlet for my frustrated creativity. My mother was loyally wearing a knee-length waistcoat I'd made her, and Bobo a cable knit sweater, but once the children were born, my creations took longer to appear – the classic example being a stripey sweater I started to knit for Anita that was only completed just in time for Tabitha.

Eventually Bobo capitulated and I returned to Italy in triumph on 17 July. My mother insisted on accompanying me to the air terminal in Cromwell Road and carrying my suitcase for me, even though she was sixty-three and I was twenty-four. Bobo met me at the airport and that evening we had friends round to celebrate the *Festa del Redentore* (Feast of the Redeemer, one of the main celebrations in the Venetian calendar, with most of the population taking to their boats, eating elaborate dinners on board and watching the dazzling, municipal firework display). Bobo's mother had been told of my pregnancy and was very kind to me, the weather was beautiful and all seemed to be sweetness and light.

It didn't last of course. Bobo still had black moods and seemed to have become very jealous of me even though, as I wrote in my diary, 'Is he really so stupid as to think I'd be faithful to him for two years and then choose the time when I was pregnant and nauseous with my first child to start playing around with other men?' But basically we had turned a corner. I looked on my pregnancy as an act of God and loved and wanted my baby. All my doubts about living in Venice disappeared. Fate had stepped in and made up my mind for me. My pregnancy was now known and accepted and I had my dear friend Suzanne in Venice to support me.

My morning sickness wore off surprisingly quickly. By 30 July I was writing that I felt 'remarkably well, with only about half an hour's nausea all day'. With less than perfect timing, I decided to do a degree in English by correspondence course. In those days, to take a degree in English, you had to have a GCE O level in Latin. I'd dropped Latin with much relief at the age of thirteen, so this necessitated a correspondence course in preliminary Latin at which I excelled, followed by the O level course at which I did not. By the time I finally got a place to read English at London University in 1986, Latin wasn't necessary anyway and I never took the exam. At the same time I took an Italian O level course, and this I did eventually take and do rather well in, although not until 1975.

Looking back, I now see how the seeds of the things I did later were sown during those early childless years with Bobo in Venice; the novel written in 1971 and published in 1991, the degree embarked on in the same year and completed in 1989 and of course the voracious reading of English classical novels which I'd somehow never got round to finishing in London.

So it was a time of great creativity, but of the simmering kind that would take another twenty years to come to the boil. Was this positive or negative? Part of me thinks it was positive. I'm glad I had my children young. The births were easy and my body snapped back into shape afterwards, but as far as a career was concerned, I think I took my degree too late to be considered seriously. I remember talking to a female academic at a party in the 1990s, and when I told her I'd got my degree at the age of forty-two, she looked away briefly, but not in time to hide the slight curl of disdain on her lip.

As the pregnancy progressed, I started to feel the glow of wellbeing that the baby books promised. At five months, I was troubled with headaches in the morning. Bobo suggested I should drink a small glass of red wine when they came on. I did, and they disappeared. When, thirty-five years later, I mentioned this to Victoria, she told me the NHS forbade expectant mothers to drink any alcohol at all. It made me feel very relieved to have got through my pregnancies before the era of the Nanny State.

The only cloud on our horizon was our divorces. At first Bobo's seemed more likely to be straightforward than mine, since Ruth had started divorce proceedings when she left him in 1969, but when she heard about me, her interest in divorcing him waned. Since I appeared on the horizon so shortly after she left, she may have suspected initially that I'd been around for some time, but Venice is such a gossipy city, with everyone knowing each other's business, that she must quickly have realised that I didn't meet Bobo until after she'd left him. That being the case, I could never understand her hostility towards me. I didn't expect her to be my best friend or anything, but since, under the terms of her agreement with Bobo, her children spent a month a year in my care, I would have thought it was only rational and in her own best interests as well as theirs for her at least to be civil to me.

Because of her delaying tactics, nothing at all had been resolved between Ruth and Bobo by the time I became pregnant. Having children with a lover when you were married to someone else was still, potentially, quite a serious matter in Italy. Although divorce had been legal there for a few years, great efforts were made by the extreme right to abolish it and a referendum was held on the topic in 1974. In theory the cuckolded spouse of a man or woman who parented an illegitimate child could denounce him or her and even have him thrown into prison. In practice, people had illegitimate children all the time and found numerous ways of getting round the situation. Some people were able to get Swiss divorces, but the chief route of the unmarried pregnant in the 1970s was to London. These included Bobo's older half-brother, Alessandro, known for some inexplicable reason as Ping Ping, for whom we had organized a gynaecologist and hospital bed the previous year. He was the President of the Bank of America, about fifty years old and married, but childless. His girlfriend, a vivacious factory owner, was pregnant with Ping's first child, and he was both terrified and besotted by her. Bobo and I were actually in the hospital when Pino, as she was called, gave birth to a beautiful little daughter, Giovanna.

We had also organised numerous referrals of friends to my GP in London, some to have babies and others for terminations. The advantage of England was that any child born here – at least at that time – was automatically given a British passport and could take its father's surname (or indeed any surname) no matter what the parents' marital status was. Ping wasn't even the first of Bobo's brothers to take advantage of the situation. Ucci's eight-year-old son Barnaba had also been born in London. Barnaba's mother, Pupa, was married when she met Ucci and hadn't yet obtained her divorce when she became pregnant. To my amazement, I discovered that she and Ucci, who was single, had been able to marry in the Catholic Church, which didn't recognise her civil marriage. They did this so that Pupa would be allowed contact with her daughter from her first marriage since, for the Church, Pupa's marriage to Ucci was the only one that counted.

What I'm saying is that although Bobo potentially had the right to be dismayed and alarmed by my pregnancy, he actually knew perfectly well from the example of his brothers and numerous friends that the situation could be got round very easily. Besides that, we had the added advantage that I *was* English and that, thanks to my mother, we had a home in London that we could stay in for as long as we liked.

Bobo's doubts and fears undoubtedly added stresses and strains to my pregnancy, as did Ruth's procrastination. I felt much happier and calmer about the situation when we were in London, where my mother was a tower of strength, having gone through the same situation herself in the 1940s.

My divorce, potentially far more complicated than Bobo's, in the end came through sooner. I married Ken in December 1968 and, under English law, divorce proceedings couldn't even be started until three years after the marriage. There were then only two sets of grounds for starting divorce proceedings less than three years after the marriage – extreme mental hardship and exceptional depravity.

I really wanted to go for extreme mental hardship. Tony Greenburgh sent me to a psychiatrist who listened to my dismal story and backed me all the way, but my solicitors would have none of it. They said it had to be exceptional depravity, and so the lurid details were regurgitated again and written down in my so-called 'discretion statement'. It was all, of course, a tremendous bluff. If Ken had contested the case, it would have been heard in open court with every detail of our transgressions reported to the public. In that case, I would naturally have backed down, in which case my only hope of a divorce would have been under the new law that had just come in whereby it was possible to divorce without the consent of one's spouse after five years separation. Under this law one could also divorce after two years separation by mutual consent, which I very much doubted Ken would give.

My solicitor persuaded me to go ahead with the depravity charge on the grounds that Ken was fifteen years older than me and much bigger – both taller and heavier. He said a judge would be unlikely to believe I had corrupted him.

Ken's solicitor was the notorious Ronnie Schulman who was found guilty of forging the so-called 'shilling will' of their mutual friend Clive Raphael and absconded, probably to South America, before he could be sentenced. Clive had been killed in a plane crash. The only will that was found was typed on an envelope above Clive's signature. The envelope contained nude photos of his estranged wife, the teenage actress Penny Brahms, and the will left the photos and a shilling to Penny on the grounds that she'd left him. The balance of Clive's fortune, about £500.000, was left to Ronnie Schulman. It later transpired that Schulman had found an envelope with Clive's signature on it and dreamed up the whole scheme himself.

Although I quite liked Ronnie, who'd been to dinner with Ken and me several times, I didn't find his code of morals particularly reassuring. I was still afraid that he and Ken would call my bluff and contest the case in the hope of a large pay-off. Ken did in fact cobble together a defence, saying that I'd used physical violence against him, locked him out of the house and caused him great distress by buying pornographic books on a trip to Paris. My solicitor said Ken's defence was ludicrous, but I found it deeply upsetting.

I didn't back down, however, and just before the summer recess Ronnie Schulman wrote to say that owing to financial problems Ken had decided not to contest the divorce provided each party paid its own costs. I'd won, but only by the skin of my teeth. If Ken had known I was pregnant, he might well have hung on for a settlement.

I flew to London in October 1971 and was granted my decree nisi on the 13th, the absolute to follow six weeks later. I travelled to London alone, as Bobo was busy in Venice and had his own separation hearing in December. By now I was five months pregnant, but luckily it hardly showed. There were photographers waiting for me outside the High Court, and I was glad not to have to appear in front of them in a billowing smock. I wore a camel coat by Ted Lapidus that Bobo had bought me in Paris. It was just above the knee and had a leather belt that I was still able to do up. I actually looked rather good in the photos and I don't think anyone would have known I was pregnant if I hadn't had to confess it to the judge in order to get my decree absolute speeded up.

The judge was a woman, Mrs Justice Elizabeth Lane, though, as my counsel naughtily remarked, you would never have guessed the fact by looking at her. My case was heard in the early afternoon, and I spent the morning sitting in the courtroom listening to other divorce cases and wondering when the woman judge I'd been told about would appear. It wasn't until some time later that the penny dropped, and I realised she'd been there all the time.

At first I was fairly calm, but as the case in front of mine ended and I realised my hour had come, I had a moment of terrible panic and thought I might faint. This passed reasonably quickly, and when I was offered a chair to sit on because of my pregnancy, I was able to decline thinking, mistakenly, that I would win the judge over by my bravery.

Mrs Lane didn't like me. This became apparent when my counsel questioned me about my state of mind during the marriage and I remarked that I was reduced to tears almost every day.

'And what effect did this have on your husband?' he asked sympathetically.

'None,' I replied, self-pityingly.

'Except perhaps to bore him?' Mrs Lane interjected acidly.

Her dislike was compounded no doubt by my discretion statement, which she took a very long time to read, while I stood in the dock watching her and wishing I hadn't turned down the offer of a chair.

Dislike it as she might, however, there was nothing the judge could do to prevent the divorce. She tried to make it as awkward as possible, though. My counsel had asked for the absolute to follow in two weeks and she extended it to six. This was reasonable enough as my baby wasn't due till February, but added to the suspense of waiting. She expressed distaste at the fact that I was expecting a child by 'a married man' and when she finally granted the decree nisi, she prefaced it by saying, 'with some hesitation.'

Looking back at my younger self, I can see what a God-awful

mess my situation must have looked from the outside. Yes I was married to a violent brute. Yes I was pregnant by another man. Yes the father of my child was technically married to someone else, and yet how very simple it had all seemed on that day in 1969 when I stepped into Bobo's boat.

*   *   *

I arrived at Venice station with four hours to kill before I was due at Bobo's. I decided to go to *La Madonna dell'Orto*, a church I'd never visited. Amongst the treasures there, were six paintings by Tintoretto, two of which, *The Golden Calf* and *The Last Judgement*, I found absolutely stunning. Tintoretto is the painter who, to put it crudely, turned me on to art. When I first moved in with Bobo, he took me to endless galleries and stood with me in front of paintings exclaiming in wonder, 'Guarda come respira – com'è vivo!' ('Look how it breathes – how alive it is!') while I shifted from foot to foot and wished we could move on because my back was aching. It wasn't till I went to the Accademia Gallery with Felicity and Peter Osborne who came to see us in Venice in 1972 when Ingo was a baby that I suddenly understood. I'd left Ingo with Balbina for an hour to sneak off and meet them, and we were standing in front of a painting called *The Miracle of St Mark Freeing the Slave*, one of a series by Tintoretto on Venice's patron saint. A figure in the centre of the painting, the executioner, was standing with his back to us, three quarters on, with his arms upraised in wonder and one muscled calf exposed in an almost balletic contrapposto. Suddenly I became conscious of his vitality and strength, the blood flowing through his veins and the miracle of being part of that turbulent scene. We moved on to the next painting, *St Mark Saving a Saracen from Shipwreck*, and I almost fainted. I was caught in the terror of the storm, the delirious vertigo of standing upright above the waves and the fear that I would sink into them once more and be overwhelmed. I finally understood what Bobo was on about, although ironically it had taken an occasion when he wasn't there for the penny to drop. Still when I look at paintings, particularly modern ones, I ask myself if Bobo would approve of them before I make up my own mind. He gave me my appreciation of art, but whether I see it through my own eyes or a combination of my own and his, I'm still not entirely sure.

I lit a candle for Bobo at a miraculous statue of the Virgin and left the church on foot, following signs to Rialto. I didn't know this part of Venice at all, but having ranged its streets from end to end for six years, first with Bobo and later with the children, I was entirely confident that I'd find my way. Eventually I reached a picturesque canal with two or three restaurants along the side of it. I sat down gratefully at an empty table and ordered a quarter litre of sparkling wine and a very expensive salad.

When I finished lunch, I still had time to kill, so I continued my walk, directing my way through the tourist highlights of Venice, Rialto, Piazza San Marco, and the newly restored opera house, *La Fenice*. Just before my affair with Jeremy Isaacs came to its abrupt end in 1996, we'd been planning an illicit trip to Venice together, the only possible pretext for which was to attend a performance at *La Fenice*. Shortly after we were separated by the flash of a paparazzo's camera, *La Fenice* was gutted by fire. Strangely I found this rather comforting. It seemed an appropriately cataclysmic end to all our hopes.

From there I took the Gritti traghetto across the Grand Canal and walked past Bobo's old studio in *Campiello degli Incurabili* which he'd bought in 1972. At that time it was a factory for repairing boats' engines and crammed to the ceiling with rusty machinery. Bobo was clever enough to realise it had the potential to become the best artist's studio in Venice and bought it on the spot for the equivalent of about £5000. I think he had some idea of escaping domesticity by working there and returning home at night when Ingo was safely in bed, but I wasn't having any of that, and insisted on moving there too. Commuting to the

Giudecca was no longer fun with a baby, pram and shopping in tow. Bobo capitulated with good grace and built two bedrooms and a bathroom on the mezzanine for us and Ingo and continued to live there for thirty years after we left, only recently having sold up and moved back to the Giudecca.

The studio was shut up and the mural Bobo had painted on an adjoining wall had almost eroded or been chipped into invisibility. I took a photo anyway. I'd been back there many times since our separation, both with Anthony and without him, and even though I'd visited Bobo's new home with Anita two years before, it was strange to walk past the studio and think that Bobo was no longer there.

By now I was no longer nervous at the idea of seeing him. Either the sparkling wine had done the trick, or Venice – the city where people never seem to age – had wrought its magic and I was once more a twenty-something model, about to visit a famous artist in his new studio. I took the motoscafo across to the Giudecca and arrived at Bobo and Hélène's house on the Riva di Bigio on the dot of four.

Ingo opened the door but Bobo wasn't far behind, descending the steps from his atelier into the inner courtyard. I'd been warned he was very thin, but apart from that, there was nothing particularly worrying in his appearance. He seemed strong physically, moving around without difficulty, and his expression was full of its customary vitality.

He made tea, and I produced a tin of shortbread from Partridges in London. It was the only present I'd been able to think of. He used to like it when we were together, and we'd even tried making it ourselves, rather successfully.

To my pleasure he ate a piece and seemed to enjoy it. I told him I was reading a book by his friend Donna Leon, the acclaimed American crime writer. I'd never met Donna, but Bobo and the children knew her well. She used to take them to the American Army base to buy jeans during their summer vacations. I'd come to her books late, but was now utterly hooked. The one I was reading currently, *Through a Glass Darkly*, actually contained a description of Bobo's former studio and praised the Ferruzzi paintings hanging on the walls.

Bobo smiled. He wasn't a great reader and Donna's books weren't translated into Italian since she had a home in Venice and didn't want to offend her neighbours. But he told me that one of her characters, an *eminence grise* named Lele Bortoluzzi, was based on him. I'd already noted similarities between Bobo and Lele and was delighted. Our conversation moved to reminiscences, and Bobo seemed in great form, although I noticed that occasionally he would start an anecdote about one person and end it talking about another.

Ingo sat quietly in one of Bobo's antique chairs, and I thought how strange it must be for him to be alone with his parents in his father's house, a situation that probably hadn't occurred since Bobo and I parted when he was three. I've always adored Ingo. My happiness when he came home from Bedales in the holidays used to prompt Anthony to say, only half jokingly, 'He's your man, isn't he?' But rather than embarrass him, I tended to copy the character in Agatha Christie's *Death on the Nile*, who adopted a stern (in my case read neutral) expression whenever she looked at her son in order to disguise her extreme affection for him.

Although the experience of fatherhood seemed to have created in Ingo a certain grudging respect for my own efforts, I was sure that most of the time he thought of me as a pathetic old has-been. It was therefore strangely satisfying for me to see him sit so quietly and respectfully listening to Bobo and me. For a few minutes our roles were reversed again and I felt a surge of parent power that was strong enough to make me wonder how my life would have turned out if Bobo and I had never parted.

Life on the Giudecca is governed by boat timetables. On arrival, I'd told Bobo the time of my train to Assisi, and he'd called Roby, also a native of the Giudecca, to check with him which boat I needed to catch to the station. All of a sudden, seemingly in mid-sentence, it was time to go. I was flattered, if slightly alarmed, when Bobo announced that he was going to accompany me to the boat stop. Ingo came too. The boat was already visible, just leaving the island of San Giorgio, and Ingo was sent ahead to make sure it didn't leave without me, though Bobo was able to keep up a good pace by my side.

We got to the boat stop with a minute to spare. I kissed them both hastily and stood on deck waving till they were out of sight. The sense of grief and apprehension I'd felt that morning had completely vanished. I felt sure somehow that I'd see Bobo again.

CHAPTER THREE

10 May 2009

My mother died in 1999, and once a year my children and I meet in the Garden of Remembrance at Golders Green Crematorium to remember her. We tell affectionate stories about her and have lunch or dinner together afterwards. Today we were going to Tabitha's, stopping to buy lunch at the supermarket on the way.

Tabitha was going to bring Anita and Juliet. We'd arranged to meet at 12.30, but as I arrived, I had a call to say they were running late. I didn't mind at all. It was a beautiful day, and as usual being in the garden had lifted my spirits, which were now at a low ebb because of Bobo's illness. I was also feeling sad because Juliet had told me a few days earlier that she and her boyfriend were going to have a trial separation. As mothers do, I invited her back to stay in her old room for as long as she wanted, and although part of me was delighted to have her home again, I worried that tricky times lay ahead.

As always on arrival in the garden, I went first to study the marble wall plaque we'd put up for my parents in 1999. Although my mother loved my father very much, she never created a memorial for him nor, as far as I know, visited the garden. After her funeral, I asked for her ashes to be scattered in the same place as my father's and when we arrived for the ceremony, the attendant said, 'I've found your father's ashes!' which, to our amazement, had been standing on a shelf for forty years awaiting instructions. We were all thrilled at the thought that my parents would finally be reunited. It turned what could have been a very sad day into rather a joyous one.

After inspecting the wall plaque, I went and sat on what we thought of as our bench. It was Anita who started the tradition. One year we happened to be the only two who could meet there on my mother's anniversary, so she told me that if she got there first, she'd be sitting on the first bench on the left at the far end of the lawn. I have a very clear picture of her now, sitting waiting for me in the sunshine and waving to me as I approached her.

Once in a creative writing class, I was asked to think of two things my father had told me. I remembered sitting on his knee aged five, after my first term at Francis Holland, and saying I didn't want to go back because I was being bullied. In the art class, one of the girls had told me my drawing was scribble, and on another occasion she'd turned round in the corridor and stuck her tongue out at me. My father persuaded me to give the school another try. He said that if anyone told me my drawings were scribble, I should say, 'I was just copying you,' and that if anyone stuck out their tongue at me, I should say, 'You look better like that!' I don't know what an assertiveness trainer would have made of his advice, but I followed it and all bullying ceased. I already considered my father to be my hero and the handsomest man in the world, but after that, he was the fount of all wisdom as well.

After converting to Catholicism in 2003, I attended a series of spiritual meetings, at one of which I was asked to think of an incident that summed up my mother for me. I remembered a time when I was probably even younger than five, when we were walking in Park Square Gardens near Regent's Park. We were key holders, and I spent a lot of my childhood there. At the time they seemed vast, a sort of Elysian Fields, but years later, when Anita was working for the Prince's Trust, we visited the gardens in her lunch hour and I found that though they were enchantingly pretty, they were actually quite small. The incident with my mother must have been in winter, because it was getting dark very quickly and there was no one else there. I suggested we should walk in opposite directions round the perimeter of the large lawn near the entrance gate and meet on the other side. She agreed and we set out, but somehow it got dark before we completed our circuit. I couldn't see my mother anywhere and was lost in the dark. I left the path and ran in the direction I thought she'd gone. A moment of blind panic ensued and I started to cry.

My mother must have heard me and started walking towards me. The relief I felt when I saw her was indescribable, and from then on she was enshrined as my protector and nurturer. She kept this role almost to the end of her life. When Anthony walked out, in 1995, she was the only person I could confide the full extent of my feelings to. I'd sit in her flat drinking coffee and chain smoking while she listened to me sympathetically. Afterwards I felt certain that I wouldn't have survived the whole thing without her.

When she died, several of my friends described her to me as a great lady. She certainly never thought of herself as one. She was a doctor's daughter. Her parents were originally from Scotland, but had settled in Kentish Town where my grandfather practised. My mother was dark, pretty and petite. When she was young she was told that she resembled the actress Merle Oberon. She studied and later taught ballroom dancing with a famous teacher of the era, Josephine Bradley, and was twice sent on cruise ships to South America as a professional dancer with her mother as chaperone. The second of these trips proved a great spur to my father's affections. He declared himself on her return, and they set up home together. What I never thought to ask her when she was alive, was why a respectable doctor's daughter should have chosen the path of mistress rather than wife. Her sister, my Aunt Dorothy, also had quite an exotic career. She worked as a swimming teacher in the South of France where she mingled with the Scott Fitzgerald set, married an actor, Neal Arden – still wonderfully alive at over a hundred years old – and divorced him at a time when it simply wasn't done.

I suppose my mother would have said that having once seen my father (on a station platform with two women in mink coats, one on either arm), there could never have been anyone else for her. Certainly she never looked at anyone else after he died, but she cared enough about getting married to urge me to do so from when I was about eighteen to when I was just twenty-two and married Ken, after which she realised, I suppose, that there were worse fates for a woman than being unmarried after all.

After about twenty minutes my daughters arrived with Petal and Snowy squirming in Anita's shoulder bag. Anita had just returned from Venice and told me she'd visited her half-sister Nora to try and bring about a reconciliation between her and Bobo. Nora and Hélène had fallen out after Bobo fell off a ladder while decorating the new house on the Giudecca. Nora had rebuked Hélène for letting Bobo do too much, and somehow the quarrel had escalated and Nora hadn't spoken them for several years.

Nora was a talented painter, but now appeared to have given up painting and was working in a shop near *La Fenice*. Anita had gone to visit her there, but no sooner did she walk in than Nora's mother, Ruth, appeared and Nora virtually pushed Anita out of the shop. I like to think that Nora did it to protect Anita from the row that might have ensued if Ruth had realised who she was. I'd had my spats with both of them and sympathised, but although Nora and I had made up, and she'd even been to stay with me and Anthony in London, I felt sure that the inter-vening years had done nothing to soften Ruth's dislike of me. Perhaps she had a point. When the chips were down, Bobo and I had been too slick for her.

* * *

On the day of my divorce, Ronnie Schulman remained silent except to remark plaintively at the end that he'd had absolutely no idea of my (pregnant) condition before the hearing and neither had his client. Afterwards he said goodbye to me in quite a friendly manner and melted away, soon to disappear forever into the depths of the Amazon rainforest, or some equally exotic location.

My decree absolute came through on 25 November 1971 and I changed my surname to Bobo's on 6 December. Bobo cut things even finer. His separation hearing in Venice wasn't until 14 December. I stayed in London. Since I had no legal status in Bobo's life, we were looking for a house that could be put into my name in case anything happened to him before we could marry.

Bobo got his legal separation although Ruth refused to let him backdate it to the day she had actually left him. I was bitterly disappointed that Bobo had given in on this point, but he said that if he hadn't, she would have walked out of the courtroom. His solicitor assured him that when the time came for the divorce (five years after separation under Italian law), it would be easy to prove when she had actually left, and at least there was now nothing she could do to prevent it coming through, and no further need to conceal my pregnancy. Looking back I can sort of understand how galling it must have been for her when she found out I'd had a baby just two months after the separation hearing.

Bobo flew back to London a few days later and we spent a happy Christmas with my mother at Queen's Gate. All the unpleasant symptoms of pregnancy had now passed and I felt happy and well, studying, going for short walks, seeing friends and house-hunting.

We found the house we wanted in January 1972. We got home one afternoon to find an urgent message from our estate agent about a £14,000 house in Bevington Road off Ladbroke Grove. Bobo and I drove straight round to see it, climbing through a window and looking round by candlelight. It was exactly what we had been looking for, a pretty, little end-of-terrace house on three floors with four bedrooms, two bathrooms, a patio garden and a terrace. The street, just off Golborne Road, was considered quite rough at the time, though now, of course, it's tremendously fashionable. Bobo and I were thrilled. When we got home that evening he immediately started drawing up plans.

The only stumbling block was my mother. The plan was that she'd move in with us and that the house would be her home while we were in Venice, though it would be in my name to avoid death duties as well as any attempts by Ruth to have it included in Bobo's estate. My mother was currently renting the large and lovely flat in Queen's Gate that we'd moved into in 1964. We planned that I'd put down the deposit of £3000 by selling some shares my mother had given me, and get a mortgage for the rest, which my mother would pay off, while Bobo would do all the work on the house.

The problem was that for the enterprise to succeed, we all needed each other, and my mother, while seeing the financial sense of the equation, and wanting to help me own my own home, kept getting cold feet at the idea of moving to such a rough area. Now I understand her qualms only too well. Then, however, I thought she was being snobby and ridiculous, as did Bobo, and the situation led to rows and tensions that eventually caused my mother's relationship with Bobo effectively to break down.

Ingo was born on 19 February at the Princess Beatrice Hospital in Finborough Road. It was a terribly easy birth. He was a biggish baby, 7 lbs 13 ozs, but I managed to produce him in only an hour and a half. I stayed in hospital for ten days as was the custom in the 1970s. The nurses taught me how to breast-feed and bath Ingo and kept him in the nursery for the first six nights so my sleep would be unbroken. For several days I was the only mother in the private wing and relished those quiet, solitary mornings alone with Ingo in my room overlooking the

Brompton Cemetery where the juxtaposition of birth and death seemed entirely harmonious.

We completed on the house in March. My mother's doubts had taken second place to her adoration of Ingo, and there was so much work to be done that she knew we wouldn't be moving there for at least a year.

Bobo and I went to Kensington Registry Office together to register Ingo. The surname I put on his birth certificate was Ferruzzi-Balbi. Balbi was Bobo's mother's maiden surname that she'd reverted to after her wartime divorce from her first husband, the father of Ping Ping. She never married Bobo's father and told me that as a contessa in her own right and the last of her line, she was entitled, under Venetian law, to confer her title on her three Ferruzzi sons by passing the name Balbi to them. Thus all three had the surname Ferruzzi-Balbi, which apparently made them counts. For painting purposes Bobo was known solely as Ferruzzi.

Since the whole point of me changing my name to Bobo's was to avoid the sneers on the faces of foreign concierges when we travelled together, I had changed my surname to Ferruzzi-Balbi too. Balbina was delighted. She told me that Ruth 'voleva fare la democratica' and had been known merely as Ferruzzi. Frankly I wasn't displeased by the thought of distancing myself from Ruth in this respect, and actually rather enjoyed being a contessa, even if only a bogus one.

Bobo appeared quite happy when we were with the Registrar, but when we got outside, he blew up about me giving Ingo the surname Balbi and said I was a snob. I didn't think that was fair, when all I wanted was for the three of us to have the same name.

It was the first serious row we'd had since Ingo was born. We drove home from the Registry Office together, then Bobo stormed off. I confided in my mother, who tried to soothe me by saying Bobo was probably frightened because the name Ferruzzi-Balbi could so easily be traced to him if Ruth decided to make trouble. This didn't actually comfort me at all. I'd been led to believe we were safe from any legal repercussions now Bobo had his separation, and the fact that he might be frightened of Ruth merely made me despise him as a coward.

It was in this mood that I went to tea with Felicity Osborne, 'taking Ingo,' as I wrote, 'who had his first historic meeting with Gideon (George), who's now enormous and has four front teeth and a divine smile.' Although I was right about the historic meeting that took place that day, it wasn't the one between Gideon/George and Ingo, but the one between me and Anthony Russell-Roberts who had just moved into the house opposite the Osbornes, and was living on the top floor with his wife while builders gutted the rest of the house. They currently had no hot water, and Anthony'd come over to have a bath.

Flee was busy in the kitchen and left me to entertain Anthony, chaperoned by the presence of the two sleeping babies. I actually found it quite awkward to be talking to a man on my own. Bobo was very jealous, so I had learnt to protect myself from scenes by displaying a sort of outer layer of unavailability. By the time I met Anthony, who was just three years older than me, this outer layer was so well established that I think I must have appeared rather dull. But I do remember thinking how sympathetic and unthreatening Anthony was, and wondering what it would be like to have a young, uncomplicated English husband like him. After that I put him out of my mind and didn't see him again for two years until just after Anita was born.

It seems to me I've written an awful lot already and haven't even got to Anita's birth, but since this book is dedicated to her, I think she'd quite like to know how I met her father and how the situation was between us before she was born. I know I always enjoyed it when my mother told me stories about my father and the fun they had during World War Two. After she died, I found some of his letters to her, addressing her as Dearest Child (he was nine years older than her), and though they were very short and not at all sentimental, I found them all the more poignant for that.

When we got back to Venice in April, I had a nasty shock. My mother was no longer there to help me with Ingo, and Bobo, having previously spent almost every waking hour with me was suddenly, now I had a baby, nowhere to be seen. I wasn't alone, however, since Bobo's mother came to live with us for eight months. She was eighty-three and had been ill during the winter, and it was my idea she should come and stay. If it occurred to me to wonder why none of her other sons invited her, I rationalised that it was impossible for Ping Ping, who was now living with Pino on the top floor of Timothy's palazzo up hundreds of steps. Lillo, as a ship's captain, was away seven months of the year. Ucci had his father's palazzo, but his father's last girlfriend Vittoria, had an apartment there, and Balbina loathed her with a passion.

At first things went well. Balbina took over the running of the house, which suited me since Ingo was still feeding at night and it meant I could go back to sleep with him after the early feed. Problems only occurred later when I tried to resume my former role. Roby and Nora came to stay for a month in June and, to our horror, Bobo's ex-wife Ruth and her paramour José moved into the annexe of our near neighbours the Sacerdottis. Bobo and I tried to avoid them by taking the children on boat trips, but there were inevitable encounters. Ruth found out I was using the name Ferruzzi and told me she was going to sue me, José tried to break into our house, Ruth screamed that I was a *puttana* and Balbina, relishing the excitement of two warring daughters-in-law, tried to play us off against each other. Bobo's reaction was to spend ever longer hours away from home, working on the new studio.

When Bobo and I split up three years later, he blamed his mother for our parting and boycotted her. A friend of ours, an American academic who, I suppose, recognised the dangers of the thwarted creative urge in me, blamed Bobo for not encouraging me to work, but although these were both contributing factors in the demise of our relationship, to my mind the real problem was that Bobo didn't want children with me and that once Ingo was born, he never smiled at me or looked on me with approval again.

The studio was ready for us to move into by November and Bobo held an exhibition there on the 11th, which was a huge success and sell-out. He'd built a bedroom and shower room for Balbina downstairs, but in the event she never lived there. She'd always said that she wanted to go into a retirement home, and a splendid new one was being built on the Riva degli Schiavoni. We heard, whether it was true or not, that even in the home she became a tremendous stirrer and soon had all her contemporaries at each other's throats.

Bobo and I left for London in December. My mother was still at Queen's Gate and the house in Bevington Road, to quote my diary, had 'been used as a dumping ground for rubbish by all the neighbours and has been broken into a few times and has all the pipes cut and people shitting on the floor.' Bobo was about to embark on another epic conversion. He also had his first, highly successful exhibition in London at the Langton Gallery off King's Road, the owner, Rob Stuart, having been introduced to us by two of my dearest friends, David and Sue Hill-Brookes.

I'm not sure exactly when the idea of desperately wanting a second child entered my mind, but some time between the winter of 1972 and the spring of 1973, it became an obsession. I wanted one for Ingo's sake. I saw how he loved watching and playing with other children and I remembered my own loneliness as an only child – not so much when I was small, because I had Dicky to play with but later, after my father and grandmother had died and Dicky and Dorothy had moved and I'd left the safe dullness of Francis Holland and all my old friendships to try and realise my dream of becoming a classical dancer.

I also wanted Ingo to have a sibling so he wouldn't be emotionally dependent on his parents as I had been. My father was forty-seven when I was born and died when I was twelve. Bobo was forty-four when Ingo was born, and although physically extremely fit and young for his years, I'd already tempted fate by allowing an older man to father my child, and didn't want to create another unit of three out of which, if one parent died, half the child's world would be gone.

Bobo refused absolutely to have a second child, so of course my longing intensified. I saw how happy Ingo was to be in London with my mother, and now I owned a property of my own that we would soon be able to live in, I conceived the idea of just going ahead and having the child anyway. Even if Bobo abandoned me, which I didn't think he would, he would be a more than adequate sperm donor. I didn't stop to think that in mentally preparing for a fatherless family unit, I was in fact recreating the one I myself had grown up in. Nor did I think about money. I had my house and I had my mother. I would go out to work and support my children myself.

I determined that my second child would be a girl. There was no particular logic to this, only instinct and the desire to recreate my own childhood only better, by providing my daughter with the older brother I would have liked for myself. I read an article in *Nova* magazine, entitled 'Choosing your Baby's Sex,' and followed it to the letter. So not only did I deceive Bobo into giving me a second child, I also choreographed the event with military precision.

After the hideous events of the previous summer, I'd extracted a promise from Bobo that he wouldn't invite Roby and Nora to stay in 1973. I now see that this was cruel and unreasonable of me, but at the time I felt I was justified and believed in his promise, so was stunned when he called them from London in March and asked them when they were coming to Venice. When I tackled him about it, he said his promise to me had been a forced one and therefore not valid, and stormed off into the night.

Instead of deterring me from my plot, our quarrel made me all the more determined to carry it out. My logic was on the lines of, 'If he's going to be so unfair to me, I'll bloody well be even more unfair to him!' Anita could be extremely argumentative – I used to think she'd make an excellent barrister – and I sometimes wonder if my mood of fury and rebellion at the time of her conception could have had something to do with it.

On 13 March 1973 I wrote in my diary, 'Spent the night in a state of fury, bent on revenge. At 10.15 I went chez Tony (Greenburgh) and had my IUD taken out. I'm going to tell Bobo it must have fallen out (Tony says they sometimes do without anyone knowing). I'm giving him a sporting chance though. If it doesn't work this month, I'll have another put in and think again next year.' (I wanted my child to be a Sagittarian like me, imagining that we'd thus be able to live together in perfect harmony.)

D-day for my plot was 25 March. Bobo and I were in the middle of a quarrel, because he considered I'd been too friendly with an ex-boyfriend of Suzanne's at her twenty-first birthday party the night before. He spent the day working at Bevington Road and, according to my diary, came in at five, extremely moody, 'but I just pretended to ignore it and talked very brightly, as if to a lunatic, which I've discovered is the best way to get him out of it. We had an early night and made up the quarrel. (I had to really, it was D-day for my plot.) I can hardly believe myself capable of such a thing. Now we have to wait and see if it works.'

The short answer is that it did. I was supremely confident that it would and I was right. The pregnancy was confirmed on 29 May and I broke the news to Bobo over lunch with Jim Lee at our favourite *pizzeria* in Gloucester Road. I wanted Jim to be there as a witness because I knew Bobo would take the news badly. It was a sad time for Jim, because his marriage had just broken up, but he managed to be pleased for us, and the fact he was there meant Bobo couldn't behave as badly as he might have otherwise.

After lunch Bobo went back to Bevington Road to work, but called me in the afternoon to say he was going to leave me unless I had an abortion. I remained unmoved and told him he must do whatever he wished. Later he called again to ask me to take his razor and pyjamas to Bevington Road (I used to pick him up there most evenings and drive him home to Queen's Gate). This led to a long discussion during which he told me what a lousy mother I was and criticised me for my calmness over the pregnancy (the time before, he'd criticised me for my hysteria).

I *was* calm. Forewarned is forearmed and in a convoluted way I felt justified over having deceived him because of the cruel and unfair way he'd treated me when I'd found out I was expecting Ingo. I also resolved to tell absolutely everyone we met that I was pregnant so there'd be less danger of him trying to bully me into an abortion.

Bobo finished the house in early June and a friend of my mother's, a maternity nurse from New Zealand called Christine Sloane, moved in soon afterwards so it wouldn't be left unguarded. Bobo, Ingo and I left for Venice on 15 June. The house on Giudecca had now been sold and we were living in the new studio which, though it didn't have a garden, was set back from the canal in a biggish square where Ingo could play with his toys while I sat on the front step and watched him. He soon attracted a group of local boys in their early teens who played with him and looked after him as no English boys would have done, and I was lucky enough to find a circle of English and American girls married to Italians. One of them, Denise Bacci, lived right opposite us and had a son, Gregorio, who was only a little older than Ingo. She told me of a café at a place called Catecumeni which was moderately safe – no canals in sight – where we often used to meet with our children and their toys and bicycles, and sit nursing cups of tea while our *bambini* disported themselves. This circle of friends was a real lifeline to me, and made me less dependent on Bobo who did, however, cheer up a lot once we were back in Venice.

Various friends came to stay that summer including Roby, who arrived without Nora at the end of August, having grown about a foot. He became Bobo's right-hand man, doing everything with him and behaving very sweetly to me and Ingo, who took an enormous fancy to him. My relationship with Bobo improved during this period. There were far fewer quarrels and the tone of my diary occasionally, though not very often, reverted to the affectionate tone that characterised it before my 1971 pregnancy.

On 17 November I departed for London by plane with Ingo for Anita's birth. She was due on 23 December, so I was way past the safe date for flying, but Bobo had swung things with his doctor by giving him a painting in return for a medical certificate. Ingo and I were met by my mother at Heathrow. We took a taxi to the new house which my mother had moved into a month before and turned into a luxurious home. I was thrilled to be back in London and in my very own house with nothing to do but await the arrival of my very much wanted and fought for second child.

*   *   *

We spent about half an hour in the Garden of Remembrance, then went back to Tabitha's for lunch, stopping on the way to buy food at the big Sainsburys on Ladbroke Grove. Tabitha, Juliet and I went in, leaving Anita and the dogs in the car. As well as shopping for lunch, we all had bits and pieces to buy for ourselves, and inevitably the whole process took longer than we'd intended. When we got back, Anita commented on how long we'd been and, to my dismay, another family quarrel ensued. I vainly tried to assert my ever-diminishing authority, but could see our memorial lunch degenerating rapidly before my eyes.

The situation was saved by our timely arrival at John's. He was entirely ignorant of the quarrel, and the need to behave in a civilised manner in front of him enabled us to chat pseudo-amicably while helping him prepare lunch. Soon everything calmed down and we were able to have a pleasant meal after all.

Anita had exchanged contracts on her flat and was in the process of buying one in Warrington Avenue. I was concerned. She'd be taking on a large mortgage, and although she was earning extremely well, she was self-employed and a recession was looming, so the situation could change at any moment. None of us had seen the new flat, but Anita assured us it was enchanting. It was on the second floor and had access to communal gardens, but, unlike her previous flat, there was no outside space for the dogs.

After lunch, Anita called her solicitor, David Goodman. The vendor of the flat in Warrington Avenue was pressing for exchange, but at the same time being evasive about the searches. David advised Anita to visit the property herself and talk to the neighbours. Tabitha offered to lend us her car. Anita, although to my mind a competent driver, had never managed to pass her driving test. She'd bought a licence in Sierra Leone and driven herself around there, but been too law-abiding, or perhaps too cautious, to convert it into a European licence at the end of her stay.

We left at about four with Juliet, who we dropped home on our way. I stayed outside the new flat and walked Petal and Snowy up and down the street while Anita went in. She emerged some time later looking shocked. David's caution had been well founded. She had spoken to one of the people living in the house and discovered that the entire outside of the building was due to be painted that year – a considerable expense that the vendor hadn't bothered to mention to Anita.

At five, she had a commitment at an AA meeting in Portobello Road. She'd been clean for nearly nine years now, and her AA attendance had certainly paid dividends in terms of her looks as well as her social life. I quite envied her the networking side of the programme, and the way the members looked out for each other. When one of the student priests in my parish complained that he'd been in London for a year, and never seen anyone famous, I instantly recommended that he attend a meeting of AA.

I dropped Anita at her meeting and took Tabitha's car back to John's. Juliet was due to move back with me in just five days, and Anita in ten. Sad as I was about Juliet's break-up, I couldn't help feeling excited and happy at the thought that two of my four chickens were coming home to roost.

CHAPTER FOUR

20 May 2009

Anita came home at 8.30 in the evening, having spent the day clearing her flat. Juliet, having moved in five days before, had gone off to visit Anthony in France for a long weekend.

Anita was flushed and excited when she arrived. She'd sold her flat well and was looking forward to the adventure ahead. Kyle, her dog walker, arrived at the same time with Petal and Snowy. He lived in Willesden and didn't normally pick up or deliver dogs to my area, but had made an exception in Anita's case as she was such a good client and would hopefully soon be back in his loop.

He stayed and chatted for a while. Anita was sitting on the sofa and seemed in good spirits, but I noticed she was rubbing her stomach as if it was hurting her. She kept up the movement throughout our conversation, seeming unaware of it, as if she were so used to the pain that she had stopped noticing it. I found it a little embarrassing in front of Kyle.

As soon as he'd gone, I asked her if she'd like a hot water bottle to put on her tummy. She was later to cite this remark of mine as one of the joys of being back home with her mother, and accepted it gratefully and went to bed. She was sleeping in Tabitha's old room, as hers had been converted into a study after she bought her flat, and was presently the dumping ground for her and Juliet's possessions.

My flat, which I bought in 2001, is one of three in an Edwardian house in a quiet street in Pimlico. It's on two floors and has four bedrooms and a paved garden. When I got my divorce settlement, I promised each of my children the sum of £50,000 to put towards a property at the age of twenty-eight. I chose twenty-eight because it's the time of the first Saturn return – the moment when the planet Saturn returns to the place it was in the birth chart at the moment of birth. Most people are gripped by restlessness and dissatisfaction at this time and, lacking self-awareness, project these feelings on the people close to them and seek fundamental changes. I'd never even heard of the Saturn return until I was in my fifties, but when I did, a lot of things fell into place, and I was determined not to give my children their money until they were over the worst of it.

Unfortunately I miscalculated. Both Ingo and Anita left their jobs almost the instant they'd bought their first flats, and a hair-raising period ensued before they found their true vocations. Fortunately neither Tabitha nor Juliet were ready to buy until they were older and their horoscopes had settled down.

Ingo bought his first property – an ex-council flat in Pimlico shared with his friend from Bedales, Bill Nuttall, in 2000 – so by the time I bought my flat, I only had my three daughters at home. After a depressing week looking at duds, I found it in the *Times*. It was being sold privately, and the moment I read the advertisement I knew it was the one. The entrance is on the ground floor, which consists of a sitting room, kitchen, bathroom and bedroom. I decided to give that bedroom to Juliet because she was away at university most of the time, and when she wasn't there it could be used for guests.

Anita, Tabitha and I slept on the lower ground floor, which had three bedrooms and a bathroom. I bagged the front bedroom because it had the most cupboard space, and Anita the back bedroom with French windows on to the garden. It seemed practical to give it to her because she was twenty-seven and planning to buy her own flat the following year. Tabitha was sandwiched into a cosy little room between us. To my surprise and delight, my furniture, inherited from my mother, fitted exactly into the sitting room and my books into the bookshelves as if they'd been ordered by the yard.

When the girls moved out, Anita in 2002, Tabitha so gradually I barely noticed it sometime after and Juliet in 2005 when she took over Anita's flat, the law of nature abhorring a vacuum came into force. Dicky's daughter Clare, who was starting work in the theatre as a wardrobe mistress, came to stay when she had a London run and was an adorable guest, getting me wonderful tickets to all her shows from *Footloose* to *King Lear*. Various friends of friends who needed rooms in London once or twice a week joined the throng, and at the moment I had an old friend from the 1960s, Dr Serge Beddington Behrens, who lived in Gloucestershire and worked a few days a week in London as a psychotherapist. Anita very sportingly agreed to move out of her room and share with me one night a week so Serge could continue his visits.

Shortly after she'd gone to bed that first evening, I heard Anita's Blackberry ring. She came upstairs a few minutes later to tell me that the flat in Warrington Avenue had fallen through. The vendor had got fed up with her (entirely reasonable) delays and gone with another purchaser. She didn't seem unduly cast down, and I, although sad for her, felt secretly relieved, because I had always felt she would be overstretched financially if she took it on.

'You're just going to have to put up with me for a bit longer!' she said good-humouredly.

I assured her truthfully that I always loved having her to stay and that she could remain with me for just as long as she wanted.

*   *   *

Anita was born on Wednesday, 19 December at 2.20 pm in the same room as Ingo in the Princess Beatrice Hospital. She weighed 6 lbs 12 ozs and was the smallest of my babies. This was probably because she was induced. Mr Denny, my gynaecologist, was going away for Christmas and wanted to deliver her before he left. I saw nothing wrong in this. Her due date was 23 December and it would be convenient for me too, and give me time to prepare for Christmas. Later I started to read articles saying it was always better to let a baby come to full term, and now I torture myself with the thought that if she had, her destiny might have been completely different. At the very least, she wouldn't have been born under the angry Scorpio moon that at times made her so disapproving of her mother!

I was given a general anaesthetic at 9.30 am, and woke an hour later feeling very sleepy. My membranes had been ruptured, a drip put in my hand and an epidural in my back. Mr Denny went off to St Stephen's Hospital down the road, and my anaesthetist, Dr Wiggins, to get his hair cut. I didn't think much of being abandoned, wired up to the bed. The Sister in charge of the delivery, who I'd previously thought of as an ally, was very stingy about topping up the epidural and actually uttered the horrible sentence, 'I'd *never* have an epidural – I know too much about all the things that can go wrong!'

Anita had a talent for one-liners, and if she'd been old enough to do so, I'm sure she'd have thought of a suitably crushing retort. I was merely stunned by the inappropriateness of the remark and remained silent and too stoned by all the drugs they'd given me to really care. About 1 pm I started feeling a horrible pain in my pelvis. Mr Denny and Dr Wiggins were back by now, and discussed the phenomenon across me as if at a medical seminar. It turned out that the baby's head was rounding the bend and pressing on a nerve, and that the epidural had no effect on this, even though I could feel no pain anywhere else. It was quite hellish and lasted a good hour. I began to feel very disillusioned with epidurals in general, but Mr Wiggins told me kindly that without one I'd be climbing up the walls.

I was eventually given another injection. Whatever it was, it worked. The pain passed and I was into the second stage of labour which took just twenty minutes, with no pain to speak of but just enough feeling to be able to push. They told me the baby was a girl and I felt full of joy at having created my dream child and of gratitude to Bobo for having supported me, however unwillingly, and for being with me now. This mood continued for the rest of the day as I drifted in and out of sleep. Anita was whisked away to the night nursery and I didn't really get a chance to meet her properly until the following morning when I fed her for the first time.

She was a very neat looking baby with delicate features, lots of black hair and a composed manner like a little queen. When she was put into my arms for the first time, I remember thinking, 'You're going to be all right,' which I'd remind her of during stormy periods of her life as a reassurance to us both that things would get better.

I was allowed home the following day, forty-eight hours after delivery. Now this doesn't seem at all remarkable, but for the 1970s it was quite brave. Chris Sloane, the maternity nurse who was living at Bevington Road, was standing by to help me – a good thing as Anita was slightly jaundiced and still didn't have a name.

Bobo chose the name Anita, saying as justification that all the Anitas he'd ever known had been beautiful. I wasn't too happy at the thought of all the beautiful Anitas Bobo had known. Before meeting Ruth, he'd spent three years in Oslo, where he apparently enjoyed dalliances with a number of Scandinavian ladies, but somehow the name Anita didn't go away. I liked the idea of having a beautiful daughter, as indeed she turned out to be, it went well with the surname Ferruzzi, it was the only name on our shortlist that Ingo could say and, above all, once we'd known her for a few days, we felt it suited her, so Anita she became.

After our row over Ingo's surname and because Bobo had dropped the surname Balbi on his new passport, and was now registered simply as Roberto Ferruzzi, I decided to, as I thought, please him and register Anita simply as Ferruzzi. Imagine my distress when we came out of the Registry Office and Bobo told me I should have registered her as Ferruzzi-Balbi. It sounds immensely trivial now, but he upset me so much that I cried all the way home.

Although I didn't realise it at first because I had a string of helpers, I discovered when we got back to Venice that having two children is very different from having one. With one child, it's possible to make him fit into your routine and take him more or less anywhere. With two, it isn't. A children's routine has to be set up and the parents have to fit in with that.

This wasn't apparent immediately. Chris was a wonderful maternity nurse and kept Anita immaculately turned out with the exquisite little black nighties I'd bought her at Biba beautifully ironed and her black hair brushed silkily to one side. Standards slipped a little on Chris's day off and, at the risk of sounding like Marie-Antoinette, I'd like to say what an excellent investment it is to have a maternity nurse for the first six weeks of a baby's life.

Anita used to get very restless after the ten o'clock feed. I'm not sure if it was wind or hunger, but she'd draw her little legs up and cry pitifully while I alternately fed her, winded her, walked her round the room on my shoulder singing, or rocked her in her pram. I was even desperate enough to push her through the streets in her pram at midnight to try and soothe her, but was frightened off by running into a very alarming-looking man clad in black leather with a shaven head and tattoos, who sent me scuttling, terrified, back home. Our neighbours, who belonged to an Indian religious sect, and who had become good friends, assured me he was harmless, but even so I didn't venture out again at that time.

I bought a second-hand mini for the months we were to stay in England from a company called Portobello Mini Hire. It was an unmitigated disaster, constantly breaking down so that

Bobo or a kind passer-by would have to give me a push to get me started again. The car once broke down at 2 am on the Harrow Road when Bobo and I were driving Anita round to try and settle her after her late feed. This meant that Bobo, who didn't drive, had to take her home by taxi, while I waited for the AA. It was a horrible experience that put me off second-hand cars for ever.

Finally I took Dr Spock's advice and let Anita cry herself to sleep after the late feed. True to his prediction, it took half an hour the first night, ten minutes the second and no time at all thereafter. We were all much happier as a result, but naturally I felt like an axe murderer for the two nights the crying lasted.

I met Anthony again at a dinner party at Flee and Peter's in February. Once again, he wasn't accompanied by his wife, and once again I found him very pleasant and easy to talk to. All my diary says is, 'There were nine of us altogether and all the people I talked to were very nice and interesting,' showing that in spite of the all too frequent flare-ups with Bobo, adultery was the last thing on my mind. I now had my perfect little family and still hoped and intended that Bobo and I would marry and live happily ever after.

I can't remember when the subject of Bobo having a vasectomy was broached. Certainly it was I who suggested it – I don't think it was legal in Italy – but Bobo was instantly enthusiastic about the idea. I'd never have pushed it if he hadn't been. It seemed only fair to me that since he was forty-six and already had four children, and was adamant he didn't want any more, and since I was twenty-seven and faced another twenty years or so of invasive contraception just so I could be sexually available on demand, that he should be the one to take care of contraception for a change. He had the operation in March. I dropped him in Harley Street as a day patient, then took the children on to Regent's Park. The whole thing only took about half an hour, and he was given tea and biscuits afterwards, in the best English tradition.

I took Ingo and Anita back to Venice in April 1974. Bobo had gone ahead to spend time in Paris and break the news of Anita's birth to Roby and Nora. He and I had been getting on pretty well – too exhausted to do otherwise perhaps – and when he left I wrote, 'Poor Bobo. He's a truly kind, good man and he's had such an awful life with that terrible woman for all those years, turning the children against him etc., and he's really so kind and simple when you get to know him. Anyway, he's my Bobo and I love him.'

I was accompanied on my journey by an Irish girl called Marie O'Connor, who'd taken on the job of au pair with us until Christmas. She came through an agency called Universal Aunts, who always seemed to have lovely people on their books. She was only seventeen, but had experience looking after children and, I think, became genuinely fond of them. Ingo was rather cheeky and uppish with her and once, when he was out with her and Anita, ran off very naughtily in the street and came home on his own. Anita, however, loved her dearly.

One nice thing that happened just after we got back to Venice was being invited to *La Fenice* Opera House by Bobo's lawyer, Augusto Salvadori, to see Verdi's *Un Ballo in Maschera*. My experience of opera had been strictly limited until then, but Verdi was to change all that. We battled to get the children to bed by seven, left the studio about ten minutes before the performance was due to start, and scrambled into Augusto's very grand seats – a central box in the Dress Circle – with seconds to spare, Within minutes I was transported into a world of enchantment by the first tenor aria, *'La rivedrò con estasi,'* which I found myself humming incessantly the following day. One of the great joys of Verdi's scores is that you can sing along to them almost instantly. The Royal Opera House has cottoned on to this, and Friends of Covent Garden can now attend a sing-along *Traviata* in one of the studio theatres.

This was the start of a great passion for opera, which led me to book tickets for every opera going when we returned to London. Bobo accompanied me without much enthusiasm. He'd already seen most of them, didn't like Puccini and said he really preferred to listen to recordings at home, since there were always imperfections in a live performance. At the time, I thought he was just being an old stick in the mud, but now I understand far better and sort of agree with him, though in my case it's more that once you've seen what you consider to be the definitive performance of an opera (or ballet, play or film for that matter), subsequent performances can only be an anticlimax.

In May there was a referendum on divorce. Marie and my new English friends had no idea that Bobo and I weren't married, so although I was full of apprehension about our future together, I couldn't say a word to anyone. Remember I had no status in Italy beyond my model's looks and the fact that I was under Bobo's protection. I didn't even have the right to work there. Now that we're all Europeans and Italians have been divorcing each other merrily for forty years or more, my situation in the 1970s seems so remote as to be virtually incredible, but it was very real at the time. Fortunately the suspense didn't last long. The pro divorce lobby was always in the lead, and by 10 pm on Monday 13 May 1974 the news finally came through that they'd won and that the divorce law would remain. Bobo and I were at our favourite restaurant Montin with our friends the German novelist Erwin Behrendt and his companion Helga. There was nothing in it for them, but they sweetly shared in our relief and the bottle of champagne we ordered to celebrate our victory.

In June we rented an apartment in a village called Ca'Savio, an hour's commute from Venice – we took the boat from San Zaccaria to Punta Sabbione – and just five minutes from an unspoilt sandy beach with little straw huts to shade one from the sun. Traditionally Venetians leave the city in the summer to spend a month at the sea and a month in the mountains, but all we'd ever managed in the past was a few days in the Dolomites because of Bobo's work. He needed to be in Venice in the summer because that was when foreigners came and bought his paintings. He'd also acquired a shop or *Galleria* near the Fenice Theatre, which he disappeared to in the mornings, reappearing briefly at lunchtime, and then again when the children were safely in bed.

Ca'Savio was perfect because it was completely rural and yet near enough to Venice for Bobo to commute there every day. Bobo hated the sophisticated beaches on the Lido with their luxurious *cabane*, whereas I secretly loved them, but I knew better than to ask him to accompany me there.

It was a very happy month. Marie and I hired bicycles and took the children to the beach every day, which they both loved. Anita was weaned there and developed a huge appetite, though always remaining slim and pretty, with neat, delicate features. Gradually her black hair grew out and she eventually became flaxen blonde. It was a summer for reconciliation. The children and I visited Balbina regularly and Nora accompanied Roby to Venice in early August (we were given two days' notice of their arrival) and stayed with us for six weeks. My mother had arranged to come at the same time and was renting a neighbour's spare room round the corner from us, where Balbina had stayed after her illness in 1972, so I didn't feel too outnumbered. Nora seemed fairly disenchanted with her mother that year and made great efforts to please me and was, in fact, very good company.

It was also during this summer that three incidents occurred which convinced me my relationship with Bobo was ultimately doomed. It wasn't a decision, more a premonition, or, to mis-quote Wordsworth, an intimation of mortality. It was the last thing I wanted or expected to feel, and left me very sad.

The first occurred in August during the children's visit. Bobo was meeting some antique dealers I didn't particularly like for dinner and took Roby and Nora with him. I stayed home with Ingo, Anita and Marie, reading the newspapers. I was just going downstairs to get some food when Nora came in and went to sleep on the downstairs sofa near the kitchen. I didn't like to disturb her by starting to cook, so walked to the Zattere hoping to get a snack at one of the cafés. I found Bobo and the two dealers eating an ice cream, but nothing more substantial was available, so I left them there saying I'd try Montin – a five-minute walk away. Their kitchen was closed too. They told me the only places open at that time were Harry's Bar or Rialto. I went to Piazza San Barnaba to check there was nothing there and saw the boat for Rialto approaching, so ran and caught it and found a little restaurant near the bridge where I was able to get a pizza. I only stayed there for about forty minutes, but had to wait for a boat home where I arrived about 12.30. Bobo had sent Marie to bed and gone out looking for me, which I thought was very irresponsible of him. He came in soon after, incoherent with rage, saying I'd done it to humiliate him. He told me to go back to London and take *my* children with me, then stormed out and stayed out all night.

The second incident took place in October. Marie and I went into the Fenice Bar near Bobo's gallery with the children, and the vile old hag at the counter shouted at us to shut the door and then complained that we'd left Ingo's bike outside and it was blocking the entrance. Obviously she took us for tourists and thought she could be as rude to us as she liked, whereas Bobo was a regular customer and often took clients in there. We left and walked to the gallery where I recounted my tale of woe and asked Bobo to go to the bar and tick the woman off, which he refused absolutely to do.

Both these incidents, when recounted now, seem trivial. I can see that Bobo must have been worried about me on the night of my Rialto excursion, and spoken in haste. If I'd known it was going to take me so long to get a pizza, I'd never have gone out in the first place, but it was the phrase '*your* children' that so upset me. Re the café, Bobo and I'd had a quarrel earlier so he probably felt disinclined to take up the cudgels for me, and may well have had a quiet word with the hag proprietress later. Certainly I never had any further trouble with her, though I can't actually remember if I ever went back there.

The third incident was the one that finished me off, even though looking back it was largely my fault for not being assertive. My birthday has always meant a lot to me. With small children in tow, it was for years the only chance I had to feel pampered and special. My mother was always brilliant at birthdays. I think Aries women have a particular talent for choosing presents, and it became a tradition that Bobo and I would travel back to England each year in time for my birthday, so that I could be pampered, if not by him, at least by her.

I don't know why it became so important to Bobo to break with this tradition. He and my mother didn't get on well, so perhaps he was jealous of the fact that she was so important to me, or perhaps he just wanted to exert his power over me. He started to say what a bourgeois tradition it was to celebrate one's birthday, and how ridiculous it was of me to mind whether I travelled to England on 12 December or a few days later. Instead of standing up for myself and what was, after all, a perfectly harmless pleasure, I gave in to pressure, probably determined to show I wasn't petty or bourgeois, and agreed that we'd spend my twenty-eighth birthday in Paris and cross to London a few days later.

We stayed in the Hotel Novelty, a scruffy establishment in the Sixth Arrondissement that Bobo'd discovered shortly before meeting me and that I, in the first flush of love, had kidded myself I liked for its no-frills, student-type accommodation. Having once accepted to stay there, I felt I would lose face by admitting I found it distinctly grotty and not very clean. Ucci booked in there once on Bobo's recommendation, only to leave immediately he saw it. When I heard about this, it only increased my dissatisfaction.

On 9 December, Ingo was sick twice in the tiny bedroom we were sharing with Bobo and Anita. In the morning we called a doctor from the emergency service who diagnosed a throat infection and prescribed antibiotics. I asked Bobo if we couldn't leave immediately for England before we all got sick, but he said I only wanted to leave so I could be back in England for my birthday and threatened that if we left the next day he would come back alone for two weeks in January. I was too unassertive and in-articulate to point out that that in this case my wishes coincided with common sense, and accept with joy his offer of two weeks alone in London in January, and so we stayed on in Paris.

That night Anita developed a cough, so we decided to keep both children in all day. By afternoon they were squabbling and grizzling non-stop, and when I put Anita down for her nap in Marie's room, my back gave way, which meant I didn't sleep all night. The following day was my birthday. Bobo tried to be nice by taking Ingo out to buy me a cardigan I'd admired in a shop, but by now it was too late. Anita woke from her nap with a temperature, the emergency doctor was called again, and pre-scribed a whole new batch of medicines and said she must stay in for two days, which put paid to all our plans. Actually the virus made poor Anita very drowsy and quiet, so she was no trouble at all, but Ingo's outing with Bobo brought on a terrible cough. I lay awake all night listening to it, counting the seconds between coughs and never getting above sixty.

My thoughts that night were very bitter. I felt that if we'd gone back to London two days before, we might have escaped the epidemic that sleeping four to a room had brought on. I'd noticed in the past that a change of air often seemed to cure childhood illnesses (as indeed happened when we finally got back to London) and bitterly resented the fact that I was spending my birthday in a cheap hotel room rather than with my mother in my own beautiful house, purely so Bobo could demonstrate his authority over me.

I knew that night that my relationship with Bobo was doomed. I felt that if he loved or valued me and the children, he wouldn't have put us all through such an unnecessary ordeal, and if, as I was now convinced, he didn't, then it would be irreparably damaging for all of us to remain with him. I also felt that if we were to separate, it would be better to do so when the children were small and less likely to remember and be harmed by it.

I now think I was half right. I think Bobo *did* love us, but was only capable of expressing his love through extreme disapproval. My eureka moment came in the 1980s when I was studying Malory at university and my tutor pointed out that while we *knew* the relationship between Lancelot and Guinevere was a great love, all we ever saw was them quarrelling. I immediately thought of Bobo towards the end of our time together, watching me make an entrance in a new outfit that suited me and gazing at me for an unguarded moment full of admiration, then remembering he was angry with me and turning away sulkily. As far as damaging the children was concerned, I think that Anita was actually more harmed by our break-up than Ingo, because she was too young to remember how difficult Bobo could be, and romanticised him and our life in Venice to an unrealistic degree.

Anthony was just the opposite of Bobo. He was always charming, especially when trying to persuade me to do something I didn't want, and always careful to praise my appearance and my achievements. Even though he probably loved and valued me less than Bobo did, he put on a much better show of doing so, and made life so much more pleasant in comparison, that I was lulled into staying with him for twenty years, only to be shocked and confounded when, after unlimited protestations of love for me and the children, he walked out on us all to be with a woman he'd met three times.

Both Ucci and Anita told me that Bobo was completely devastated when I left him. I didn't want to believe this. I pointed out that he'd met Hélène within months of me leaving and was very happy with her, but they both insisted it was so. I was inclined to believe Ucci more than Anita, because he was such a cynic and far less likely to romanticise the situation unless he truly believed it.

Whatever the truth of the matter, I did take enough notice of what they both said to apologise to Bobo at the end. I'd always told myself that I could forgive Anthony if he'd apologise to me, and finally realised that if I felt like that about Anthony, it might well be the case that Bobo felt like that about me. So after Anita was diagnosed with cancer, before the biopsy but after the CAT scan, and flew to Venice the following day as planned, I accompanied her to Gatwick, taking with me a card that I planned to write to Bobo on the train, apologising for the way I'd treated him thirty-four years before.

Anita was thrilled with the idea. Sitting on the train with her, the card burning a hole in my handbag, I felt suddenly overcome by embarrassment. I couldn't think what to write, and rather hoped the idea would be quietly forgotten. Anita didn't forget, though. She urged me to get started, and so I did, sitting on the crowded train with only the limited space of the card available to put right the wrongs of thirty-four years. I can't remember what I wrote. I know the phrase 'Saturn return' came into it ('The fault, dear Brutus, lies not in ourselves but in our stars'). Actually, if you study Shakespeare, you'll see that his characters mock soothsayers and astrologers at their peril. Hélène was interested in astrology, and I knew she'd be able to explain the reference to Bobo if he didn't understand it. I wasn't prepared to take all the blame, but I knew that the awful restlessness and dissatisfaction I was suffering from in 1975 had less to do with Bobo than with my age at the time, and that I behaved very badly at the end of our relationship. I think and hope that I expressed that. I ended by telling Bobo that he'd been a good husband and father. This was at least partly true. He'd certainly been wonderful to me before we had children, and had become a very good father as the children got older, even though he'd been impatient with them when they were little.

I let Anita read the card after I'd written it, and her little face glowed with happiness, so I felt that even if I'd been lying through my teeth when I wrote it, which I wasn't, it would all have been worthwhile.

Amazingly it took only a few days from my apology to Bobo for me to get my apology from Anthony. He was on his way to visit Anita and we ran into each other in the street outside my flat. When he said he was sorry for leaving me, my jaw dropped and my eyes filled with tears. This was the moment I'd been waiting fourteen years for, but now it had come, I was hardly able to feel anything because Anita's illness overshadowed everything else.

Back in 1974, we didn't make it to London for my birthday, but at least we made it for Anita's. She slept all morning, while I rushed around running errands, then we had a tea party with Felicity Osborne, Gideon/George and his younger brother Ben. Marie, back home with her parents, dropped by with a very pretty dress for Anita and everyone said she was the image of Ingo, and both the image of me. Flee invited Bobo and me to join her and Peter for New Year's Eve at a Chinese restaurant in Soho. There were going to be six of us in all. The other two were a friend of hers called Sophie and Anthony Russell-Roberts, who was newly divorced, but still living in the house opposite the Osbornes at number 8 Kildare Gardens.

CHAPTER FIVE

21 – 26 May 2009

In the days after Anita moved back home, I was both horrified by her work schedule and concerned about her stomach pains. Her working day generally started with a private pupil at 7 am, which entailed leaving my flat at 6. Petal and Snowy weren't too happy about this, so I brought them into my room in their basket and we all dozed off again until I got up at 7 to get ready for Berlitz.

The summer months at Berlitz were far busier than the winter ones, and my schedule was beginning to hot up, so I often didn't get home till after six. Anita was usually able to pop back in the middle of the day to exercise the dogs, then taught again in the evenings and usually went straight to bed afterwards at about 9.30. She'd caught on to the hot water bottle idea in a big way, and though I was pleased that for once one of my children was heeding my advice, I was also increasingly worried by her constant stomach pains, which she told me had started soon after Bobo's cancer diagnosis.

Saturday was her only day off, and I persuaded her to see a doctor. We were in jubilant mood. Victoria'd had her five-month scan the day before. All was well and the baby was a boy. It was a long-standing joke in the family that Ingo had longed for a brother. When Juliet was born and Anthony told Ingo he had a third sister, he asked if we couldn't 'Dress her up in boy's clothes and tell people she was a boy.' His sisters teased him mercilessly about this, but we were all delighted for him when Max was born, and were sure a second son would compound his joy.

When I urged Anita to see a doctor, I had no thoughts of cancer. I was thinking of her appendix, since we have a tradition of problematic ones in the family. My mother nearly died from a burst appendix in her twenties, and I suffered regular, crippling stomach pains until I was nineteen, when I had my appendix removed privately by Philip Paton Philip and never had a stomach ache again. Ingo also had his appendix removed by Mr Paton Philip at the age of eight. In both our cases, as in my mother's, doctors had dismissed our fears. This was because all three of our appendixes were located much higher in the torso than is usual, so that a rudimentary examination of the area had revealed nothing out of the ordinary.

Anita was now between doctors, so I suggested she went to the private medical clinic in Victoria Station where the charge was reasonable and the service quick and efficient.

She went in the early afternoon. The doctor thought she might have a pre-ulcerous condition brought on by stress (Bobo's illness, moving, overwork) and prescribed a drug called Lanso-prazole. That evening I went to Saturday Mass and for a drink with my friends. I got home about nine and Anita went to bed shortly afterwards. I didn't find her tiredness alarming. To my mind it was easily explained by her early morning starts and long working days.

The following morning, Anita taught a class at the RAC Club and got home about two. I was lying in the garden sunbathing with the dogs and newspapers, and she came out and joined me saying she was feeling better. She'd taken one dose of Lanso-prazole, and also some Aloe Vera. We both had an afternoon nap, and when Anita woke she was overcome by nausea. We looked up Lansoprazole on the internet. It seemed to have some very nasty side effects, so we called NHS Direct, who advised her not to take any more but to try Paracetamol instead, which seemed to help a bit.

The next day was Bank Holiday Monday. Anita had cancelled

all her pupils but seemed in good spirits although tired. She ate a slice of cake for tea and her stomach, which had been feeling better, started cramping again. On Tuesday she went to see Dr Ali of the Integrated Medical Centre. He'd helped her when she was twenty-one and suffered whiplash after a car accident. He said Anita was suffering from candida. He gave her a stomach massage and recommended a colonic irrigation, which caused us to giggle nervously. Although Dr Ali failed to diagnose her cancer, as I think anyone would have done without the aid of a scanner because of her apparent radiant health, I believe that the two colonic irrigations she had at his clinic probably helped rather than harmed her condition.

Anita told me the stomach massage had made her feel better. Once again, I went to bed feeling reassured. It was impossible to believe there could be anything seriously wrong with Anita. Apart from a couple of childhood illnesses, she'd enjoyed robust good health since having her tonsils removed at the age of six.

*   *   *

I recognise the notebook that my 1975 diary's written in without looking inside because it has a great rip in the cover where Bobo tried to tear it in half after reading about my affair with Anthony. This was towards the end of the year. At the beginning things still seemed fairly normal. The New Year dinner with the Osbornes and Anthony wasn't particularly successful. The menu at the Chinese restaurant was hopeless for vegetarians, and Saturn was gnawing at me again and making me feel boring, unattractive, inadequate and that my life was over.

Things improved a bit in the spring. Anita started walking at the beginning of February, and I got tickets for everything I possibly could at the Royal Opera House and London Coliseum. Bobo had his own studio in the house, a kiln to make ceramics and the proximity of the auction houses. We ought to have been happy, but somehow we weren't.

Bobo's moods were particularly black that winter. It seemed to me that he was always complaining. I began to wonder if the vasectomy could somehow have affected him psychologically and read articles about the unknown health risks associated with the procedure, which made me feel extremely guilty for having suggested it. As we know, Bobo went on to have a long and happy life, so I hope and trust that it had no long-lasting implications on his health.

In the early hours of 16 February 1975, the day Bobo was to die thirty-five years later, Anita, who I'd taken into our bed around 5 am because she had a temperature and was very restless, stood up and then fell across me and started gasping for breath like a fish out of water. I called an ambulance and we were taken to our nearest hospital, St Charles's, which at that time didn't have a very good reputation. When I mentioned this to the ambulance driver, his chilling reply was, 'Let's put it this way, I wouldn't let a child of mine go there!' Our first impression, however, was favourable. Anita was examined promptly and we were sent home. They told us she'd had a febrile convulsion and that although they were terrifying to watch, they were quite common in children aged between one and two. My mother told me that I'd had one myself when I was sixteen months old. The only advice the hospital gave us was to give Anita Junior Disprin, and she seemed to make a remarkable recovery, playing and laughing with Ingo and her cousin Barnaba who'd arrived in London the day before.

I'd always believed that a child with a fever should be wrapped up warmly and allowed to sweat it out. The doctor at St Charles's hadn't told me anything to the contrary, so that evening I put Anita to bed in a woolly all-in-one from Mothercare, and the poor little thing had another convulsion at 2 am. This time we drove her to hospital ourselves. We went to St Stephen's, Fulham Road, who couldn't admit her because they didn't have a children's ward, but arranged for her to be sent to Charing

Cross Hospital by ambulance. Bobo accompanied her, and I followed in our car. They decided to keep her there until her temperature returned to normal. She was taken to the children's ward and stripped down to her nappy. The staff pointed an electric fan at her and started sponging her with cold water, which upset her so much that she had another convulsion. (Later my mother devised a method of getting her to play with cool water when she had a fever, so she effectively sponged herself, which was far less traumatic.) After that she was given a bone marrow test for meningitis, which was mercifully negative, dosed with aspirin, antibiotic and sedative, and finally managed to sleep, with me on a camp bed beside her. She remained in hospital for three nights, and was allowed out for Ingo's third birthday. She was put on the anti-convulsant, Phenytone, for a year.

At first no side effects were apparent, and Anita seemed back to her old self – playing and fighting with Ingo like two little dogs. I have to say that my master plan of providing a companion for Ingo to play with hadn't really worked, since for the first eighteen months of Anita's life, they did nothing but fight. Anita's first word was, 'Mia!' which means 'Mine!' in Italian and was no doubt a response to Ingo snatching her toys.

Shortly after leaving hospital, Anita started to become very restless and disturbed at night, with periods of being worryingly limp and languid. Worst of all, she stopped walking, although she continued to pull herself up into standing position in her cot. She had an EEG at Charing Cross Hospital in February and an assessment in March at which it was decided to take her off the Phenytone. Blood tests showed that the dose she had been put on was far too high, and that the symptoms that were worrying me so much were equivalent to extreme drunkenness.

Although it was a great relief to take her off Phenytone, it also felt like an awesome responsibility. Although febrile convulsions are rare after the age of two, they can continue up to the age of five. I'd lost an awful lot of confidence in myself as a mother and felt I wouldn't have a quiet moment for the next four years. Taking her off Phenytone wasn't straightforward either. She perked up immediately and started walking again, but three days later seemed to suffer a nervous reaction, trembling for no apparent reason and spending her days either sleeping or clinging to me and crying. I realise now that the poor little girl was going through the equivalent of a cold turkey detox and think it would have been more responsible of the doctors to give me some warning and advise me to take her off the drug gradually rather than all at once.

Some years later, I embarked on one of those writing courses that promise your money back if you haven't earned it through writing by the time you finish. The way they get you is by dragging the course on interminably so that nobody ever does. I was no exception, but I did write an article about Anita's convulsions which I sent, at my tutor's direction, to *Mother and Baby* magazine, who published it without changing a word. Apart from a book review for an American magazine, this was the first thing I ever had published. I'd always wanted to be a writer, and it was thanks to Anita that I finally found a way to begin.

In March Anita developed another high temperature, which we managed to bring down successfully with sponging and Junior Disprin. Having been very supportive when she was in hospital, Bobo started to argue with me again about what Anita should wear when she had a fever. I was for following the doctors' advice and keeping her in nothing but a nappy, but Bobo maintained she'd catch pneumonia if we didn't at least put a vest on her. My diary entry at the end of March lists one such altercation. At the end I wrote, 'I'm feeling very depressed at the moment. Our relationship is bad. I dread Venice.'

In April we went to dinner with the Osbornes at the Standard, Westbourne Grove, our favourite Indian restaurant. Anthony, who we hadn't seen since New Year's Eve, was also there and spent most of the evening talking to me. 'Nice evening,' I wrote in my diary. 'Found myself rather fancying A.'

What strikes me reading through my diary is how very adolescent my attitude was. I went to tea with Felicity on 6 May and must have confided in her because, 'she said she'll fix up a foursome with Anthony next week,' (when Bobo was going to Paris). It reads exactly as if I were young, free and single. I suppose that technically I was young (twenty-eight), though Saturn was making me feel extremely old and careworn, and certainly I was single (as in unmarried, which I have to say, still rankled), but by no means could I have been described as free.

The dinner with the Osbornes and Anthony was at Kalamaras Restaurant in Inverness Mews. Anthony told me about his desire to change careers and work in the arts. His uncle was the famous choreographer, Frederick Ashton, but his father, who had recently died, had been very anti the world of theatre. Now he was gone, Anthony was determined to change his life.

At 10.30 he mentioned that there was a midnight gala at the Royal Opera House and asked if I'd like to go. I longed to, but protested that I couldn't because I was wearing jeans. Anthony overruled me. Obviously I didn't protest enough. And in fact I was looking reasonably smart, having made a great effort to look good for my first date in years.

Nothing happened that evening, but then Felicity told Anthony of my feelings for him, even though I had expressly asked her not to, and it did. I confessed to Bobo and made two trips to Venice, ricocheting between him and Anthony. Anita had a fourth and last convulsion in June, which compounded the hideousness of the situation, and I was persuaded, against my will, to put her on 30 mg of Phenobarbitone a day.

In September I discovered that Bobo, too, was having an affair, and it became clear that our relationship couldn't be repaired. I returned to London and Anthony. Felicity's mother, the artist Clarisse Loxton-Peacock, advised me not to marry him because she thought he was the sort of man who would fall in love with someone else after twenty years and run off with her, but I was in the grip of a powerful infatuation and ignored her advice. Anthony and I married in Paddington Registry Office on 12 December 1975. For our honeymoon we went to Marsh Barn, Anthony's cottage in Norfolk, with Ingo and Anita.

CHAPTER SIX

31 May 2009

Just as Mother's Day was the moment when everything started
to go wrong, 31 May was the last time that everything appeared
to be going right for us as a family. Anita'd had her colonic
irrigation and was feeling better, and we were all gathered in the
garden of Ingo and Victoria's house for Sunday lunch.

I'm very fond of my own garden, which is tiny and paved and
perfectly adequate as somewhere to sunbathe and read, but Ingo
and Victoria's is something else. They moved there just after
Max was born and when I visited them for the first time I was
enchanted by my first glimpse of the sunny expanse of lawn and
well-established plants. There was even a vine growing round
the French windows, complete with bird's nest. At that moment
I felt so proud of Ingo. He'd achieved it all: lovely wife, beautiful
baby and the perfect home for them all to live in.

These feelings returned on the day of the lunch, directed
towards all my children. Anita was in good spirits, regaling us
with tales of her treatments, and looking radiant. Tabitha and
John, recently returned from a holiday in France, were bronzed
and well and assisting capably with the new barbecue. Juliet,
who had also been in France, was looking brown and beautiful
and seemed in excellent form. Her friends were rallying round
after her separation, and she was inundated with invitations.

Victoria had gone back to work part time, and I looked after
Max on Tuesdays. Sometimes, sitting in the garden with him,
I'd get the feeling of being fully present, at one with nature and
full of a sort of ecstasy of joy and love for the little boy beside

me. I had the same feeling that Sunday. This was my beloved family. The long years of being a full-time mother stroke drudge had paid off, as had the struggle I'd had to keep them all – and myself – on the rails after Anthony's departure. Now I was witnessing the fruits of my labour in the shape of my four clever, beautiful and successful children.

*   *   *

While I was trying, unsuccessfully, to salvage my relationship with Bobo in the summer of 1975, Anthony achieved his ambition of working in the arts. He was offered the role of Assistant Stage Manager at Glyndebourne Festival Opera for the 1976 season. Sometimes, when he was working backstage in jeans during the festival, he ran into old friends from Eton in their dinner jackets, who gaped at him in astonishment. When he explained what he was doing, they looked at him admiringly and exclaimed, 'Good for you! I'd love to do something like that for a year or so.'

The job signified a huge salary drop for Anthony, and I used to joke that I'd fallen in love with him when he was rich, but been lumbered with him now he was poor. I was still supremely unworldly however and certain the universe would provide as it always had before.

In June 1976, I sold the house in Bevington Road and paid off Anthony's mortgages in return for a half-share of his house in Kildare Gardens. My mother was given the use of the self-contained garden flat for life. This was wonderful for me and the children and by no means a bad deal for Anthony, who acquired someone he could trust to look after the house in our absence and unlimited baby-sitting on demand.

Anthony's mother Edith had married Harold Grenfell, a former neighbour from Norfolk, and lived with him in some style at Clobemon Hall in Ireland. I met them soon after our wedding. Edith and Harold were staying at the Ritz, and invited us to dinner. Edith met us in the reception area. She was sitting on a sofa in a very chic black, sleeveless dress with a full pleated skirt, which was spread out around her. After a few minutes' conversation, she reached under the pleats and produced a jewel box containing a beautiful ruby and diamond ring, which she gave me and which fitted me perfectly. Anthony said afterwards that she was waiting to see if she liked me before giving me the ring. I've no idea if that was true or not, but I loved Edith instantly, and I don't think we ever exchanged a cross word during the fifteen years until her death in 1990.

I met the legendary Frederick Ashton soon afterwards at a Christmas party given by John and Anya Sainsbury for the luminaries of the ballet world. Everyone was so nice and kind to me that I quite forgot to be shy. Fred simply held out his arms and said, 'Welcome to the family!' Wayne Sleep was the only person to say what everyone else was probably thinking. I was wearing a loose-fitting, vintage red velvet dress from Hindu Kush, our favourite shop on Portobello Road, and he immediately exclaimed, 'You're pregnant!' and put out his hand to feel my stomach. For once I wasn't guilty, and enjoyed confounding expectations.

In April we moved to Sussex for the start of the Glyndebourne rehearsal period. We rented a three-bedroomed farm cottage near Ringmer, with a pretty garden and vegetable patch, for five pounds a week. The children loved it instantly. I enrolled them at a nursery school in Lewes for the summer term. Ingo was now four and Anita two and a quarter. Anthony used to drop them there in the mornings on his way to work, and I'd pick them up at lunchtime. Because she was with Ingo, Anita had none of the qualms usually associated with a child's first day at school. The children sat in the back of Anthony's Renault 16, joyously unencumbered by seat-belts, and when he pulled up at the school, Anita dived head first on to the front seat, so eager was she to get inside and join her classmates. This pattern was to continue throughout her education. Anita was lucky or good-natured enough to enjoy every one of her schools and to fit in easily and make friends at all of them. It was the second of two brilliant summers in a row. The first had been ruined for me by the Bobo / Anthony triangle, and the second was ruined by the most virulent attack of hay fever. Everyone was suffering that year, but I suffered more. What should have been a succession of sun-kissed days, *dejeuners sur l'herbe* and barbecued dinners, was ruined by itchy eyes, a streaming nose and incessant sneezing. I'm sure at last some of it was psychosomatic.

I was feeling very mixed up. Madly in love with Anthony, but at the same time missing Bobo and feeling guilty at the way I'd treated him. He called me just one week after we arrived at Glyndebourne, to tell me his mother had died that morning. Ironically the date was 3 May, Anthony's mother's birthday. The symbolism wasn't lost on me and only compounded my guilt. I never said goodbye to Balbina. I'd been meaning to write to her for some time, but hadn't got round to it. Bobo, who somewhat unfairly blamed her for our split, hadn't seen her since my departure the previous September. Years later Ucci told me that he, probably the least close of all her sons, was the only one to attend her funeral. Unusually for an Italian, she chose to be cremated. A plaque was put up on the cemetery island of San Michele which I visited in 1988, when I spent a month in Venice as part of my Italian degree.

My Aunt Dorothy died two days after Balbina. There had been a silly quarrel over my mother's move to Bevington Road, and the coolness had lasted a year or so. Dorothy was diagnosed with cancer of the lymph glands in 1975, and for a long time just carried on as normal. In March 1976 she slipped a disc and was rushed to hospital, after which her decline was very rapid. Everything was made up between us, and my mother and I visited her every day.

Anthony was supportive through these sad events, and both

my mother and Dicky visited us frequently, but I couldn't help feeling that I'd caused untold misery – not only to Bobo, but to three or four close female confidantes of Anthony who had erupted into fury and hostility at the news of our marriage – and uprooted my children and myself, only to exchange one prison for another. A great part of my unhappiness with Bobo had been because I longed, once the children were born, to live in London, and now here I was, stuck in the depths of the country, often not speaking to another adult between 9.30 in the morning when Anthony left for work and 10.30 at night when he returned. It gave me far too much time to dwell on my faults and failings. I'd shown the novel that was to become *A Darker Shade of Love* to an agent, Anne McDermid of Curtis Brown. She said I had talent, but was worried by the libel implications and wanted me to work on something completely new. Unwisely I didn't listen. I spent the summer working on it in a desultory way only, when I finally delivered it to Anne way after the agreed deadline and not, I think, much improved, to have her turn it down.

I now decided that the answer to my problems was to have another baby. Children were definitely part of the deal with Anthony and Tabitha was conceived at our first attempt. Anita was still on Phenobarbitone and I noticed a slight clumsiness, which might not have been caused by the drugs, and some mood swings. In August 1976 Anthony was given a week's holiday and we drove to Newhaven with the children and crossed by ferry to Dieppe for a happy week in Normandy. During that time I ran out of Anita's medicine, possibly because I was pregnant and had lost my memory or possibly because I simply didn't want to give it to her any more. Her clumsiness disappeared, and she seemed generally so much happier that I simply couldn't face putting her back on it again.

I dreaded having to confess to the team at Charing Cross Hospital, but finally did so in October. I was lucky enough to see a sweet young doctor, who listened to my story and said, 'Good for you! There are two schools of thought on the Phenobarb question.' He asked if Anita'd had a convulsion after coming off her medicine. She hadn't but I felt very betrayed that nobody had warned me this was a possible side effect. The doctor assured me that of course the team would see her again if she was ill (one of the things I'd been worried about) and we left the hospital in triumph never, thankfully, to return.

The Glyndebourne season ended in September and Anthony got a job working for Kent Opera, a young touring company with an excellent reputation. Ingo and Anita started nursery school together in London, and once again the presence of her big brother gave Anita confidence. Several friends remarked on how protective Ingo was of her during this period. Their relationship improved no end after I married Anthony. Seeing us all lovey dovey together inspired them to act in the same way, and eased my life considerably. I no longer had to act as a permanent referee to two antagonists, but instead got great pleasure from witnessing their touching displays of courtesy and affection.

Early in my pregnancy Fred Ashton told us he could divine the baby's sex if I pulled out some hairs, looped them through my wedding ring, and lay on the floor while he held it over my stomach like a pendulum. Fred concluded that the baby was a boy. Some instinct, however, made us decide we really ought to have a girl's name ready just in case. Near the end of our name book we both had a eureka moment when we came to the name Tabitha, which we both loved so much that I began to hope the baby might be a girl after all.

In March we were invited to the Royal Opera House to see Jon Vickers as *Otello*. Anthony's mother had a long love affair with Kenneth Clark, later Lord Clark of *Civilisation*, and his daughter Colette was a good friend of Anthony's. She was the only woman on the board of directors at the Royal Opera House and thus entitled to invite guests to the Royal Box, which has its own private dining room. On this occasion we were seated in great style with Lord Clark and other friends. I started to have contractions, and had to pay an embarrassing number of visits to the royal loo, but I told myself they must be psychosomatic, brought on by the emotion of the opera. They continued the following day, but I waited till the children were in bed before calling the hospital, who told me to come in immediately.

On this occasion, I was booked into St Theresa's Hospital, Wimbledon because my gynaecologist, Frank Denny, was on the verge of retirement and now only delivered babies there. My diary account reads: 'Had a strange time – in some ways the best birth ever, because the epidural worked and I hardly felt a twinge, but in others the worst, because poor baby's head was retroverted, and though I was fully dilated from about eleven on, and it should have been born by twelve, no progress was made and, though I didn't realise it, they were preparing the theatre for a Caesarean. Mr Denny was alerted at ten and fell asleep, fully dressed, on his bed, waiting to be called when I got to the second stage, then knew nothing more till he woke at 5.45, rang the hospital in a panic and came straight over. Of course, once he took charge, all was fine. He ruptured my membranes and made me push and babe started coming. Just near the end, the poor little heart slowed down, so he used the forceps just for a second, but I did the final push and, lo and behold, a girl! I'd been sure it was a boy, but finding the name Tabitha had made me want a girl and Anthony wanted one all along, so we were thrilled. He had been sweet and heroic, sitting up with me all night and refusing to lie down in my room. He was far more worried than I was about the non-appearance of the head, as I was all valiumed up, and apparently came into my room and prayed, which I found terribly touching.'

Thanks to Anthony, I at last experienced what it was like to have a baby with someone who wanted one as much as I did – something every woman should experience, and that I shall always be grateful to him for.

When Tabitha and I were all cleaned up and asleep, Anthony ate my breakfast and went straight off to work in Tonbridge Wells. I dozed on and off and fed Tabitha at one with no problems. Anthony brought my mother and the children to visit about five. My mother loved Tabitha and the children seemed to and got all excited and made her cry.

Because of the more difficult birth, I stayed in hospital for four nights. Anthony was on tour the following day and couldn't visit, but my mother struggled over by public transport, bringing magazines and treats from home. Ingo and Anita visited me again on the Saturday. They were very sweet and got into bed with me and cuddled me, but Anita cried in a very sad, not naughty, way when it was time to go, which convinced me I should leave next day and return home.

The Kent Opera tour finished in May, and we heard that John Tooley, the Administrative Director of the Royal Opera House, Covent Garden, was looking for a new Personal Assistant. John had been the PA of the previous General Administrator, David Webster, so the position was one to be coveted. I was all in favour of the idea. It would mean that Anthony was working in London again and earning a regular salary.

In April 1977, Ingo and Anita started school at Bassett House, a Montessori school for boys and girls between the ages of three and eight. Ingo was now five, and Anita three. The uniform was royal blue and grey and they both looked adorable in it. They went in bravely, if a little subdued. Their first day finished at 12.15. Anita was fine when I picked them up, but Ingo was tearful and belligerent. It was his first day of serious study. 'Awful to think there's no end to it now until he retires,' I wrote in my diary, 'unless he becomes a gigolo.'

The years at Bassett House were extremely happy ones. The children made good and lasting friendships and I reconnected with girlfriends I'd known before going to Italy. Bunty Lampson, who'd been Deb of the Year in 1963, the year before I did the season, was living just round the corner from us and shared a school run with me for over a year before going off to live in California with her husband Ian Ross and their five children to start the world's first roller disco. Suzanne Lilley, married to Julian Moulton's close friend Nick, also turned up at the school gates, setting impossibly high standards of beauty, elegance and sweetness. Suzanne was to die tragically of a brain tumour in 1981, when she was just thirty-three.

Anthony's interview with John Tooley took place in May. I thought his account of it sounded extremely promising, but we had to wait two weeks to hear he'd got the job. It was 6.30 in the evening and I was in the middle of changing Tabitha's nappy. She chose to take exception to the unscheduled interruption, and this most vital conversation took place to a background of angry yells. John and I tried to ignore it for as long as possible, but eventually there was nothing to do but burst into helpless laughter.

Anthony started the job in July. John was a charming boss and had the knack, which I envy greatly, of making everyone he met feel that they were the one person in the room he really wanted to talk to. Another great charmer I met at that time was Margot Fonteyn. Anthony was on duty one night and I found myself alone in the Crush Bar at a ballet gala. I was relieved to see Fred Ashton, also by himself, at a table at the far end of the room. I made my way towards him, but when I was nearly there, I was alarmed to see Fonteyn slipping gracefully into the seat beside him. He'd already seen me, so I couldn't retreat and went up to them feeling very awkward. Fred introduced me to Fonteyn as his niece, and she smiled at me and said, 'Lucky you to have such a lovely niece,' after which, naturally, I became her devoted admirer.

Gradually our lives settled into a routine. Anthony's centred round the Opera House, with me joining him there for performances at least once a week, and mine around the children. On Friday evenings we all piled into the car and drove the hundred miles or so to Norfolk, with the back seat down and the children in their pyjamas sleeping. Those were the years when I seemed to spend my life in the car, ferrying the children from one appointment to another. I had no help apart from my mother, who was always on hand to baby-sit, and a wonderful Spanish cleaning lady called Josie who came to us twice a week and transformed the house from squalor to sparkling splendour. In Norfolk we had Ivy, who had looked after Anthony when he was a child, and was now well into her sixties. She would walk to the cottage several times a week, and turn the electric blankets on for our arrival, prepare the vegetables for Sunday lunch and clean up after we'd left. She was also a much-loved baby-sitter.

In June 1978, shortly after her sixty-eighth birthday, Anthony's mother Edith had a stroke while working in the garden at Clobemon Hall. She was found by the gardener and rushed by ambulance to hospital in Dublin. Gardening was her passion, which she had passed on to Anthony. She had created the garden at the Barn, which was where we happened to be when the news came, and we walked round it sadly as we discussed what to do next.

Various tests were performed over the next few days. It was discovered that Edith had a large blood clot on her brain, which was successfully removed though the surgeon who performed the operation said there was very little chance of her surviving. In fact Edith would survive another twelve years and eventually outlive all the men in her life – Harold, Kenneth Clark and Fred Ashton. She spent several months in a coma in Ireland, then was flown to London, to St Thomas's Hospital, where they succeeded in waking her. A long stay in a London nursing home followed. She had a very grand room there and a special nurse who she adored. I used to visit her two or three times a week with whatever children were around. She still loved smoking, and I'd enjoy an illicit fag with her and keep her posted on what was going on within the family.

In July, Anita and Tabitha caught measles. Ingo had been vaccinated, so he escaped, but we must have decided not to vaccinate Anita after her febrile convulsions. She was ill for four days with a high temperature before the rash appeared, but seemed so cheerful that I wasn't terribly worried about her. She wasn't yet five, so the spectre of convulsions was still present, but increasingly remote, and by the time the rash appeared, we were relieved to be told by the doctor that the worst of the illness was over. There was a parents' evening at Bassett House that week, and I was told that she was making good progress, writing, doing sums and reading 'Janet and John' books.

Two days after Anita's rash appeared, Tabitha started to get red and grizzly, and wanted to be held all the time. By now Anita was getting better, but still had periods when she had to lie down with the electric fan on her and be sponged. By the third day her temperature was back to normal and the rash almost gone, with only a cough hanging on, but Tabitha was a pathetic sight with livid patches all over her face, and eyes all runny and ringed with red.

As always, my mother was a rock in times of trouble, and after a week, both girls were well enough to travel to Norfolk, where the change of air seemed to get rid of the last traces of illness. Our summer holidays were spent at the Barn, with regular short trips to London to see Edith. Anthony kept a small sailing boat in the creek outside our window and on 21 August, I wrote in my diary, 'Anthony took Ingo out sailing early and I slept on till 9.30. I thought Anita had gone too, till I came into the dining room and saw the poor little thing sitting pathetically on the dresser looking across the marsh to where the boat was gone and sucking her thumb. She was fully dressed but hadn't eaten, and had been quiet as a mouse so as not to disturb me.' Anita was the only one of the children to suck her thumb. She used to twiddle her hair at the same time or, if she was sitting on my knee or my mother's, twiddle our hair, which we both found very soothing, almost hypnotic. Long before it became a problem, however, she gave up sucking her thumb, seemingly from one day to the next, showing great willpower, rather as she did when she later gave up alcohol and cigarettes.

In October I got talking to Greta Chaffer, one of the mothers at Ingo's gym class. It turned out that I'd modelled for her husband, the photographer Martin Chaffer, in 1968, and indeed shared a flat in the house he and Greta lived in with my model friend Debbie Slater. Greta told me that Martin was looking for someone like me for an advertising shot he was doing in November and asked if I'd be interested to go along to a casting. I'd never shone at big castings believing, rightly or wrongly, that they were just pretexts for a group of men to chat up pretty girls when they'd probably already decided who they were going to use, so I was reluctant to get on that treadmill again. Greta persuaded me, however, and I was chosen. They also needed a child model of about three. Anita was five by now, but they asked me to take her along as a stand-by, for which she got paid £15, much to Ingo's envy.

On the same day I heard I'd got the modelling job, 13 November 1978, I was rung by a friend, Robert Temple, and commissioned to write a review of a biography of the German blockbuster author, Erik von Daniken. I had to confess that I'd never heard of von Daniken, but to my relief, Bob was delighted. Apparently most reviewers became apoplectic at the very mention of his name, and he wanted someone who would come to the subject with a fresh approach.

Modelling fees had gone up considerably since the last time I'd worked – I was surprised to realise I could earn more in one day than Anthony did in his sixty-hour working week – and there was a market for women my age, known as the 'young mum' market. On the strength of that job and some lovely lighting shots Martin had taken of me and Anita, I joined an agency called International Model, who soon had me running round London on innumerable castings. Bob was pleased with my review, which also paid respectably and following that, I decided to sign up for the writing course which led to me writing the article about Anita's convulsions. Suddenly my life seemed to be opening up. I was no longer a mere bottom wiper and domestic drudge, but a working model and a published writer.

Although I enjoyed the former, especially the ability to earn decent money, it was the latter that really thrilled me. When I was a child, my father told me I should be a writer, and the idea stuck. Although most writers publish their first novels in their twenties, I never had the feeling that I'd missed the boat. I always knew instinctively that I'd have more to say and be a better writer as I got older. My heroine, George Eliot, published her first novel in her late thirties, and I had a great aunt, Marion Osmond, who became a prize-winning novelist and playwright in her fifties.

In the meantime the children were growing up and becoming more independent. When I took them to Bassett House for the start of the spring term, I asked Anita if she'd like me to accompany her into her classroom, and she looked at me in surprise and asked, 'What for?'

It was just at this moment, when the cage door had started to open for me, that I discovered I was pregnant again. I was using contraception and have no idea how it happened, but when I said this to my agent, Tom Sheridan of International Model, he got very cross and said, 'You mean you were blindfolded and raped in a dark alley?'

I now found myself understanding something of Bobo's feelings in 1973. I also began to wonder if subconsciously I'd become pregnant on purpose, in order to prevent myself from achieving the career I'd always wanted. Wanting to be alone and think about the situation, I sent Anthony and the children off to the Barn without me for the weekend, but at the last minute Anita said she wanted to stay with me, in case I was lonely. 'Actually I would have felt terribly sad if they'd all gone,' I wrote in my diary, 'so it was really sweet of her.'

Anita was going through an accident-prone stage. Influenced by some American friends at Bassett House, I'd bought a metal exercise bar that could be screwed into a doorway and hung from or somersaulted over. When not in use it was loosened, so it remained in place but wasn't firm enough to bear anyone's weight. At the end of April I heard great shrieks and sobs and rushed upstairs to find that Anita had jumped from a chair on to the loosened bar which had promptly come crashing down, hitting her on the head. At first she seemed all right. She ate breakfast with Ingo and Tabitha, but by the time we got to school, she was very pale and said she was feeling sick. I took her to the National Health Surgery in Westbourne Grove, where she was promptly sick in reception. They sent us to St Mary's Praed Street for X-rays. Poor Anita was sick again there, and they seemed to take it all very seriously. She was put into a hospital gown looking like a little ghostie and had four X-rays. She was sick twice more and they talked of detaining her overnight, but at this prospect she immediately perked up and we were finally allowed home about twelve. My mother was there with Tabby, and very relieved to see Anita looking so well. 'The two little sisters and I had lunch and Nita had an excellent meal.'

A few weeks later, bouncing on Ingo's bed, Anita fell off and landed on his train set, smashing a carriage and leaving a very sinister imprint on her bum. In May the school secretary called and said Anita had fallen over and bumped her head walking to the playground and been sick. I dashed off to pick her up. She had bad grazes on her forehead and knee, but the first thing she said was, 'Can I have a Swiss bun?' so I didn't feel she could be that bad after all. 'We came home and I put her to bed. She didn't want to go to hospital, and they'd told me at the hospital last time that in fact head X-rays really didn't show much although they were obliged by law to do them. They'd also told me the danger signals to watch out for – vomiting, excess drowsiness etc. – so I decided to bring her home and watch her there and she was fine. She ate a doughnut and drank a lurid strawberry drink and played with Tabby.' Fortunately this was the last of Anita's accidents, so perhaps it's true about things happening in threes.

All too soon, I started to feel nauseous and need an afternoon sleep. To try to combat nature, I swam regularly and bought a bicycle to use for local errands. I also made the miraculous discovery of Vitamin B6 to combat nausea. I don't know how I managed to miss it during my previous pregnancies, but at least I found it in time for Juliet. It came in small, black pellets like rabbit droppings. I took one after each meal and my life was transformed.

I decided to have my fourth baby on the National Health. This was firstly for financial reasons, secondly because Mr Denny had retired and thirdly because the staff at St Teresa's had made such a cock-up of Tabby's birth that I thought the National Health couldn't be any worse. I was offered the choice of two hospitals, Queen Charlotte's or the West London in Hammersmith. The latter practised the Leboyer method – soft lights, baby handed to mother straight after birth for bonding – and even had a birthing pool, so I decided to go there.

My article on Anita's febrile convulsions, published the previous month, ended on rather a smug tone, rejoicing in her current good health. As I wrote it, I worried that I was tempting providence, and sure enough, the tonsillitis that had been the cause of her convulsions returned with a vengeance. After waiting weeks, we were sent to an ear, nose and throat specialist at Paddington Green Children's Hospital, who didn't even turn up till we had been waiting an hour, then said he didn't think Anita needed to have her tonsils removed immediately, and anyway the waiting list was several months long. By now her temperature was going up every evening and she was missing lots of school, so I bit the bullet and went privately. We saw Tony Greenburgh on 15 June and he made an appointment with a children's specialist, Mr Holborrow, ten days later. He said tonsils like hers – huge and pitted – would always be a problem, and that he would take them out in July, the first week of the school holidays, which was exactly what we wanted.

Anita was very excited about having her tonsils out. She got dressed in a new Mary Quant pink and white spotted dress, and we drove to the Westminster Children's Hospital together, arriving at 4.45 and getting a parking meter right outside the door. Everyone was very nice. Anita was in the Robert Mond Ward in her own little room, and a camp bed was put up for me. There were two other little girls having their tonsils out in the morning and they were very friendly. She had supper and all sorts of people came and asked her questions and Anthony came to see us both. I rang home and talked to Ingy and Tabby then Anthony went home to kiss them good-night and Nita and I settled down and to my surprise she was asleep by eight. We were woken at midnight by the nurse giving her an orange and glucose drink – last food before the op.

Tuesday 17 July

We woke about 6. Nita was very jolly and coloured in a hospital colouring book before being given her pre-med drink at 6.30. After that we both dozed till 7.30, then she was rather pathetic and cried and said she was thirsty, so we wet her mouth with a flannel and she dozed off again till 8.30. She lifted her little head up and said, 'I love you,' then a second later the nurse and orderly came in and whisked her away on a trolley to the operating theatre, leaving me nearly in tears. I went to the canteen for breakfast, getting back at 9 to await Nita, who arrived about 9.30, fast asleep, (Apparently they give them a morphia-based injection straight after the op. to kill pain and make them sleep) and she hardly stirred for the rest of the day.

Nita woke in fantastic form and, to my amazement, had corn-flakes and orange juice for breakfast. She asked to see my mother and Tabby, so Anthony dropped them round before work. Tabby wasn't allowed to stay, so she and I took Anthony to work, then shopped in Victoria for colouring books and crayons for Anita. Got back around 12 and took my mother and Tabby home, then came straight back to the hospital. Ate lunch in the canteen and went to sleep for about three hours, rather to my shame. Little Anita was wonderful and didn't talk to me but just drew away and made me a beautiful book of drawings. In the evening Anthony and Ingo came to see us. Nita was thrilled to see Ingo, but he was rather horrid and offhand with her. He'd had tea with Theo and spent the whole afternoon fighting with him and Oliver Needham.

Anita spent three nights in hospital, the last of them virtually sleepless due to the screams of a neurotic Spanish boy who woke us and the entire ward at 1.25 am, crying for his mother, who was asleep in the relatives' wing. The Staff Nurse, in her wisdom, decided not to call her, so Anita, all the other children in the ward and bad-tempered, pregnant me were kept awake all night. In the morning Anita was white and exhausted and had lost all the colour she'd had in her cheeks the day before. By now we just wanted to go home, and were allowed to do so at 12. I put Anita straight to bed, gave her lunch, and played her the previous day's children's programmes on our brand new video recorder.

Anita was on antibiotics and had to stay home for five days, so we found amusements close to home. All three children joined a Bookworm scheme at the local library. They read and were questioned on a selection of books, and were rewarded with badges and certificates. Ingo learnt to ride a bicycle, and was spotted by a neighbour cycling round Kildare Gardens in full cowboy fig.

After that came my four-month ultrasound at the West London Hospital. Scans weren't routine when I was expecting Ingo and Anita, but I'd had one when pregnant with Tabitha. Until now, my antenatal care had been excellent, but today I started to have my doubts. My appointment was for 2 pm and I was told to drink two pints of water between 1 and 1.40 pm, but when I arrived, on time, for my scan, I found another mother had been booked at the same time as me and, because there was only one scanner and she had arrived before me, she was going to be given her scan first.

I proceeded to wait in extreme discomfort until about 2.40 when I was finally taken in and told everything was spot on, but I was shaken by this totally gratuitous display of sadism. Why on earth couldn't the other mother and I have been given separate appointments half an hour apart? However, I was too relieved that everything was all right and that I could empty my bladder at last to worry how I might fare at the actual birth, with this sort of ineptitude in place. I understand that it's now considered completely unnecessary for mothers to drink water before their scans, and a good job too.

That evening I joined Anthony at the Opera House for a Royal Gala. The Martha Graham Dance Company was visiting, and Graham herself gave an introductory speech. She was a very old lady by now, and sat on a chair to address us in a creaky voice. A microphone was hidden under her dress, which appeared to be made of chain mail, and crackled and rasped in a very sinister manner as she spoke. Liza Minelli was making a guest appearance, narrating the story of the Owl and the Pussycat in what I considered a very over-exaggerated fashion. This was the evening that I understood, probably for the first time, the point of wearing expensive clothes. Until then, I'd got away with vintage velvet from Portobello Road, or for special occasions, a rather splendid beaded number that my rich great aunt had picked up in the South of France in the 1930s. I'd never felt out of place at the Royal Opera House, because at that time most of its patrons were unspeakably dowdy, but that evening, as Minelli stalked the Crush Bar at the first night party in a glittering Halston dress, I saw that someone who was neither beautiful nor, based on what I had seen earlier, particularly talented, could be turned into a star by a clever designer.

At the end of August, Ingo and Anita were invited to visit Bobo in Venice. As it was the first time they'd be staying with him on their own, although he visited them regularly in London, I proposed going too, and staying on the Lido with Anthony, Tabitha and my mother. Bobo agreed, and kindly found us a flat in the Eurotel, which had its own beach. Wanting to be as unlike Ruth as possible, I said that I'd like to be introduced to Hélène, and that I thought it was important to be on civilised terms with the woman who was going to be looking after my children for the next two weeks. This too was agreed, but on the flight over, I started to get terrible cold feet and wished I hadn't made any requests at all.

In the event, however, everything was very civilised. Hélène came to the airport with Bobo and much handshaking took place. Everyone was too polite to comment on my obvious pregnancy, which I hadn't yet announced to Bobo. I wrote of Hélène, 'She was very pretty and seemed very kind and affectionate towards Ingo and Anita.' We couldn't all fit into Bobo's boat, but he took our luggage, and kindly said he'd drop it by later. Anthony, Tabitha, my mother and I got into a water taxi, while Ingo and Anita went off in Bobo's boat without a backward glance and I felt that for the first time I was being called upon to pay the price for leaving Bobo four years before.

The flat on Lido was ideal for our needs. Bobo came by in the evening with Ingo and Anita, who both seemed very happy and affectionate. At one stage I was touched to see Anita walking along with one hand in Bobo's and the other in Anthony's. It was awful when they went away again, but on the whole the holiday was a success.

My grandfather Dr Alexander Brown with, left to right, my mother Marjorie, my grandmother Rosetta Jane and my aunt Dorothy

Bobo's mother, Contessa Emilia Balbi with the twins, Bobo (left) and Lilo

With Dicky in Regent's Park

Back row, my parents and me. Front row, left to right, my grandfather Alfred Dunhill, Caroline, my great aunt and my grandfather's wife Vera

Modelling, 1966

Modelling in Rome, 1967

With Bobo at his house on the Giudecca, 1970

8. With Bobo, Ingo and Anita in the studio at Incurabili, 1974

With Anita, Sissinghurst, summer, 1976

Modelling with Anita, 1979

With my mother, Ebury Street, 1997

Ingo and Victoria's wedding, 2004. Left to right Juliet, Anita, me, Ingo, Victoria, Tabitha, Anthony

Anita in Sierra Leone with Petal and Snowy, 2006

Left: Anita modelling, 2007
Above: Anita and Jeff, 2008

Anita and Bobo, 2009

We got into a routine of going to the beach in the morning, sightseeing in Venice in the afternoons and having dinner there in the early evenings. The first time we went into Venice I wrote, 'Felt terrifically spooked at being there again. I'd always been rather shocked at myself for forgetting Bobo so totally and with such ease, but now I realise it may have had a lot to do with leading a completely different life. It all came back very vividly being in Venice.'

The following day we went to Montin for dinner. The two brothers who owned it, Giuliano and Adriano, were very friendly and sweet, as was the waiter, Gino, who said Ingo and Anita had been in the day before and Ingo was *stupendo* and Anita *bellissima*.

My English friend, Denise Bacci, arranged a reunion tea party in her house, just across the canal from Bobo's. Anita spent a lot of the time cuddling Tabitha, who had missed her terribly and I began to see what an advantage it would be to have a fourth child who would keep Tabitha company when Ingo and Anita were with Bobo.

At the end of tea, Bobo collected Ingo and Anita and rowed them across the canal and they stood rather forlornly on the other side, waving to us as we left for the *vaporetto*. When Anita was dying, she reproached me for the feelings of being torn in two that she'd experienced during her holidays in Venice, and I was aghast that she still minded so much. At the time I tried to rationalise by writing, 'I hope the visit will broaden their horizons and make them realise they have other people who love them besides me, my mother and Anthony' – no doubt a subconscious reference to my own childhood and the devastation wrought by my father's death.

We returned to London on 15 September. Bassett House went back on the twentieth, and Ingo caught chicken pox shortly afterwards, followed by Anita two weeks later, and Tabitha at the end of the month. The baby wasn't due till 1 January (prompting one of the mothers on the school run to ask if it had been conceived on April Fool's Day), so I was glad to get the epidemic over before giving birth.

My aunt, Mary Dunhill, published a book around that time entitled *My Family Business*. Although it contained many references to my father, and some to his previous girlfriends, Mary had left out all reference to my mother and me. My father and Mary had fallen out over money and not spoken for many years, so it's possible she didn't even realise my parents had married. My mother was upset enough to write to the publishers asking that the facts be corrected in subsequent editions of the book, and they wrote back and apologised, but said there probably weren't going to be any. It would certainly never have occurred to her to sue. She simply wasn't that kind of woman. Some years later, however, the *Sunday Times* published an article about my grandfather, Alfred Dunhill, which stated that my father had died childless. This time we showed it to the lawyer Anthony Rubinstein, who acted with commendable swiftness. An apology was printed in the newspaper and my mother and I received a cheque for £1000.

After this, there really was nothing left to do but to wait for the baby. It seemed to be the season for them. Five other Bassett House mothers and one neighbour were having babies between October and April. On 15 December, while getting ready for bed, I started to shiver violently. I was having strong frontal pains and losing a lot of fluid, so we called the hospital who told me to come in at once.

That evening, my worst fears about having a baby on the NHS were confirmed. Anthony and I were greeted by a midwife who told me they'd lost my notes. She asked me if my membranes had ruptured and I said they hadn't, but were leaking, and she said, 'That doesn't happen.' A hospital bracelet was put on me and I was told I must spend the night on a narrow trolley with no sides. I asked if all the beds were full and the woman said, 'I'm afraid I can't discuss the other patients with you.' I was terrified of falling off the trolley and knew I wouldn't sleep at all if I stayed, so I signed a form saying I was leaving against medical advice and went home in floods of tears. Once safely in the car, I tore the plastic bracelet off with my teeth and told Anthony there was no way I was going through an NHS delivery at that hospital. I'd rather have the baby on the kitchen floor at home.

The following day was a Sunday. I slept all day, then got cracking on the Monday. On Tony Greenburgh's recommendation, I asked Mr Sims, my NH gynaecologist, if he'd deliver the baby privately. He sounded vastly amused by my tale and agreed to do so, though he wasn't sure he could get me a private bed at the West London.

The next day was spent rushing around doing shopping for Anita's sixth birthday. Her tastes were always very feminine. Inspired by Germaine Greer, I'd tried dressing her in dungarees and giving her educational toys, but she would have none of it. She liked pink dresses and frills, and when a friend gave her a very ordinary-looking first doll, she fell on it with love and delight. This year we were giving her a doll's house, and my mother and I drove to Parsons Green to buy furniture for it at a shop called the Singing Tree. It was the last day of term at Bassett House, so I went out again afterwards to get presents for the children's teachers. Tabitha and I then had our afternoon rest, and afterwards she came into my room and said casually, 'Where's Juliet?'

'Who's Juliet?' I asked. I'd never heard her mentioned before, and as far as I was aware, Tabitha didn't know any Juliets, but she just repeated the question more insistently.

Fred Ashton had done his trick with the pendulum again and told me the baby was a boy. I'm not sure why we believed him after the time before, but for some reason we did, and had decided to call it Frederick after him. We were so sure that we hadn't even bothered to think of a girl's name, but I suddenly felt shaken. Tabitha's question seemed almost uncanny. Did she know something we didn't?

The following day, 19 December, was Anita's sixth birthday. She was up at the crack of dawn unwrapping presents, and then, at 10.30, our neighbour, Magsie Adie, came to collect Ingo and Anita for the Bassett House school party. Ingo went in his judo outfit, and Anita wore a tutu with tinsel in her hair and a magic wand. After they'd gone, Tony Greenburgh telephoned to say he'd very cleverly managed to fix me a private bed at Queen Charlotte's Hospital. At 1.30 I was due to collect Tabitha from nursery school and go on to Bassett House to collect Ingo and Anita. I stood up to go at 1.20 and my membranes ruptured. What seemed like gallons of water poured over the kitchen floor.

My first call was to Magsie, who kindly agreed to collect Tabby and said she'd go on to Bassett House and keep all my three children with her for the afternoon. Thankfully we'd arranged to give Ingo and Anita a joint birthday party in January, so I wouldn't be letting her down on that front. I called Queen Charlotte's, who told me to get an ambulance and come in immediately. Waiting for the ambulance I managed to get hold of Anthony, who said he'd join me at the hospital. My mother came up and packed my suitcase for me, and I walked to the ambulance wrapped in a towel, and set off, sirens blaring, for Queen Charlotte's where I was rushed straight to the delivery room.

The baby, a girl, was born at 6.39. She weighed 7 lbs, had dark hair and was very pretty. I remembered Tabitha's mysterious question from the day before and instantly said, 'This is Juliet,' to which Anthony happily agreed. She was put into my arms and I lay holding her while the day staff went off and the night staff took over. I eventually got to my room about nine and fell into a delicious sleep.

The next day the children came to visit. I told Anita that Juliet was her birthday present and teased her that next year she'd have to share her party with a lot of babies in nappies. Juliet stayed in my room all day and was very sweet and contented. I also thoroughly approved of the hospital policy of giving her only water at night, unlike St Theresa's, where they'd pumped Tabby full of formula milk without asking me, just as she was due to feed.

Anthony collected me the following evening. We dressed Juliet for the first time and drove her home through falling snow. Ingo was still awake. Anthony told me he'd been horrid about the baby being a girl, but he was very affectionate towards her, and I could see he was secretly fairly smitten.

That night she was very good, and fed like clockwork at two, six and ten. 'I think we're in luck this time,' I wrote in my diary the following day.

Juliet proved to be a very easy baby. I felt that at my fourth attempt I'd finally discovered the secret of having a perfect pregnancy and a baby to match. It was ironic that the moment I acquired these skills was also the moment that they became obsolete.

Because we hadn't been expecting her until January, we'd accepted various invitations and bought theatre tickets for the whole family as a Boxing Day treat. Juliet was so easy going that rather than leave her at home I decided to slip her under my djellaba and take her with us. By the time she was supposed to have been born she had already attended three parties and a pantomime, sleeping angelically in my arms throughout and only waking if we attempted to put her in her cot. This was actually a fairly clear indication of her character. Juliet remains a party animal to this day.

CHAPTER SEVEN

16 June 2009

Tuesday was my day with Max and we were going to Wands-
worth Common to a music group organised by a lady called
Amanda, who tossed sackfuls of musical instruments at the feet
of the assembled children and danced wildly to encourage them
to do the same. Usually it was held at a café on the common, but
today the weather was particularly beautiful and the class was
being held outside in a field. At one point the children had to
race up to a line and then race back, but Max just held his face up
towards the sun and kept on running into infinity. I made a half-
hearted attempt to bring him back, but it really didn't matter. A
quick glance showed me that the entire field was safely enclosed.
I didn't have to worry about roads or lakes or bicycles or any of
the usual hazards.

When the class finished, we stayed on. There was some kind
of games pitch and men in vast, municipal machines were
mowing and steamrolling it. This was just to Max's taste and
mine too, since it kept him spellbound and safe. When they
started to repaint the white lines on the pitch, our happiness
was complete.

I'd read several accounts by women journalists of the joys of
being a grandmother, and wondered if I would experience them
too, but somehow doubted it. I thought my days of looking after
babies were well and truly over. I'd witnessed my own mother's
love for her grandchildren, but thought it was something to do
with her particularly selfless nature. Balbina, too, had told me a
story of stumbling on a bridge in Venice while carrying one of

her grandchildren. She couldn't put her arms out to save herself because it would have meant dropping the baby, so she'd ended up on her knees, her legs grazed and bleeding, but even then, I hadn't really understood.

Now, thanks to Max, I did. Our first meeting wasn't terribly auspicious. When I first held him, on the day he was born, his head was sore after a long labour and a botched delivery, and he started to cry, but things had improved since. I adored him, and he appeared to love me and be gratifyingly excited when I came to look after him. Just as my mother had with my children, I longed to spoil and indulge him. A parent's job is to bring a child up for the world, but a grandparent's, I believe, is to provide a refuge from it. When he cried, I felt as if I was being pierced by a sword, and when his parents imposed necessary discipline, I longed to defend him. In short, I found that I was turning into my mother. And was that really, I wondered, such a very bad thing?

While we were still in the field, my mobile phone rang twice. The first caller was Juliet, the second Anita. Both had been busily flat hunting – I'd visited a flat in Camden with Juliet the day before and liked it a lot – and both had offered the asking price on their chosen flats today and had it accepted. I was thrilled for them both. I hadn't seen Anita's flat, but she'd shown me photos of it. It had a large living room and terrace and looked very attractive. I felt proud of them both for their initiative and also rather amazed by the coincidence of them sharing a birthday and now finding flats, Juliet's first and Anita's second, on the same day.

*　　*　　*

The 1980s was a decade of moving. Just before Juliet's birth, Anthony was deputed by John Tooley to entertain Bernard Lefort, who was due to take over as General Director of Paris Opera in 1981. Lefort was most impressed by Anthony, but when I was introduced to him at the performance that evening, he looked at me as if I were something the cat had brought in. He was evidently not a ladies' man.

In January he offered Anthony the position of Artistic Administrator of Paris Opera, starting in June 1981. The plan was that he would go to Paris six months before, to learn the ropes from his predecessor, Gérard Mortier. It was obvious to me that Anthony must accept it. It was his dream job and would provide invaluable experience at three times the salary he was currently earning. I saw equally clearly that the children and I shouldn't accompany him to Paris. He would have to go to performances almost every night, and we'd hardly ever see him. In addition, he'd need to travel frequently to other European countries to audition singers. In London we had my mother to baby sit, but in Paris I'd have to pay a stranger every time I wanted to attend a performance with him.

Besides that we had opted to educate the children in the British system and I felt it would be harmful to their future prospects to drop out now. I was sure we could manage if Anthony moved to Paris on his own, and the children and I joined him there for half terms and school holidays, with him flying to London for term-time weekends whenever he could. The journey from *L'Opéra* to Kildare Gardens could be accomplished, door to door, in three hours – about the same time it took us to drive to Norfolk. I broached this to him, but because we had nearly a year before we needed to worry about it, we probably didn't discuss the matter in enough depth.

In June we went to Paris to do a recce. On our first morning we visited the British School in Bougival, an attractive building in a large, fairytale garden. A relocation agent met us at the gates and showed us various properties for rent in the area to give us some idea of what we could expect if we decided to live near the school. Afterwards we took the RER back to Auber, the stop for Paris Opera, and were most impressed by the speed and cleanliness of the service.

That evening we went to see *Boris Godunov*, produced by Joseph Losey, at *L'Opéra*.

Losey had rented Marsh Barn while filming *The Go-Between*, and loved it so much he wanted to buy it. His production of *Godunov* was most original, with the orchestra on stage dressed as Russian peasants, but on the whole I found the atmosphere at *L'Opéra* the opposite of cosy. People were guarded in their approach to us. I felt they were saying, 'I won't be too friendly towards you until I see if you make good,' and was accordingly depressed.

Anthony started work there in January 1981. He flew to Paris on the 7.30 am flight and the rest of us followed by car for a one-week stay in a service flat near the Eiffel Tower, after which Anthony was going to share a flat in the Fifth Arrondissement. We had a lovely time showing the children the sights of Paris. Anita and Tabitha liked the British School at once, though Ingo was more grudging. Somehow, without ever having actually made the decision to move, I appeared to be drifting into a commitment to relocate the whole family in the autumn.

We went to Paris again for the Easter holidays. My feelings about *L'Opéra* were still very mixed, though Lefort was obviously making an effort to be friendly. At a lunch for staff and their wives, 'he actually shook my hand, met my eye and smiled,' as I wrote incredulously in my diary, and when we took the three older children to a dress rehearsal of *Don Giovanni*, he seemed to take a great fancy to them. He swooped down on Tabitha like the Wolf in *Little Red Riding Hood* and said, 'Do you like opera?' in a terrific French accent. To counterbalance this, when Anthony and I attended a performance of *Le Grand Macabre*, and parked quite legally in the small staff car park, we came out at the end of the evening to find someone had let our tyres down.

Normally all the singers I met in Paris were very friendly, but I had some beginners' luck in reverse that Easter. A singer called

Maria Ewing, the girlfriend of Sir Peter Hall, had been engaged to sing Zerlina in *Don Giovanni*. Anthony asked her to do two extra performances, and she asked for more money. He explained that he could only pay the same fee per performance as he had before, and on the day before the opening night she suddenly announced that she was ill and didn't know if she could perform next day. It was Good Friday, and Anthony had to spend the whole day on the telephone trying to find a replacement, since opera houses never employ understudies for principal roles, because of cost.

Finally, just before midnight, he found a singer in Brussels and went to the airport to meet her next morning. When Ewing heard she had a cover, she announced that she was well enough to sing after all. People kept coming up to us in the interval and saying things like, 'Was she really ill?' and 'There doesn't seem to be anything the matter with her at all!' Peter Hall was in the audience and appeared quite cowed. When we made some reference to the tensions of the past two days, he rolled his eyes and said, 'Wasn't it awful?'

Perhaps the best summing up of the situation came from a colleague of Anthony's who asked me if I was having a good weekend. 'It's been rather spoilt by Maria Ewing,' I replied, whereupon he shrugged his shoulders and exclaimed, 'She ees a *beeech!*' in a delicious French accent.

The following day we were invited to lunch by Kiri Te Kanawa, who was appearing in Strauss's *Arabella* and had rented a lovely house in the Seventeenth Arrondissement. She couldn't have been more charming or hospitable and we all, children included, had a wonderful time. As I say, my feelings were very mixed, but Anthony had now given the statutory term's notice at the children's schools in London, so it was too late for me to draw back.

We were back in Paris a month later for the children's half term. We decided to travel by train and ferry and I was proud of how helpful Ingo and Anita were, carrying their belongings like little grown-ups. We were only going for four nights, and Anthony's flat mate, Jean-François, who was going away for the weekend, said the children and I could stay in his flat.

Anthony met us at the Gare du Nord and we went straight to the flat where we faced a highly embarrassing situation. Jean-François was having an affair with a married woman and they had just been settling in for a romantic tryst when the baby-sitter we'd ordered for the following evening, from the highly respectable *Agence Catholique*, turned up a day early and insisted on staying with them until we arrived.

After a flurry of embarrassed explanations, we sent her away and fled with the children to an enchanting restaurant in the Rue Mouffetarde. The main purpose of this visit was to flat hunt and Anthony had found a splendid apartment in the Rue François Ier, just off the Champs-Elysées, currently occupied by the outgoing President of IBM.

I was disappointed not to be visiting any homes near the British School, but it poured with rain all weekend and we were all dazzled by the flat in Rue François Ier, so I didn't insist. In the evening another baby-sitter arrived and Anthony took me to what turned out to be the most exciting event I was to experience in all my time in Paris. We were seeing Montserrat Caballé as *Turandot*. I'd already seen her as Leonora in *Il Trovatore* at Covent Garden, and was a huge fan.

Her Turandot was equally magnificent, but to our horror, halfway through her big aria in Act II, two live chickens, tied together by their ankles, were flung down from the flies and exploded on to the stage at Caballé's feet. One of them was killed outright, but the other set up a pathetic, blood-stained flapping, till a member of the chorus removed it from the stage and wrung its neck in the wings.

Anthony's seats were on a gangway by a side exit, so he could slip out easily in an emergency. On this occasion he was gone almost before the chickens hit the stage and I watched alone as Caballé finished her aria, held her high C for a thrilling length of time and swept her cloak disdainfully through the chickens' blood before making her exit.

In the interval she came into Anthony's office to call her agent and brother, Carlos Caballé. She was extremely courageous and dignified and spoke to him in English 'so that Mr Russell-Roberts and his charming wife (you can see why I liked her so much) can understand.' It was agreed that she would continue the performance, and fortunately there were no more dramas, although I heard afterwards that a large bag full of horse shit and red roses had been found waiting in the flies.

Two days later we returned to London for the end of the school year. We were planning to be in Paris for two to three years, so Ingo would be able to return to his prep school, Sussex House, but Anita, who was now seven and a half, would have to start afresh. With this in mind I went to an open day at Francis Holland School, Graham Terrace. I myself had attended the other Francis Holland in Clarence Gate, but they'd closed their junior school, whereas Graham Terrace took girls from five to eighteen. At that time there was no entrance exam to get into the senior school from the junior one and pupils' sisters took priority. For a mother of three daughters, this was a godsend. 'I was most impressed,' I wrote in my diary, 'and would be very happy for all the girls to go there when we get back.'

One good thing about Paris Opera was that everyone got six weeks holiday in the summer. Anthony's started on 10 July, so he was able to be with me for all the end of term events at the children's two schools. With little time to be sad, we dashed off to Marsh Barn in July for a month's holiday, after which it was to be let for a year. During that same holiday, we visited Chandos Lodge, Fred Ashton's beautiful home in Suffolk. A former hunting lodge, rumoured to have been the home of one of Edward VII's mistresses, Chandos was surrounded by a crinkle-crankle wall and had enchantingly pretty grounds with an artificial lake and a little island in the middle. Fred's partner, Martyn Thomas, had built a deliciously warm indoor swimming pool in a nearby outhouse. He was there to entertain us and took a lot of trouble with the children who had a picnic lunch on the terrace while the grown-ups ate in state in the pretty circular dining room, full of Fred's favourite Wemyss china.

We returned to London on 17 August and Ingo and Anita flew off to Venice the following day for three weeks. On their return they would be flying direct to Paris.

Three days later it was our turn to leave – Anthony, my mother, Tabitha, Juliet and I. The ferry journey was distinguished by the fact that I nearly lost Juliet, who ran off as I was disposing of her soiled nappy in the ladies' room. I wasn't worried as the door was very heavy and I knew she couldn't open it on her own, but when I went after her, she was gone. Some exceptionally intelligent person had obviously decided it was a good idea to hold the door open for a twenty-month-old unaccompanied child and leave her to roam freely around the ship.

As I searched for her I found myself, in my panic, accosting strangers in languages like Spanish and German that I didn't even know I spoke. Someone advised me to try the Purser's Office. On my way there I suddenly saw her, sitting on a seat looking very grown-up and composed. But her obvious relief at seeing me showed that her new-found independence had started to wear a bit thin.

When we arrived in Paris, we had to reverse down the Rue François Ier, which was one way, as we still hadn't discovered the correct way in. All our stuff was piled in the hall, and our removal man, the wonderful Jack Ward, had thoughtfully assembled our bed in the wrong room. There was no light as the French removal men had taken away all our predecessor's light fittings. It was hardly an auspicious start.

Anthony went back to work two days later and was stunned to

be told that Lefort had broken his Achilles tendon playing tennis and would be off work till January. Gérard Mortier had now departed for Brussels, various essential documents seemed to be missing, and soon afterwards Lefort departed to Switzerland for a sleep cure, his last words to Anthony being, '*Surtout, ne me téléphone pas!*' To all intents and purposes, Anthony was now in sole charge of Paris Opera.

Things went badly wrong for us in Paris, but I blame myself because I'd seen exactly how it would be beforehand and allowed myself to be talked into going. It took over three months for us to rent out Kildare Gardens, so our financial situation became untenable and after one term we had to take the children out of the British School, where the fees were three times higher than in London, and move to a smaller flat. I sent Ingo and Anita to the *Ecole Aujourd'hui* in Montparnasse, a friendly and welcoming school for one hundred and twenty children with twelve teachers, eight French and four English, where the children worked in the morning, ate a packed lunch and could choose from a dizzying variety of workshops – swimming, football, roller-skating, dancing, music, art – in the afternoons. For Tabitha and Juliet I found the Lennen School on the Quai D'Orsay for children from two to seven, where I was shown round by a kind American lady who told me Tabitha could learn to read and write there in either English or French. Juliet had been getting very bored alone at home with nothing to do but crawl on the kitchen table where I sat head in hands poring over the bills, and loved going to school with Tabitha. Tabitha was less enthusiastic, but soon made friends with a little American boy called Mark from whom she became inseparable.

Anita blossomed at the *Ecole Aujourd'hui*, where she soon became one of a gang of little girls and was always being invited out to tea or to stay the night. I saw that the French mothers were delighted to cultivate her friendship in the hope that she'd teach their daughters English. Ingo was very scornful about the whole set-up, but fortunately made good friends with an American boy called David whose parents were in Paris for a year, and they spent a lot of time in each other's homes.

I became very fond of Americans during this period. I'd met some kind British ladies, become part of a lively conversation group, joined an organisation called the British and Commonwealth Women's Association and even written for their magazine, but their attitude was very stiff upper lip. If they suffered over moving to Paris, they took anti-depressants and shut up about it. Americans, on the other hand, seemed to understand what I was going through. They used expressions like 'culture shock' and I found I could let my hair down far more with them than with my compatriots.

For our move, we didn't use a grand relocation agency. I just bought the *Figaro* newspaper every morning and trailed round the flats listed, often bumping into the same people at each. We eventually settled on a flat in the Rue Joseph Barra, near the children's favourite *Jardins du Luxembourg*. It was on the ground floor and, most unusually for Paris, had its own private garden. It was near enough to the *Ecole Aujourd'hui* for Ingo to walk there in the mornings and on a direct Metro line to *L'Opéra*.

John Tooley came over while we were in the midst of all this turmoil and invited us to dinner. I told him how much I hated living in Paris and said I almost wished Anthony would be sacked so we could come home. Naturally my remarks had nothing to do with it, but three months later, he came up with an offer for Anthony to return to London in 1983 as Administrative Director of the Royal Ballet, a newly created post that would take a lot of the day-to-day pressures of running the company away from the Artistic Director, Norman Morrice, who had been suffering from ill health. In his 1999 book, *In House*, John states merely that Anthony's time working for Bernard Lefort 'was an invaluable experience for him'. Indeed.

Although we had now sorted out our economic situation, and

even, finally, managed to rent out Kildare Gardens, I knew that for the children's sake as well as my own, we should return to London at the end of the academic year. If Ingo was to pass the highly competitive Common Entrance exam, he couldn't afford to take any more time out. Much as I like the Lennen School, their method of teaching was far more relaxed than the British system, and Tabitha undoubtedly struggled with her reading when she got back, while poor Juliet caught a virus, which turned into pneumonia on a visit to London for the February half term. She had to spend a week in the Westminster Children's Hospital and it took her many months to recover fully.

The only one of us to escape comparatively unscathed was Anita. She had the knack of making friends easily wherever she went and was able to pull out the stops academically when the occasion demanded it, and pass her exams with a sort of casual brilliance and the minimum of work. At the end of May, the entire *Ecole Aujourd'hui* went to Normandy for a two-week *Classe Verte* or School Camp. Anita told me afterwards that a lot of the children were homesick and crying in the evening for their mothers but that she wasn't at all unhappy, because she'd got used to being away from me when visiting Bobo. I think she intended this as a reproach, but I chose to take it as a compliment.

Bernard Lefort quit his job at *L'Opéra* after one year. Anthony and I were invited to a farewell dinner at his apartment. On entering, I was bemused to find myself one of only three women present among twenty or so young men, all wearing jeans, perfectly pressed Lacoste T-shirts and cashmere sweaters knotted around their shoulders. Lefort, who now seemed like an old and dear friend, was being replaced at the start of the new season by Massimo Bogianckino and Anthony was going to stay on till January to assist the hand-over. The children and I were returning to London in September for the start of the school year.

Ingo went back to Sussex House and I was able to organise a nice school run for him with two neighbours. Anita was now too old for Bassett House, and Juliet too young, though I got her into a lovely nursery school, the Acorn, in Portobello Road. One of Anita's best friends from Bassett House was now attending Fox School, the state primary school in Notting Hill. Her mother was enthusiastic about it and we eventually decided to send Anita and Tabitha there, rather than have the children at four different schools.

As usual Anita coped with aplomb. She wasn't in the same class as her friend, but soon made new ones and was very good at defending Tabitha. At her funeral, Ingo described how an obnoxious little boy in Anita's class kept threatening to beat her up, and how she laughed at him until he threatened to beat Tabitha up, at which point she administered a strategic kick, whereupon all threats ceased. Anita was becoming very grown up and helpful. At the Barn that summer she'd run errands for me at 10p a time, then walked into the village with one of her friends and spent the money on sweets.

She suffered a setback at the beginning of September when I took her to her first ballet class at Merle Park's school in Chiswick. She was put with a group of five year olds and they were all better than she was. Merle told me Anita should really have started at the age of four. Anita was tearful at the end and said she didn't want to do ballet any more, even though it had been her ambition for years. I felt very mean at having unwittingly let her in for this ordeal, and surprised, as I had always been led to believe that it was OK to start ballet up to the age of ten.

In October I was invited to the Fox School to watch Anita's class perform a play about how the world began. Anita was the moon, and looked very beautiful. She'd recently become a vegetarian like me, which I found very touching, and stuck to it for fifteen years until tricked into eating meat by her husband. Tabitha and Juliet were to follow her several years later, as was my mother, but for many years it was just Anita and me versus the carnivores.

After the play, the parents were invited up to the children's classroom for coffee. Anita's teacher, Miss Moore, was there, but made no effort to circulate. She sat slumped in a chair talking to one of the parents, a famous soap actress, and later deigned to acknowledge a daddy who happened to be a militantly left-wing Labour councillor. When I approached her and asked her how Anita was getting on, she replied, 'She's very lazy, isn't she?' which left me feeling infinitely depressed.

There was another disturbing incident a few days later. I'd made friends with a mother who lived round the corner from us, and we'd arranged to share a school run. On this occasion, she forgot to pick up Anita and Tabitha, and I rushed trembling to the school forty minutes late. Pick-up time was 3.30 and the school policy was to leave the playground open till four and then turn any remaining children out and lock the gates. My two little daughters aged eight and five were standing in the street alone in the gathering dark.

I think I knew after that that I couldn't leave them at the Fox School much longer, but the October parents' evening confirmed it. I looked through Anita's folder and realised that the standard of the maths she was doing was lower than it had been at Bassett House two years before. Miss Moore explained that her pupils weren't taught how to solve maths problems, but expected to work them out for themselves, and that similarly they were no longer taught how to read, but that books were left lying around so that they'd teach themselves.

'But there's no *harm* in teaching them, is there?' I said aghast.

'You're very black and white, aren't you?' she replied, which I still think is a *non sequitur*.

The next day I called Francis Holland. I'd put the girls' names down for 1984, but regarded this as an emergency. Initially the answer was no, there were no places for the following term, but four days later I was electrified when they called me back and invited Anita in for a test.

In a last-ditch attempt to salvage the situation at Fox, I tried speaking to Miss Moore again in the company of the deputy head, who had a much better bedside manner, and spouted a lot of helpful sounding jargon about the 'new maths' which, if listened to carefully, was no more than theorising. Miss Moore told me she didn't want to show me the children's books, which were in 'a bit of a mess', and that if I didn't like it, I could take Anita away from the school. 'And I will,' I wrote in my diary that evening.

The following day, I took Anita and Tabitha to Francis Holland to meet the headmistress, Jennifer Anderson, who I liked enormously. After Anita died, she wrote me the sweetest letter, remembering my 'three beautiful daughters'. Of course it made me cry, but I appreciated it very much.

Mrs Anderson said Anita's written test showed that she wasn't up to the standard of the class they'd hoped to put her in, which had a vacancy, whereas the class below had no vacancies. There was, however, the possibility of putting her in the higher class anyway, where she would be one of the youngest, and letting her repeat the year if necessary. I privately felt sure that this would not pose a problem and that she would soon catch up with the other girls because of her ability to rise to the occasion. We were taken on a tour of the school and both Anita and I hoped she would be able to go into the higher class where, because of her height, the girls looked more her age group. Neither of us wanted to repeat the harrowing experience at the ballet school. 'The headmistress was so nice,' I wrote, 'and seemed really to want to help. She'll be writing to me on Monday. Let us pray.' When I didn't hear from the school by the Wednesday of the following week, I telephoned and was told that Anita had got in and would be starting in January.

Anthony came home from Paris on Christmas Eve and started his new job at the Royal Opera House on 4 January 1983. As part of his job, he now got two stalls tickets for every ballet performance and two for each new opera production. That evening I joined him at the Opera House for a triple bill. The first ballet was *Konservatoriet* with Rudolph Nureyev and Marguerite Porter. 'I haven't seen Nureyev dance for twelve years,' I wrote, 'and oh the difference. Such stiffness of leg and shoulders, and wriggly hips in the *batterie*. Life is cruel to dancers . . . We went backstage afterwards and Anthony abandoned me in Nureyev's dressing room while he went on an errand, to my abject terror. I saw his office, which was tiny compared to *L'Opéra* and came home. He said everyone had been sweet and the day had gone well.'

Anita started at Francis Holland on 12 January. 'I've never seen her so nervous,' I wrote. 'Always before, she's been to a new school with Ingo or Tabby or both. We went upstairs with her, the poor love looking more and more nervous. To my great joy, she was in Class 2A, the nicer of the two I saw. Her teacher, Mrs Bown, has great charm and charisma and gave her a lovely welcome. I saw Nita melting on the spot . . . Later I collected Nita. The other mums looked promising, and Nita was bubbly and happy and chattering all the way home. All the other girls had wanted to look after her, and she'd been voted deputy form captain and made lots of friends. She thought Mrs Bown was a much better teacher than Miss Moore and had enjoyed the work and not found it too hard.'

I hope I fully appreciated just what Anita had done for us. By being accepted at Francis Holland, she had also won acceptance for Tabitha, who would join her there in the autumn and Juliet, who would start in 1984. The next time any of my daughters would have to worry about where they were going to be educated was when it came to university entrance.

On the home front, too, we had arrived at a period of calm. We were back in our family home and Anthony was back at what I felt was his spiritual home, the Royal Opera House. The children were sorted educationally and a period of peace and stability beckoned.

CHAPTER EIGHT

19 June 2009

It had been a strange few days. For the first time in eight years working at Berlitz, I'd forgotten to put my availability in the book, and hadn't worked all week. It had turned out to be a lot of fun. An old friend, the photographer Philip Townsend, was exhibiting his photos at the Albert Studio Gallery – part of a picturesque enclave of studios off Albert Bridge Road – so I'd gone along there and spent time chatting to Philip and got a copy of his new book which contained four photos of me modelling in the sixties and some very flattering comments. Still on the 1960s' theme, I'd been invited to the private screening of a film called *Popdown* that I'd apparently appeared in with my friend Debbie Slater in 1967, though neither of us could remember anything about it. I went along to check and, sure enough, there I was in close-up, for all of five seconds, wearing my Ossie Clark leather jacket.

On the Friday, feeling very decadent, I went to the Curzon Mayfair at twelve noon to see *Shadows in the Sun*, a touching, award-winning film set in Norfolk and featuring the old wreck on Brancaster Beach that the children and I used to make an excursion to every summer. The walk took about half an hour and we were always very careful to return to the beach before the incoming tide cut us off. On one occasion we were confronted by a deceptively deep and fast-flowing channel of water that I was hard put to struggle across. The older children must have swum, clinging to my legs, while I carried Juliet in my arms. I remember emerging from the waves triumphant with my babies intact, glowing with the sense of omnipotence I used to feel when they were little and their lives depended on me and I knew with absolute certainty that I'd never let them down.

After the film I went swimming at Dolphin Square, returning home about three to dry my hair and make myself presentable. I was standing in front of the bathroom mirror when Anita rang. Fed up with not getting a proper diagnosis, she had decided to go back to our old friend Tony Greenburgh. He was away, but his locum, Peter Ryan, who I'd known almost as long as I had Tony, took blood and stool samples and told Anita that it was entirely normal for a son or daughter to manifest the same symptoms as a terminally ill parent. Yesterday he had arranged a liver test, which proved negative, and today he'd sent her for an ultrasound in Harley Street. The ultrasound had revealed lumps in her liver, and she'd been sent straight away for a CT scan at University College Hospital. They had told her the news might be bad and to have someone with her when she went back to Harley Street at five for the results. She was calling to ask if I would accompany her.

My usual reaction when I'm told one of my children may have something seriously wrong with them is anger. I felt anger now at the way the doctor had told Anita the news, but curiously winded and lacking in fight. I told her I was sure it was nonsense and that they had no business to frighten her like that, but that of course I'd come and meet her. She was in a Pret-a-Manger off Tottenham Court Road.

Tabitha had lent me her car as she was going to Italy for the weekend to attend a wedding. I tied back my wet hair, flung on some clothes and set off immediately. I knew the roads round University College Hospital well from the dreadful period when Tabitha had been diagnosed with Idiopathic Thrombocyto-paenia Purpora after a routine blood test at the Eastman Dental Hospital prior to having her wisdom teeth extracted. Her platelet count was dangerously low and the specialists at UCH thought she might have leukaemia. They recommended a bone marrow test and gave us half an hour's grace to discuss it. We'd gone to an Italian café in Tottenham Court Road, and afterwards the test had proved negative so now, remembering, I headed back there instinctively, hoping the place would bring us luck a second time.

I found a parking space and called Anita to ask her to meet me at the Italian café. As I gave her directions, I saw her walking towards me, slim and graceful in her summer clothes and smiling and waving as she spotted me. No, I told myself, disbelievingly. It's quite impossible there can be anything seriously wrong with her.

I hadn't eaten lunch, so I ordered a home-made sandwich and we both had diet cokes. To outsiders it must have looked as if we were on a jaunt – a mother and daughter on a shopping trip, perhaps. We must have seemed normal at least, because a young mother who came into the café with her toddler in a buggy asked us if we'd keep an eye on the child while she went to the toilet which was down a steep staircase.

Naturally we agreed. We were proud to be chosen, and the child was very good, staring at us unblinkingly while the mother went downstairs. Inside, I was bargaining with God. 'You see what nice people we are. I'm a good mother. I help other mothers. I do kind things for strangers without seeking reward. Please don't let my daughter have cancer.'

We were in Harley Street punctually at five to see the liver specialist, Steve Pereira. I put less than an hour on the meter because Anita was due at the RAC Club at six to teach Pilates.

Mr Pereira kept us waiting, which seemed a bit curious because there was nobody else in the waiting room. Had I allowed myself to think that way, I would have seen it as a bad sign that for some reason he couldn't bring himself to face us, but of course I twisted it and told myself he wouldn't be so cruel as to keep us waiting if there was anything seriously wrong. When he appeared, we only had about fifteen minutes left on the meter and were starting to wriggle. He told us they'd found a 5cm tumour in Anita's pancreas and several smaller ones in her liver. Until Bobo's diagnosis, I'd hardly heard of the pancreas and still didn't know what it was for. Because we had so little time left, we concentrated on practicalities. Anita was due to fly to Venice next day for a week to see Bobo. Ingo was already there, due to return on Wednesday. Mr Pereira wanted to do a liver biopsy on Anita. It would take some time to organise so it was agreed that Anita would go to Venice as planned, but return early, with Ingo, and have the tests next Thursday or Friday. The results would come a few days later. Although she had originally seen Mr Pereira as a private patient, he told us that after the ultrasound he had switched her to the NHS.

Our meter had run out and all we could say was thank you and goodbye and dash to the car. I drove Anita to the RAC Club, where she taught her class. It was a short journey and most of it was taken up with finding the best route. At that stage we were allowing ourselves to be optimistic. OK, so she might have cancer, but cancer was curable nowadays, wasn't it? And Anita was so fit and healthy.

I said I'd pick her up afterwards and drove home. Juliet was in, so I told her the diagnosis and she came with me to collect Anita after her class. On the way home, Tabitha called and Anita told her the bad news herself. She apologised to Anita for every quarrel they'd ever had and said that Anita had been right in all of them. She then came dashing round to my flat to see her.

Back home, Anita called Hélène. They agreed not to tell Bobo, who was very ill, but Hélène told Ingo, who called Anita back in great distress. If I hadn't been so distraught myself, I would have been happy and proud to witness the children's devotion to each other. Dr Ryan then called and said that if Mr Pereira wanted to perform a biopsy, it must mean there was some doubt as to whether or not Anita had cancer. This gave us a bit of hope. We persuaded Anita to eat some scrambled eggs, but she was in a lot of pain afterwards. Eventually Tabitha had to leave. She felt bad about going to Italy, but Anita was going to Italy herself and they would be back on the same day. The rest of us went to bed about 11.30.

The following morning Anita came into bed with me at 7.30. We were both feeling very sad, but we tried to be positive. I made porridge for her breakfast and Juliet changed her return flight for her so she and Ingo could come back together. Later I drove Anita to Victoria and we took the Gatwick train, where I wrote the card apologising to Bobo. Anita was looking very elegant in skinny jeans and a lovely navy blue cardigan. She told me she wasn't in pain or nauseous, only very tired from lack of sleep. I stayed with her while she checked in and watched her through customs where she turned, smiled bravely at me and waved goodbye, as she had so many times before.

*   *   *

In fact there was a period of nearly two years when Anita didn't go to Venice. When Ingo went to Sussex House, he said he'd like to be known as Russell-Roberts instead of Ferruzzi – in those days it was still quite unusual for children to have different surnames from their parents – and since Bobo had never once been to Bassett House or shown any interest in the children's schooling whatsoever, Anthony and I agreed. We didn't think it would matter or, frankly, that Bobo would ever find out.

We were wrong. A friend of Bobo's from Venice had moved to London and had a son in the same class as Ingo. I already knew the family and the boys became good friends. I didn't ask the parents not to say anything to Bobo about Ingo's surname. In my experience, when you ask someone not to do something, it immediately becomes almost irresistibly tempting to them, so I said nothing and hoped for the best. Alas! In May 1983 I received a furious letter from Bobo demanding that Ingo should be known by the name Ferruzzi at school, which frankly I found very annoying. Of course I should have sent him a tactful reply, but I didn't. Instead, I said something along the lines of, 'He who pays the school fees gets to choose the name.' Bobo disregarded school fees. His line was that schools in Italy are free, and that if I sent the children to him, there wouldn't be any school fees to pay, which I thought was below the belt, because he knew I never would. After my reply, there was an ominous silence that went on and on and on. Bobo stopped sending any money for the children (our arrangement had always been unofficial and erratic anyway) and it began to seem as if we might never hear from him again.

It was Anita who broke the impasse. She got Anthony, ever more tactful than me, to call Bobo in June 1984 and say she wanted to see him again. It was arranged that she would fly to Venice all by herself for two weeks in July. She was just ten years old. Anthony and I took her to the airport. She was very brave, but admitted she felt nervous and clutched my hand tightly. She called me from Venice at lunchtime to say she was there alone with Bobo, but that the others were returning from the mountains that evening. By now Roby and Nora had left Paris and were both living in Venice. Bobo always used to say that daughters were particularly dear to their fathers and sons to their mothers. After his quarrel with Nora, I think Anita was probably more dear to Bobo than anyone in the world. Or as she put it in her novel, 'He had in her [Anita] another chance to love her mother in a relationship that was devoid of the destructive passion he had felt which had almost driven him mad.'

Tabitha and Juliet came with me to collect Anita from Heathrow at the beginning of August. She'd bought us all lovely glass animals from Murano and my mother made a mouth-watering sponge cake in her honour. We were thrilled to see her again. All by herself, little Anita had broken the impasse with Bobo. Diplomatic relations were resumed and child maintenance restored.

That autumn, Anita moved up into the senior school at Francis Holland. As I had predicted, she soon caught up with the rest of her class. In the exams at the end of her first year, she came out somewhere in the middle, which wasn't at all bad considering she was the second youngest in the class and had only been studying the curriculum for two terms instead of three. She made lots of friends, one of the first and most important being Alice von Stauffenberg, who was to prove so loyal and devoted during her final weeks. Tabitha left Fox somewhat reluctantly, but soon made friends at Francis Holland. We had to work very hard on her reading for a term or two and she never read with as much pleasure as her siblings – a fact I blamed on our year in Paris – but Anita kept an eye on her and reported that she always seemed perfectly happy when she thought herself unobserved. For Juliet, the transition was easy, since she was nearly five and had to leave Acorn anyway. On her first day she entered the school without a backward glance, and when we passed her classroom a bit later, we saw her sitting cross-legged on the floor, listening to a story and totally oblivious to her parents, which of course was entirely as it should be.

Once the girls were settled, I tentatively resumed the academic ambitions I'd put on hold when Ingo was born and enrolled at Paddington College to study A level English. Our class met once a week on Monday evenings and did fun things like go to pubs and theatres together. I sat the exam in June 1983 and was thrilled to bits to get an A. Once again, I dared to dream of getting a degree in English. An added incentive was that I would be setting a good example to the children. When the time came for them to go to university, I didn't want any of them to be able to turn round to me and say, 'Well, *you* didn't go,' as an excuse for dropping out.

A friend suggested the Open University, and sent me the relevant information. I loved the sound of the Arts Foundation Course and the way the OU courses didn't restrict themselves to the literature and culture of just one country, but included, for example, French philosophy and Italian opera. I did two Open University modules and found them excellent, but soon realised that the structure of the courses, which ran from February to October, was designed for people in full-time employment and wrong for a someone in my situation, since it meant revising for the exam during the children's school holidays. I saw that I'd be better off attending a normal university, where my schedule would be more compatible with the children's.

Ingo went to Bedales in 1985. I'd never intended him to go to boarding school, but our year in Paris had put paid to his chances of getting into the highly competitive London day schools. Three of his friends from Sussex House went with him and the pupils were allowed home at weekends. In fact he blossomed in the relaxed atmosphere and got into Cambridge at the end, which made us all very proud of him.

One night I had a vivid dream that I was reading English at Bedford College, part of the University of London. As a child, living near Regent's Park, I often used to walk past Bedford College and sometimes see female students reading in a little summer house by the lake. My dream was so vivid that I went along to Senate House, the London University HQ, to look up courses, and found that Bedford College had been merged with Royal Holloway College in Egham. The Royal Holloway campus, Victorian Gothic in beautiful grounds, looked idyllic, and offered a combined honours degree in English and Italian – a course that represented my interests perfectly and would enable me to realise a long-felt ambition to study Dante in the original. I established that there were still places on the course (in fact there was only one other person in my year doing it, and she soon dropped out), and bit the bullet and drove to Egham to see if I'd be able to cope with the journey.

The moment I saw the campus, I fell in love and knew I just had to study there. Driving home along the motorway, I was thrilled to discover that the door-to-door journey against the traffic took only thirty-five minutes. I applied for the course, was accepted, and started there in autumn 1986 at the age of thirty-nine. Fifteen years after first formulating it, my dream had come true.

Astonishingly, the realisation of another dream, that of publishing a book, was set in motion at the same time. Anthony came home from work one day with the news that the ballerina Marguerite Porter had asked him if he could recommend a ghost writer. A publisher was interested in her life story and had already approved an outline on the stipulation that she collaborate with a professional writer. Well, I was a professional – just!

As soon as Anthony told me of the project, I had one of my flashes of intuition. I knew that this one would succeed, but at the same time I felt absolutely terrified. If I wasn't up to the job, it wouldn't just be me I'd be letting down, but Marguerite as well. My fears were calmed during the course of lunch with Marguerite at *La Brasserie* in Brompton Road. I'd seen her dance many times – she was a great favourite of both Fred Ashton and Norman Morrice – but had only met her briefly in the Royal Opera House Crush Bar. To my relief she was very frank and down to earth. Beautiful and elegant, but at the same time modest and self-deprecating about her achievements, she told me stories about the goings on in the Royal Ballet Company that made my eyes pop. I could tell at once that it was going to be a fun project.

Marguerite was about to get married to the actor Nicky Henson, so we were able to proceed at a leisurely pace, which suited me, since I was due to start at Royal Holloway on 29 September and take my Open University end-of-year exam on 20 October.

We used to meet for lunch, generally at her house in Fulham, and chat about whichever period of her life we were working on at the time. We taped our conversations and I, or a professional typist, would transcribe the tapes, after which I'd write the whole thing up. The first chapter was completed by Christmas 1986 and I delivered it by hand to Marguerite in fear and trembling. Almost as soon as I got home, she called to say she loved it. The publishers, Pavilion Books, approved, and we were assigned an editor, Rachel Stewart, who worked closely with us every step of the way.

Writing the book was a very happy experience. I was given a year to do it, which put me under quite a lot of pressure since it coincided with my second to fourth terms at university, but I seemed to thrive on it. Of course I had my wonderful mother to help me. She used to prepare the girls' supper in the evenings so that when we all got back from school, we could disappear to our rooms in peace and do our homework. If I got behind, I had the long university vacations to catch up in.

In 1986, Anthony Dowell succeeded Norman Morrice as Director of the Royal Ballet. I was sad to see Norman go. Through his policy of not inviting any guest artists to dance with the Royal Ballet for the two years between 1978 and 1980, he had created a whole new generation of English ballerinas as well as being a man of great integrity and a good friend. He told us how, at the beginning of his period as Director, he had been approached by various warring factions within the ballet world and invited to side with them, and how his refusal had earned their universal enmity. One night, after the premiere of Jiri Kylian's *Return to the Strange Land*, Anthony and I gave Norman a lift home, and he entertained us on the way by telling us what each of the ballet critics was going to write about the piece, based on their political standpoints. In the morning, when I read the reviews, I was stunned to see that Norman had been one hundred per cent right.

In 1987 Anthony took over the organisation of Royal Ballet tours from Paul Findlay and negotiated a ticket for me to accompany him once a year. Inevitably this brought about changes. We couldn't go to Norfolk at weekends now that Ingo was at Bedales because the time was too short, and in any case Anthony often had to work, and we couldn't go there for Christmas because of Edith, who was now a widow. Ivy had retired and although we tried various alternative housekeepers, nobody could really replace her. Eventually we decided to sell the Barn and buy somewhere cheaper in France that we could rent out for most of the year. The house we got was near a small village called Le Thoronet, half an hour from the coast and wonderfully secluded.

That summer I accompanied Anthony on the Royal Ballet tour to Moscow and Leningrad. I'd always wanted to visit the USSR since reading the ballerina Beryl Grey's account of dancing there in the 1950s. Another incentive was the fact that Marguerite, who had now left the Royal Ballet, would be appearing as a guest artist in *A Month in the Country*. We would be able to continue work on the book, which included inter-views on different aspects of ballet training with the Russian ballerina Irina Kolpakova and the American Cynthia Harvey, and with backstage staff, teachers, physios and the wardrobe mistress.

As a vegetarian, I think I would have starved to death in Moscow if I hadn't modified my regime. Breakfast and dinner were provided at our hotel, the Rossia, and the dancers could have lunch at the theatre – not, alas, the Bolshoi, which was closed for refurbishment, but the much smaller Operetta nearby. Since there were then virtually no restaurants in the city I was forced, not that I needed much forcing, to buy a huge black market tin of Beluga caviar from one of the hotel waiters for twenty dollars and eat guilty spoonfuls of it during the day to sustain me. On our return, Anthony Dowell spotted the same tin on sale in Fortnum and Mason for £700. The ballerina Galina Samsova had a fridge in her room, and kindly stored it there for me between binges.

Others of our party, Colette Clark and Adrian Ward-Jackson,

who was on the Board of Governors, were much cleverer than me and managed to secrete generous portions of breakfast about their persons to eat at lunchtime.

Leningrad, now St Petersburg, was a different proposition and much more civilised. Contrary to all expectations, the weather was beautiful, and we witnessed the legendary White Nights. The company was performing in the Maryinsky Theatre where, entering into the spirit of ghost writing, I joined them on stage one morning for daily class. Never again! Although I was the same age as many of the principal dancers, my legs were trembling so much that I quit at the end of *barre* work. At least the experience had the salutary effect of making me realise how unfit I was. I determined to commence a daily exercise regime and have managed to continue it to this day.

Once Ingo left Sussex House, the school run departed with him since there was no one at Francis Holland to share the driving with. Although the three girls started school together in the morning, they all came out at different times, added to which Tabitha and Juliet had half day on Fridays and Anita didn't. I tried to make the waiting period tolerable for the little girls by taking snacks and books with me and, before Juliet joined the school, I was able to practise Tabitha's reading with her in the car, but the time was really too short to do anything constructive in, and too long to do nothing at all. I worked out that taking into account my two and sometimes three round trips to the school, I was averaging about two and a half hours a day in the car. I began to think seriously about moving nearer to Francis Holland.

When Anita turned fourteen, I sometimes entrusted her with the job of bringing her sisters home by tube from Sloane Square to Bayswater, our nearest stop. I tried picking the girls up from there, but didn't like the idea of leaving them standing in what was then a dodgy area. On one occasion, Juliet's jacket got caught in the train door when the girls got out. Anita managed to wrest it off her, and it disappeared into the tunnel, but the story horrified me. I felt that Anita was far too young to have such a responsibility forced on her.

In January 1988, we put Kildare Gardens on the market and sold it almost instantly to the actor Simon Cadell and his wife. We asked for a three month delayed completion, and an almighty scramble ensued as we hadn't even started to look for anywhere else. Ironically it was the long delay between picking Tabitha and Anita up from school that enabled me to find our dream home. It was 22 February and Anita had a detention, so was going to be particularly late. I decided to pop round to an estate agent in Cadogan Gardens to see if they had anything available.

They mentioned a house in Ebury Street that was selling for exactly the same price we'd agreed for Kildare Gardens, though on a very short lease. It was a house I'd spotted some months before and liked the look of, but I was told it had been taken off the market. Yes, the agent said, it had been off the market for several months, but had just come on again yesterday.

The agent showed us round that same evening and we were all bowled over. From the outside it looked like an ordinary Queen Anne terraced house, but at the back was an enormous garden in which the previous owner, Charles Worthington, a former director of Ballet Rambert, had built a magnificent studio room for entertaining the company, with a flat roof that caught the evening sun. It was romantic in the extreme, like having a country house in the centre of London, and the garden actually backed on to the Francis Holland playground. From being one of the furthest mothers from the school geographically, I would now be the nearest, with not even a road to cross between home and school.

The short lease wasn't something we'd encountered before, but it was explained to us that once we had lived in the house for three years, we would have the legal right to enfranchise (buy the freehold). This would probably take several years to negotiate, but the price would be fixed at the time we served the notice, so we wouldn't lose out. If the price of the freehold proved too high for us, we could sell the property plus the right to buy the freehold or borrow the money, buy it ourselves and sell it as a freehold.

The attraction I felt for the house almost frightened me. I knew immediately that this would be a house in which things happened, whereas Kildare Gardens was a house in which things almost happened, but never quite came to fruition. I also knew that not everything that happened would be good, but I felt that this was *my* house, and that whatever price was demanded of me for living there, I would be prepared to pay it.

After five years at Francis Holland, Anita was considering going to a co-ed school for the sixth form. I was quite happy with the idea. Having been to an all girls' school myself, I felt that possibly it wasn't the best preparation for adult life. Bedales would have been the obvious choice, but since Anita, through being one of the youngest in her class at Francis Holland, was only one year behind Ingo educationally, it would have meant them being in the sixth form together, and this he refused to contemplate. Anita was very good about not wanting to cramp his style. Bunty Ross had told me about a school called Frensham Heights in Surrey, very near Bedales and run on the same principles. Anita and I went to an open day in May 1988 and loved it. The building and grounds were beautiful, the pupils charming and positive, and when the headmaster, Alan Pattinson, interviewed Anita, he was amazingly perceptive and sensitive and I felt he really liked her. She was due to take her mock GCSEs in the summer, and the offer of a place at Frensham would be conditional on the results.

We moved into Ebury Street on a sunny day at the end of May. The children went to school as usual and returned to the new house, first Ingo, home for half term, then the three girls, who had walked from school. I was sunbathing on the roof terrace when they arrived and feeling blissfully happy. I had been liberated from the school run at last and was now confident I could bring my projects – my degree and my book – to completion.

Four days later, Anthony flew to Melbourne to consolidate the details of the Royal Ballet tour to Australia in July. It was the first tour he'd organised since taking over the job and the children and I were going with him, leaving my mother in charge of the house and pets, while supervising extensive building works on her flat. I saw it as a unique opportunity for the children, and in any case couldn't have contemplated travelling so far without them. We got special permission to take them out of school early on condition that the girls wrote a holiday diary describing their experiences.

We flew out on 1 July, a few days after the company and spent a week in Melbourne.

On 13 July we flew to Alice Springs for a four-day tour of the Red Centre which, to my mind, was the highlight of the trip. On 16 July, in the days when it was still allowed, we climbed Ayers Rock. 'We were up at 6.30 again,' I wrote. 'After breakfast, most of us caught the 7.15 bus to Ayers Rock, but I was determined to see the sunrise from the hotel observation platform at 7.30 and Tab stayed with me. There were lots of other people with cameras on the small platform, so it wasn't that magical, but one nice man showed us Venus, Jupiter and Mars, which I found thrilling. I felt like Dante having just emerged from *Inferno* into the undiscovered Southern Hemisphere and seeing Venus as the morning star instead of the evening one. After some hassle Tab and I got a lift to Ayers Rock, arriving about half an hour after the others. This was a climbing trip. Serious stuff. Ingo, Anita and Juliet were nowhere to be seen, but Anthony was there to greet us having got chest pains and a swimming head a little way up. The bus driver had said it wasn't advisable for people with high blood pressure or heart trouble to do the climb, so we agreed he'd stay down. I couldn't wait to get started, but I must say the first bit was a nightmare. There was a chain on poles stuck in the rock and I was clawing my way up it, bent double and gasping for breath. The coach driver said that at the top of the chain there was a place called Chicken Rock (for obvious reasons) which was only a third of the way to the summit, and that most people turned back there. I decided I definitely wasn't going to make it further than that. Also the whole climb was supposed to take an hour and just that bit took me an hour. Tab and I met Anita and Juliet near the top of the chain. They'd got to Chicken Rock, where there's a sort of plateau to rest on and take photos, but it was incredibly windy and Anita said Juliet shouldn't go any further as there was nothing to hold on to, and was bringing her down. I took a photo of them on the slope, looking adorable. Anita is wonderfully protective to the little girls. Tab and I got to Chicken Rock, where a nice lady took photos of us both. I felt guilty (and worried) about Ingo as I had his camera and thought what a shame it would be if he got to the top and couldn't take a photo. Eventually we decided to struggle on a little further, hoping to run into him. It was much less steep after the chain, and I could breathe again, but the wind was terrifying. One very experienced-looking climber said it was the worst he'd ever known it. Quite soon we saw Ingo sitting on a ledge. He didn't come down to meet us, so we went up to him. He'd been to the top and, to our amazement, said it was only about ten minutes away, so we decided to go on, with him as our guide (though you can't miss the path because some angel has painted dotted white lines all the way along it). On we went, clinging to each other and throwing ourselves to the ground whenever there was a specially strong gust of wind. Finally we made it and signed our names in the climbers' book at the top. The sense of achievement and exaltation was wonderful. Took hundreds of photos, then had to charge down to catch the bus. Ingo went ahead to tell Anthony we were OK, but in fact we were so pleased with ourselves that we went skipping down like mountain goats. Descending the chain was hard on the backs of the knees, but nothing like the horror of coming up. A man was being lowered down on a stretcher. His face was covered, only his calves and climbing boots were sticking out, so I realised he must be dead. (Later we were told he was 'oldish' and had had a heart attack. His family was waiting at the bottom.) Felt strangely unmoved. There was something about the rock that made the sacrifice of life seem appropriate, and there couldn't be many better places to close one's eyes on the world. Compare the awful street in Norwich where my father died.'

I've reproduced this episode in full because, to my mind, it perfectly encapsulates the children's characters: Ingo = independent, Anita = protective of her younger siblings, Tabitha = protective of her parents, and Juliet = adventurous. Perhaps it sums up mine as well = maternal instinct pushing me to feats of daring I would never have contemplated on my own.

After Alice Springs, we rejoined the company in Sydney for two weeks. Sadly they weren't able to perform at the Opera House, because the stage was too small, but we went there for a reception on our first day and found the view of the harbour quite breathtaking. The party was in a room with a glass-bottomed floor so we felt as if we were standing on the waves. In Sydney we renewed acquaintance with old friends and saw some thrilling ballet performances, notably Jennifer Penney's final *Manon* with Anthony Dowell, after which John Tooley and Kenneth Macmillan made emotional speeches from the stage and most of the company were in tears. John Tooley was retiring at the end of the season, nobody quite knew why, to be replaced by Jeremy Isaacs, the former Chief Executive of Channel Four, who knew little about opera and even less about ballet, so there was a general feeling of wariness and uncertainty.

The highlight of Brisbane, our next stop, was cuddling a koala called Boysie in the Lone Pine Sanctuary. Afterwards we made a quick trip to Cairns and spent a day snorkelling on the Barrier

Reef, before flying to Hong Kong on 8 August. Our last stop was Thailand. We spent two days in Bangkok, then flew to Phuket, where we stayed at the Yacht Club and felt we were experiencing a foretaste of paradise.

The thought of leaving was almost unbearable, but at the very last minute, when Anthony went to reception to pay our bill, he was given a telegram from Jeremy Isaacs telling him that Frederick Ashton had died in his sleep the night before. The girls burst into tears, and suddenly we all longed to be home. Dear Fred, a consummate professional to the end, had timed his death perfectly so as not to disrupt the tour.

CHAPTER NINE

22 – 24 June 2009

I went back to work on the Monday after Anita flew to Venice, but fortunately it wasn't an arduous day – just three lessons with a Japanese student. Tabitha had advised me not to research pancreatic cancer on the internet, presumably because she knew how serious it was. I tried not to. The official line within the family was that until Anita'd had her biopsy, we didn't know if she had cancer or not, and were going forward on the assumption that she didn't. I couldn't resist a peek however. It seemed that some pancreatic tumours were operable – the operation was called the Whipple procedure – but that others, depending on the proximity to vital organs, weren't.

This bewildered me. I knew of course that people died of cancer, but assumed that this was only after years of treatment. I had no idea that there were some cancers for which there was no treatment at all. After that my mind veered away again and I told myself sternly to remember that it was entirely possible that Anita didn't have cancer at all.

The news from Venice wasn't all bad. Ingo and Anita were sharing a room as they had as children, and Ingo was practising Reiki on her. He'd completed the Reiki course parts one and two as a student and treated my mother when she was in hospital during her final illness, bringing her great serenity and comfort.

Hélène, too, had a soothing presence. Before Bobo's illness, whenever he got difficult, she would withdraw to another room and meditate. I wished I'd thought of doing that myself. Hélène had also taught Anita to meditate, and on the Sunday when

Anita was feeling upset, Hélène accompanied her to the beach and talked to her until she felt better.

Victoria had gone to Brighton for the weekend to visit her mother but was returning on Monday evening in order to go to work on Tuesday. The fire alarm in their house had gone off at 3 am on Friday and given her a fright, so Ingo asked if Juliet or I would go and stay with her till he got back.

In the end we both went over at about eight with the dogs. Max was in bed and it was a beautiful, mild evening, so the three of us sat in the garden for an hour or so drinking wine (Victoria drank water) and keeping up the façade of normality.

The next day Victoria went to work and I took Max by bus to Wimbledon to the house of a former student, Petra, whose husband's company had paid for her to have a course of Berlitz lessons, which had now finished. I never normally socialised with students for fear of breaking the Berlitz rules and being accused of poaching, but I liked Petra and felt bad about the way her course had ended so abruptly when the money ran out. Besides, her son was exactly Max's age and his name was Moritz and Max and Moritz are a famous duo in Germany, so I hoped they might be friends.

I said nothing to Petra about my worries over Anita. Even though she was no longer my student, I felt it would be inappropriate, and anyway it went against our official line that Anita was cancer free until proved otherwise.

It was a beautiful day and Max loved Moritz's toys. Moritz was unexpectedly shy and hid his face on his mother's shoulder while Max made free with his possessions. After an hour or so, Max got into his buggy and said, 'Go home.' Victoria told me afterwards that he never lasted more than an hour in someone else's house, but at the time I was mortified. Offers of drinks and biscuits were refused politely but firmly and off we set again in the bus to Tooting, where Juliet was working on her computer and keeping an eye on the dogs.

We gave Max lunch and put him down for his nap, then took him for a walk on Tooting Common with the dogs in the afternoon. Victoria got back about five, simultaneously with the window cleaner, who was a huge success. Max followed him around the house for the next hour, spellbound with admiration.

I'd planned to go home in the evening as I was working at Berlitz the following day, but suddenly I couldn't bear to. The flat would be empty and I'd be alone with the nameless dread that I'd been keeping at bay since Friday. After Max had gone to bed, Victoria cooked a delicious stir fry, which we ate in the garden together.

My lessons finished at 1.30 next day, the same time that Ingo and Anita's plane landed at Gatwick. She and Ingo were catching the train to London together. He was getting off at Clapham Junction and returning home, and I said I'd meet Anita at Victoria. We kept in touch by text and, almost as soon as I'd parked the car by Warwick Square, I saw her walking towards me looking very beautiful but alarmingly thin.

She had a photo session that afternoon at the RAC Club. She'd bought some Pilates machines at her own expense for the use of her pupils there, and was to be photographed demonstrating them. These were the last photos ever taken of her.

She came home for some lunch, then I drove her to the club and picked her up again after the session. She was having all her tests – blood and biopsy – the next day at University College Hospital. Juliet was going to accompany her in the morning and I was going to take over in the afternoon when I finished work.

Anita had just said goodbye to her father for the last time and was about to find out if she had a terminal illness, but we didn't talk about any of that. She, Juliet and I watched an hour of TV together and went early to our rooms.

*   *   *

After Fred's death, Anthony and I got caught up in a whirl of reflected glory. We had always believed he was going to leave Chandos Lodge to Martyn Thomas, but Martyn was killed in a car accident in November 1986. Fred was deeply upset, even though, by that time, his relationship with Martyn had become semi-detached, and he had a new friend, Tony Dyson, who we were all very fond of.

Two days before we went to Australia, Fred came to lunch at Ebury Street. Sadly I couldn't be there, and he and Anthony ate alone. It was the first time Fred had been to the house, and he told Anthony to congratulate me for having found it. 'I'm going to leave Chandos to you,' he said with typical generosity, 'and you can sell it to buy your freehold or do anything you like with it.'

Fred died at Chandos. His friend, the former dancer Alexander Grant, was staying and had been trimming the topiary in the garden for him. They sat up late after dinner talking. Finally Alexander went to bed. Fred said, 'I'll just have one for the road,' and remained downstairs. In the morning Alexander and the housekeeper, Mrs Dade, found him dead in his bed.

Anthony went to Chandos the day after we got back from Australia to organise Fred's funeral. I saw Ingo and Anita off to Venice and joined him there two days later. Late that evening a beautiful bouquet of flowers arrived from the Queen Mother, delivered by two flustered ladies in a Moyses Stevens van, who had got hopelessly lost.

Fred had enjoyed a close relationship with the Queen Mother. They used to spend her birthdays together in a foursome, with Sir Martin Gilliat, her private secretary, and Ruth, Lady Fermoy, the grandmother of Princess Diana. For the Queen Mother's eightieth birthday in 1980, at her request, Fred had created a new ballet for her, *Rhapsody* (named after *Rachmaninov's Rhapsody on a Theme by Paganini*) starring Mikhail Baryshnikov and Lesley Collier, and he was a regular house guest at Sandringham.

The funeral, at Yaxley Church where Fred's mother was

buried, was like a Who's Who of the ballet world. Dame Ninette de Valois, aged ninety, looked frail but gallant and was driven down by Merle Park's husband, Sidney Bloch. John Tooley, Anthony Dowell, Antoinette Sibley and Lynn Seymour were all present, while Fred's closest friends, Alexander, Tony, Michael Somes, Leslie Edwards and Bryan Shaw followed the coffin and Somes read the lesson from Corinthians with a breaking voice.

Fred's memorial service took place at Westminster Abbey on 29 November. It was attended by the Queen Mother and Princess Margaret and the congregation was so large that many people had to be seated in St Margaret's Westminster, next door. Princess Margaret was President of the Royal Ballet, and took her responsibilities seriously, attending first nights and foreign tours, especially in America, where a royal presence ensured good ticket sales. She had given a dinner party at Kensington Palace for Fred's eightieth birthday in 1984, to which Anthony and I were invited. Fred enchanted everyone with his very short speech of thanks beginning, 'Who would have thought that little Freddy Ashton from Lima, Peru would be given a birthday party by a Royal princess?'

Hours of preparation went into the memorial service. Both Ninette de Valois and Margot Fonteyn were asked to give addresses, but in the event Fonteyn was too ill to come and her tribute was read by Michael Somes. Fred had requested that Hans Werner Henze, who had composed the score for Fred's ballet *Ondine*, should conduct the Andante from Mozart's *Piano Concerto K.467* at the service, which he did, most movingly. One of the most touching moments for me was when the head boy and girl of the Royal Ballet School walked up the aisle with Fred's decorations – CH, CBE, OM, *Legion d'honneur* – on velvet cushions. For the reading, the Abbey gave us various ideas, but none seemed entirely apt. Ruth, Lady Fermoy, had invited Anthony and me to dinner at the beginning of November, and among the high-powered guests was Sue Lawley, who was then presenting *Desert Island Discs*. Thinking about the dinner next day, I remembered listening to Fred on the programme some years before, talking to Roy Plomley. For his book, he had chosen the complete works of Proust. Skimming through the last volume, I found a passage about truth in art that seemed most apt. I edited it ruthlessly, cutting out all references to Madeleines, and showed it Anthony, who luckily shared my enthusiasm. Anthony Dowell was given the task of reading it, and did so most beautifully.

Anthony and I were invited to lunch at Clarence House after the service by the Queen Mother. There were about twenty people, some of whom – Princess Margaret, John and Anya Sainsbury, Lady Fermoy – we knew already. The Queen Mother was most gracious and welcoming, 'like a teeny, little ballerina, beckoning us into the room'. Princess Margaret kissed us both and I felt my usual moment of fear that the combination of curtseying while bending over to kiss her would cause me to topple over and squash her. Everything ran like clockwork, with hordes of equerries at our elbow showing us where to go. At lunch Anthony was on the Queen Mother's left, and I sat between Sir Eric Penn, husband of Princess Margaret's friend Prue, and Sir Alastair Aird, Comptroller of the Queen Mother's Household. 'Even the conversation was choreographed,' I wrote, 'with Sir E. addressing me first and then, sharply with the pudding, the Queen M. turning to address Anthony and every-one else turning at the same time, so I got Sir Alastair.' Both my neighbours were seasoned courtiers and kept up an easy, pleasant flow of conversation. At one stage I told Sir Alastair that I'd been married to an Italian, and he looked at me with great sympathy and said, 'My dear, how you must have suffered!'

At the end of the wonderfully rich and delicious lunch, after the silver cigarette box had been passed round with the coffee, the ladies were led into the drawing room and the Queen Mother beckoned me to sit on the sofa next to her.

'Isn't it difficult to find anything black in one's wardrobe?' she said. 'My dress must be fifteen years old.' I replied that my wardrobe was almost entirely black, and that my husband was always complaining about it.

'Well, it's very useful, isn't it?' she said politely, if somewhat dubiously.

Much to my surprise, I thoroughly enjoyed both the service and the lunch. Anthony and his team had coped beautifully and, most important of all, we felt Fred would have approved of our arrangements. That evening we drank a melancholy half bottle of champagne together in his honour.

In between Fred's funeral and his memorial service, I went to Venice for a month as part of my university course. Normally I would have been expected to spend a year in Italy, but because I had already lived there in the seventies, and because of my family responsibilities, I was granted an exemption.

I arranged to stay the month at Montin in a room above the restaurant. It was perfect for my needs, containing a single bed, desk, chest of drawers, wardrobe and wash basin, with a French window and a tiny balcony, covered with red geraniums, over-looking the garden. Breakfast in the restaurant was included as part of the deal, but for my other meals I had to fend for myself.

At first I was very conscious of my own lack of inner resourcefulness. Like many mothers, I had often dreamed of having time to myself, but now that I had, I didn't know what to do with it. The shock of being on my own was enormous. Eventually, however, I pulled myself together. I looked up old friends and family. Bobo and Hélène were kind and welcoming. Ucci cooked dinner for me and lent me his camera and Ping Ping, who had lost an eye in a childhood accident, most flatteringly mistook me for Anita. I formed an unofficial cinema club with four of the other students and went on trips to Urbino and the Villas of the Brenta – the start of a passion for solo travel that would lead me round the seven new wonders of the world after my divorce.

Soon after my return from Venice we received some good news about the ballet book. Marguerite and I had handed the manuscript in to the publishers, Pavilion, in January 1988. A few weeks later, we were bemused to receive a letter from Pavilion saying, 'Hi, I'm X your new editor. I really like your book, but need to meet you to talk about some changes . . . ' We later heard that Pavilion was notorious for this sort of thing, but it didn't make it any better at the time. We met, were told what changes to make and made them, but still the thing dragged on. Eventually we got lawyers in and it was agreed that we could keep our meagre advance and take the book elsewhere.

In December Anthony came home with the news that the American publisher Michael O'Mara and his wife Lesley had read the book, liked it and wanted to publish it. They had previously published a book of photos of the Royal Ballet and owned their own company, so there was no question of them having to please anyone else. The O'Maras were a joy to work with. We eventually became good friends and they went on to publish my two novels.

Anita did well in her GCSE mocks and was offered a place in the sixth form at Frensham Heights. We had mixed feelings about it. I knew I'd miss her horribly if she went, but had come to believe passionately in the importance of education, and felt she would be more likely to work for her A levels if we got her away from the distractions of London.

She was now fifteen, and getting more beautiful by the day. Model scouts were constantly stopping her in the street and giving her their cards and she was starting (shock horror) to go out with boys. The first time she went on a date, Anthony dropped her at the meeting place, taking Tabitha and Juliet in the car. Her date kissed her on the cheek in greeting, and Anita said she could see our car starting to shake as Tabitha and Juliet jumped up and down with excitement. Anthony then stepped forward, at my request, and asked for the boy's telephone number in case we needed to get hold of Anita. I'm surprised, looking back, that she ever forgave us.

All too soon it was the Easter holidays and Anita and I were on a countdown to our exams – my finals, for which I had to read seventy texts in four weeks – and Anita's GCSEs. The other children were very good and gave us peace and quiet to work. Ingo had completed his GCSEs the year before and achieved very respectable results, so now had a year of comparative calm before his A levels.

Anita's exams started on 25 May and mine on 1 June. I was quite pleased with my schedule which was spread over two weeks with a decent amount of time to revise between each exam. That first weekend, Anita and I stayed in London while the others went to Chandos Lodge. We were closeted in our rooms all day, meeting only at meal times when we tried not to get into too much of a state about the ordeal that lay ahead.

I sat my finals in the Picture Gallery, the most beautiful room in the college, though I doubt many of us were in a position to appreciate it. Founded in 1879 by the Victorian philanthropist Thomas Holloway in memory of his wife Jane, Holloway acquired seventy-seven Victorian era paintings, including works by Turner, Constable and Gainsborough, which he donated to the college at the time of its founding. One painting of a ship-wreck was deemed to bring bad luck, and was always draped in a Union Jack during finals.

My exams finished on 16 June. I had dinner at my favourite Indian restaurant, the Great India in Lower Sloane Street, then went home and watched junk TV. Anita's GCSEs finished on the 21st and we didn't see her for dust. She had one particular friend who, although very likeable, we considered something of a bad influence. This was probably unfair, since she's now a respectable wife and mother. At the time I wrote, 'we all worry about her influence. The late nights, smoking, boys etc. and, sad as it is, feel that Nita's going to Frensham just in time.'

Only my Italian oral exam now remained. I splashed out on some private lessons at the Berlitz School in Oxford Street, but in the event the exam was a gift. I asked the head of the Italian Department, Professor Aquilecchia, a question about the *dolce stil nuovo* and, to my joy, he was off with a detailed explanation of which I took in not a word (although I had very much appreciated his lectures during my course). My main desire was to keep him talking for as long as possible so I wouldn't have to, and in this I succeeded brilliantly, in spite of the other examiners' attempts to stop him. We then had to wait around for several hours before the Italian leavers' party that evening where we were given our results. I got a respectable 2:1, which was what I'd been hoping for, although I still had to wait another two months before my English results came through and confirmed my grade.

There was a parents and children's leaving party at Francis Holland on 27 June, which I rather enjoyed. 'Anita looked stunningly beautiful,' I wrote, 'and went out afterwards with Emily and a boy called Remy. Anthony and I were in the position of middle-aged parents waiting for their offspring to come home.'

In the meantime the ballet book had gone to the printers. We agonised over a title for ages, but in the end Michael O'Mara chose it for us, *Ballerina: A Dancer's Life*. To be a ballerina, you have to have danced the principal roles in *Swan Lake*, *Giselle* and *The Sleeping Beauty*, and *A Dancer's Life* referred not only to Marguerite's life, but to that of every classical dancer. I had to write a new chapter to bring the book up to date, as Marguerite had recently given birth to her son Keaton and we also had to choose and caption her photos. One of the themes of the book was Marguerite's ill-fated relationship with her dance partner Wayne Eagling, now director of English National Ballet. Nicky Henson said that since all Eagling's girlfriends were bound to buy the book, we ought to be able to count on sales of at least a thousand.

That summer we spent a month at the house in France, where we had installed a rather splendid pool in what the architect called a *dessin libre*. It had become the custom during the summer holidays for Ingo and Anita to go to Venice early on and then fly directly to France to join us. On this occasion I called Bobo to see if they'd arrived safely and was told the sad news that his twin brother, Lillo, who I hadn't seen for many years, had died the day before of a heart attack after what was supposed to be a routine operation. I asked Bobo if it was a bad moment for the children to be there, but he replied that on the contrary, they were a great comfort to him.

They joined us in France on 8 August. Nicky, Marguerite and Keaton were staying, and a few days later we all went to Simon Sainsbury's lovely house in Ramatuelle for lunch. Anita mentioned to Sian, the Sainsbury Major Domo, that she wanted to be a model, and he told us he was good friends with the director of Models One. He said he would give her a call about Anita, and told us to telephone the agency when we got back to London, to make an appointment.

I wasn't in favour of Anita becoming a model. Although she was exquisitely beautiful, she had no confidence in her looks, and I remembered from my own experience the relentless pressure to be thin that models were under, that almost inevitably led to eating disorders and an obsession with one's physical appearance. One of my favourite tricks when I was modelling was to put myself to sleep for a weekend with Mogadon, eat nothing for two days and lose half a stone. I told her that the modelling world was full of fat old men telling slim young girls that they were fat, and that ninety per cent of a model's career consisted of rejection. This was all true, but unfortunately it didn't seem to put her off.

I told Sian of my concerns about Anita's education, and he assured me that the team at Models One had great respect for education and would fit Anita's modelling assignments round her studies. Thus reassured, I accompanied her to the agency's offices in World's End when we got back to London. A young girl in front of us was being summarily rejected, but the bookers took a Polaroid photo of Anita and said they liked her very much, so I couldn't help being pleased for her.

In the end they kept her dangling for the next two years. They told us they didn't take girls under sixteen, so asked us to come back the following summer, and told Anita not to go to any other agencies in the meantime. They wanted her to lose a bit of weight (surprise, surprise) and recommended she didn't drink alcohol as it tended to make the jaw puffy. Anita was very disciplined and gave up alcohol for the next two years, which was the most positive aspect of our dealings with the agency. Shortly before her A levels, Anita visited them again and was accepted on to their books, only to be contacted again a few months later and told that because of the economic downturn, they were getting much less work than usual and weren't taking on any new girls after all.

I was furious at the way they'd mucked Anita around. They offered us a list of other agencies, but I said we didn't want it. Years later, when she was dying, Anita accused me, on the basis of this meeting, of having prevented her from modelling. I was utterly taken aback, as I thought we had resolved the issue years before. I feel that if she had been really determined, she would have gone ahead and visited the other agencies without me, and I also feel that modelling wouldn't have made her happy, but at the same time I'm truly sorry that I was the one to take the lustre off her dream and make her unhappy.

Anita's GCSE results came through on 25 August and were a respectable mixture of As and Bs. Astonishingly to her, she got an A in Science which made her very cross since she insisted she knew nothing at all about the subject. For her A levels, she decided to do French, English and History.

Term started at Frensham Heights on 4 September, but only

for the sixth form, with the rest of the school going back the following day. We set off with Anita about three, taking Tabitha with us for company. Anita said she didn't feel at all nervous until we actually arrived. She was in a room with three other girls, one of whom was also new and had never been to boarding school before. Anita was very composed when we said goodbye, but as we were driving off, I looked up at her window and saw her waving to us as we went down the drive. 'It was a sight that will always haunt me,' I wrote and I was right, since it's haunting me now. On the way home, Tabitha kept leaning forward and asking me if I was crying in an interested voice. 'I wasn't,' I wrote, 'but I felt like it.'

Anita was a weekly boarder like Ingo, so we soon saw her again. The Frenshamians came to London on Saturday mornings by coach to Waterloo, and were picked up again at 6.30 pm on Sunday. Both Ingo and Anita made their own way home on Saturdays, but were usually glad of a lift to the station on Sunday evenings.

Anita was very affectionate when she came home from school at weekends. Since becoming a teenager, she'd been increasingly stroppy. In her case this took the form of questioning every aspect of her upbringing, especially those she'd previously taken for granted, but all this stopped when she went to Frensham. Several of her new friends were from broken homes, and the stories they told her made her feel that perhaps we weren't such a bad family after all. I basked in this new approval, which was a totally unexpected and welcome by-product of her time at boarding school.

For the first few weekends, Anita socialised mainly with her old friends from Francis Holland and it was then, as she told me much later, that she started to do drugs for the first time. I had absolutely no idea. Her behaviour, as I say, was adorable, although one of my diary entries sounds ominous: 'Anita and Rose remained closeted in Anita's room most of the afternoon, burning incense.' Perhaps I was very naïve, but as a mother I had always tried to model myself on the three wise monkeys. My mother took the opposite approach and cross-examined me relentlessly over what I was doing and who I was seeing and I'm convinced that this made me even more determined to go my own way. It certainly made me dislike my mother intensely at the time.

When I was a teenager, my friend Mike Gross told me that his father had paid him an allowance for not smoking until he was twenty-one. Mike took the allowance but smoked anyway. Before I could express my shock at this duplicity, he explained that in doing so he was making both of them happy – his father because he believed Mike didn't smoke and himself because of the money. Another plus was that he ended up smoking far less because he couldn't do it at home.

It was impossible to refute his logic, and I since knew from my own experience that no parental edicts would stop my children from doing anything they wanted, I decided to adopt Mike's approach in reverse. I never cross-examined or accused my children, but tried to exude an aura of confidence in their ability to say no. I took the attitude that they were far too intelligent and well educated not to be aware of the consequences of excessive drinking or drug taking and would never be foolish enough to put their health at risk in such a way.

By and large, I believe that it worked, at least to the extent that, whatever may have gone on behind my back, none of my children ever lost the ability to function or to keep up the pretence of normality in public. I believe, but only because she told me so, that Anita was the worst offender, but even she, by her mid-twenties, had cleaned up so completely that she never drank alcohol, smoked or took drugs again for the rest of her short life.

As usual Anita made friends quickly at Frensham, and soon started to bring schoolmates of both sexes home at weekends and to France and Suffolk in the school holidays. I believe one or two wild parties were held in the studio while we were away, but once more the wise monkey approach served its purpose, since everything was more or less cleared up again by the time we got home.

Chandos Lodge was the scene of an exciting adventure in June 1990 when the Russian ballet star, Irek Mukhamedov, defected to England with his pregnant wife Masha. It had all the potential to become a diplomatic incident, so Anthony and I invited them to stay at Chandos, where it was felt they would be safe from attempted abduction or poisoned umbrellas. Irek and Masha were a good example of how it's possible to become very fond of people without being able to talk to them, although the Russian interpreter Tamara Finch, widow of the actor Peter, was with us for part of their stay. I only had one bad moment. On Sunday morning they slept very late, and I had a sudden terror that they'd been murdered in their bed. I was much too frightened to go and look, so suffered agonies until they appeared. They came back to London the following week to have lunch with us and meet Anthony Dowell for the first time at *La Poule au Pot* opposite our house. It was something of a historic meeting. We were already seated when Dowell arrived and I remember him whispering to me, 'I wish he'd stand up so I can see if he's tall enough to partner Darcey Bussell!' Fortunately he was, and a month later the two of them made a sensational debut in the *pas de deux* from Kenneth Macmillan's new ballet *Three Sisters*.

Ingo acquitted himself well in A levels, and was offered a place at Cambridge to read Theology and History of Art. He spent his gap year in Florence, taking a History of Art A level at the British Institute, which was one of the nicest educational establishments I've ever had the pleasure of dealing with. I was delighted when Anita decided to go there too, the following year, for a three-month course to brush up her Italian.

Anita had followed her usual pattern of doing the minimum

amount of work at Frensham until the month before her A levels and then pulling out all the stops and getting decent grades. She had no idea what she wanted to do as a career, but she enjoyed travelling so decided to go for a degree in European Studies, since it included a year abroad as part of the syllabus. By coincidence, Royal Holloway did a really good European Studies course, and she ended up putting the college down as her first choice on her UCAS form. She chose French as her European language rather than Italian on the grounds that she was bound to learn Italian anyway, as indeed she did.

In both Ingo's and Anita's cases, the summer after their A levels was the last time they deigned to come on a family holiday with us. In 1990 we spent a fairly horrific fortnight in the Dominican Republic, where the catch-phrase was, 'No problem!' which in our experience translated as 'You're in serious trouble!', and the food was hopeless for vegetarians. Ingo's A level results were telephoned to us there by my mother, but a message from Edith's nursing home to say she was ill never got through. She recovered on that occasion, but died peacefully in the Meadbank Nursing Home on 23 September 1990. Her funeral service was at Yaxley Church and she was buried there beside Fred. Her last years hadn't been very happy, but she had always been a kind and loyal mother-in-law to me, and the children and I loved her dearly.

Anita was convinced she'd done really badly in her A levels in 1991, but in fact she'd achieved the exact grades she needed to get into Royal Holloway. She said a sad goodbye to Frensham Heights, then flew with us all (apart from Ingo, who went inter-railing with a friend) to New York for the start of the Royal Ballet summer tour. It was the girls' first visit to New York. We were staying at the Mayflower Hotel on Central Park West, within walking distance of the Lincoln Center where the company was performing, and spent our days sight-seeing, swimming and shopping. Being tall, we found that

American clothes fitted us better than British ones as well as costing far less, so stocked up blissfully on jeans, trainers and T shirts.

Anita accompanied Anthony to the opening night of *Swan Lake*, where she caused a sensation among the young men of the company who promptly invited her out clubbing. After New York, we flew to Miami where we stayed at the Doral Beach Resort for a week and the girls learnt how to scuba dive. My daredevil days were over, so I lay by the pool and watched them. I was a bit nervous, but I knew I could count on Anita to look after them. The girls and I then flew off on our own to Orlando for three days for a long-promised visit to Disneyworld. It was supposed to be a great treat, but turned into more of an ordeal, since each five minute ride seemed to involve queuing for forty minutes beforehand in a hundred degree temperatures.

From Orlando we flew to Dallas Fort Worth, where we saw Anita off on a flight back to London. She was going to Greece with a group of friends from Frensham to celebrate leaving school. Tabitha, Juliet and I rejoined the Royal Ballet in Orange County where I was able to renew my friendship with Suzanne who offered us the most marvellous California-style hospitality – champagne under the stars in the jacuzzi – and told us all the best places to go.

That autumn we accompanied Ingo to Cambridge and Anita to Florence, where we helped her find a flat with another student from the British Institute, Miranda Harvey. As usual, she made loads of friends. One evening, which I'm glad I didn't know about at the time, sounded particularly dramatic. She was out with two friends, Brendan Douglas Hamilton and James Napier. Brendan was wearing a kilt and, for some reason decided to moon at a group of Italians who took great offence. One of them produced a gun and chased Anita's group round Florence for several hours before they managed to escape.

Just after Christmas, when Anita was back from Florence,

Suzanne came to stay with us for a week with her twelve-year-old son Simon, who the girls adored. On New Year's Eve, Suzanne and I went to see the clairvoyant Tom Corbett, who lived just off Sloane Square. It was the second visit for both of us. At the time of our first visit in 1975, Suzanne was about to marry her then boyfriend Andrew. The church had been booked and the dress bought, while I had just left Bobo and, although I was seeing Anthony, had no idea how the relationship would turn out. To our astonishment Corbett told Suzanne that she wasn't going to get married and me that I was, both of which turned out to be true. He also told me I was about to embark on something artistic (the rewriting of *A Darker Shade of Love*) and that I would succeed at it, though I was going to have to work hard. When the book was eventually published, I realised that everything Tom Corbett told me had come true, as it also had for Suzanne.

I had no particular reason to see Tom Corbett in 1991, as my life and career were progressing nicely. *Ballerina* had been received well and sold out, *A Darker Shade of Love* currently had two publishers bidding for the paperback rights and Michael O'Mara had signed me up to write a second novel. I had also embarked on a new career as an Italian translator. My Italian tutor at Royal Holloway, Dr Letizia Panizza, told me I had a gift for it and after graduation recommended me for various well-paid assignments in the academic field. I joined a team of three translators working on a *History of the History of Philosophy* which was published in 1993. I worked on this at the same time as *A Darker Shade of Love*, and found it rather soothing to turn from the appalling irrationality of the Ken character in my novel to the cool logic of the historiographers. In fact my only worries were financial ones, since the running of our three lovely houses had left us sorely overstretched.

When I went in to see Tom Corbett, he shook my hand and said, 'I've seen you before, haven't I?' which I thought was pretty good after sixteen years. He dismissed my financial worries, said he saw me speaking Italian and added one or two predictions of a generally reassuring nature before bursting out: 'I don't care if you're single, married or divorced, I see another marriage!' This, frankly, horrified me as it was the last thing I was expecting or looking for.

Suzanne and I had coffee afterwards and compared notes. Her immediate future sounded a lot rosier than mine – romance, a proposal, a ring – all of which materialised. Sadly Tom Corbett died in 1995, just when my marriage broke up and I needed him most.

Anita wanted to work as an au pair for the rest of her gap year in order to perfect her French. The choice was limited, as most au pairs worked from September to June, but in January a very nice English couple, Mr and Mrs Stoodley, who were living in Brussels with a two-year-old daughter and a baby on the way, came to see us and offered Anita a job with them from March to July. The fact that they were English wasn't ideal – Bobo was most scathing when we told him about it – but at least she would be living and studying in a French-speaking country. She accepted the offer and flew off to Brussels at the beginning of March.

Anita hadn't done any work since getting back from Florence in December and had got into bad habits – late nights and even later mornings, so I think Brussels, where she had to get up early to give the children breakfast, came as a bit of a shock. To her credit she rose to it admirably. The Stoodleys seemed delighted with her, and when the job came to an end, wrote her the nicest reference I've ever seen.

She didn't know anyone in Brussels, so at first she was very lonely. At the end of March Anthony and I were invited to Amsterdam to see a performance of one of Fred's ballets. We arranged for Anita to join us there for the weekend, as it was just a short train ride from Brussels. She was touchingly sweet and affectionate and burst into tears when she saw us, though she said her employers were very nice to her and her only problem was loneliness.

A month later we went to Brussels for a weekend and saw her again. This time she had started to make friends and seemed far happier, though still very affectionate and pleased to see us. She showed us the sights of the city, and the kind Stoodleys invited us for a drink at their lovely house in the *Rue Michel-Ange* where Anita's room was far larger and certainly far tidier than her room at home. She was very sad when we left but, 'has generally seemed much happier and more settled than when we saw her in Amsterdam. I do miss her, but I feel she's got really nice employers and adorable children to look after and that Brussels is in many ways an enchanting city.'

The Stoodleys gave Anita a two-week holiday in May when they came to England. A few days earlier my mother, walking our Bedlington terrier, Tito, round the block in the early morning, had tripped on an uneven paving stone and fallen and broken her hip. Anthony and I had just arrived in Tokyo with the Royal Ballet. I was due to stay a week, but had to turn round and fly straight home. My mother was over eighty and I was desperately worried about the consequences at her age, but the moment I saw her in hospital I knew she was going to be all right. She made a remarkable recovery and was home and as active as ever after about ten days. Anita was able to visit her in hospital and see her safely home again before returning to Brussels.

In July, Tabitha, Juliet and I took the ferry to Ostende for a long weekend at a Belgian seaside resort called Knokke, where we stayed in a 'family room' at the Hotel Lido for three nights. In the evening we walked down to the station to meet Anita off the Brussels train and the following day went down to the beach. 'The three girls went down to the sea together to swim, and looked so beautiful that it bought tears to my eyes. I felt the vision of them would remain imprinted on my inner eye forever, and prayed their lives would be happy and successful in the spiritual sense.' We filled out Anita's forms for Royal Holloway, and the next day saw her off again at the station. 'Anita's been so sweet and lovely all weekend,' I wrote, 'and such a companion and support to me. I do hope we'll be able to maintain this good relationship all our lives.' After leaving Brussels, she did consent to come on holiday with us one more time. The Royal Ballet was dancing in Sicily and Anthony and I stayed at the luxurious Villa Igiea in Palermo with its own beach and pool. Anita and Miranda Harvey came with us for a week and caused a sensation. Anthony had told the hotel to expect *'due bambine'* and they'd put cots in our room, only to be confronted by two beautiful eighteen-year-olds, one fair, one dark, and both nearly six feet tall. Trying to chaperone the two of them round Palermo was one of the scariest things I've ever had to do.

That autumn Anita started at Royal Holloway. She had a spacious room in Founder's Building, which she shared with a girl called Nathalie. She called next day sounding very happy and said her course was really interesting and she was getting on well with her room mate.

Just as I was finishing my second novel, Letizia called to ask if I'd be interested in translating a feminist Renaissance work written in 1601 by a Venetian author named Lucrezia Marinella. The University of Chicago was publishing a series entitled 'The Other Voice (the Woman's Voice) in Early Modern Europe' and this would be one of their titles. The name of the work was *The Nobility and Excellence of Women and the Defects and Vices of Men.*

I had been wondering what my next project would be, and now here it was. I arranged to meet Letizia to discuss it and went to bed that evening feeling very pleased. Little did I know that the work would take me six years to complete and that during the course of it my life as I knew it would end, and I would lose my husband, my mother, my home and my career.

CHAPTER TEN

26 – 28 June 2009

Friday 26 June was my last day at Berlitz. Anita didn't have her biopsy on the twenty-fifth. She and Juliet went to the hospital but were told that Anita's blood wasn't clotting well enough for them to do it. They were sent home and I joined them there after work. She had a sleep in the afternoon, and I started to research cancer cures on the internet.

Someone had told me that cancer treatments in Denmark were more advanced than in the UK, so I googled 'Cancer treatment in Denmark' and was directed to the Fuda Cancer Hospital in Guangzhou, where a Danish woman with cancer of the pancreas and liver had recently been treated successfully. There was a contact e-mail address, so I wrote off a list of questions.

On the Friday I taught five lessons. Anita called me during my break to say the hospital was now going to perform her biopsy on Monday, as well as an ERCP (Endoscopic Retrograde Cholangio Pancreatography – an x-ray examination of the pancreatic and bile ducts) which involved sticking a camera down her throat and inserting a stent. I immediately arranged to take Monday off work. I taught two more lessons till 1.30, then went back to the office and told them I wanted the whole week off and admitted that I was afraid Anita might have cancer. I hadn't told any of my colleagues until then because I didn't want to tempt fate and, I suppose, because I didn't want to cry in front of them. I left Berlitz quietly without saying goodbye to anyone, and never returned.

When I got home I found, to my excitement, that I'd received a reply from the Fuda Hospital:

Dear Ms Dunhill – Our hospital specialises in therapies for pancreas, liver, and lung cancer, though we treat a wide range of cancers. We have a wide range of options that are available to Anita. The biggest danger is waiting too long, as you likely know that Anita has cancers that progress very quickly. At the moment, however, we have very little information about Anita. Instead, I can tell you what our doctors recommend for patients with cases similar to Anita's

  • cryosurgery – for immediate ablation of any medium to large tumors
  • brachytherapy – for radiate any residual cancer, or tumors too small to be appropriate for cryosurgery
  • immunotherapy – for a systemic approach to cancer, prevent metastasis and recurrence, and to generally boost the immune system
  • perhaps absolute alcohol injection (PEI)

Nearly all English hospitals will recommend conventional surgery, radiation, and chemotherapy. Sometimes these work, sometimes they do not, or sometimes they cease working over a period of time. We also have these three options available, but also so much more. Our approach to cancer therapy is to have as many tools available as possible, and combine different therapies. Combining therapies increases the chances of a positive outcome.

I do hope that you can join us at Fuda. If Anita is healthy and strong enough to fly, our doctors are very optimistic that they can have a positive effect with our therapies.

I was tremendously excited by this e-mail, and wrote back with more questions, before walking the dogs. That evening Anita's friend Helen texted her to invite her to a concert at the Cobden Club where Anita had celebrated her thirtieth birthday. Anita texted back to say she had cancer, and Helen immediately dropped everything and came round. Juliet and I left the two of them to talk, and both agreed how good it was to hear them laughing together. Anita seemed as pleased as I was about the news from China, and it was agreed that we would wait till we got the results of the biopsy and then, if the news was bad, travel to China as soon as possible.

I tried to carry on as normal at the weekend, although my fears for Anita afflicted me at intervals like stab wounds. She bravely taught her regular 10 am class at the RAC on Sunday morning, which she said energised her, and afterwards the entire family came to lunch. Anita lay down and rested afterwards while I cleared and that evening, with the horrible banality of tragedy, we sat together and watched TV before early bed.

*   *   *

After Anita's cancer diagnosis I looked back over her medical history to see if there were any indications of ill health that I ought to have picked up on. There were, of course, the febrile convulsions when she was one and the inflamed tonsils which were removed when she was six. She suffered from excruciatingly painful periods for some years, but these were finally cured by an iridologist, who recommended her to take 1000 mg. of oil of evening primrose three times a day, after which, to our great relief, the pain stopped. The next health crisis in her life was her car accident in April 1994, when she was twenty.

It was a worrying time for the whole family. Financial considerations had forced us to sell Chandos Lodge in 1993 and Ingo had been ill for a year with ME, which necessitated him dropping out of Cambridge for two years and spending the winter of 1994–5 in Australia for his health. Tabitha had been diagnosed with ITP, (Idiopathic Thrombocytopenic Purpura or low platelet count,) in December 1993 during the course of a routine blood test, and we were told that the only treatment available was for her to take high doses of steroids for an indefinite period. Anita was in her second year at Royal Holloway, sharing a rented house in Windsor with friends. She was going out with an extremely handsome and charming Nigerian boy called Oby who she'd met in a pub when she was seventeen and been seeing on and off ever since.

Anita's friend from Florence, James Napier, invited her to his twenty-first birthday party near Petersfield. The next day Oby called to say Anita had been in a car crash with her friend Emily, coming back from the party at 4 am. They had been driving through mist when a stag appeared in the road and Emily swerved to avoid it. She lost control of the car, which turned over twice and was a write-off. A lorry driver saw the accident and called an ambulance. Emily was able to get out of the car, but Anita was trapped inside. The ambulance took them both to hospital, where Anita signed herself out and got a friend to drive her to Oby's because she didn't want to worry me.

Juliet and I rushed over to Oby's flat in Maida Vale. When writing *Ballerina*, I had interviewed the Royal Ballet physio, who emphasised the importance of catching injuries when they were fresh. The company was on tour in Florida, but I managed to get hold of Anthony who called back in the morning with the physio's recommendation, Sarah Mottram, who she said was one of the best neck people in London. We made an appointment to see her the following day. 'Anita went in like a lamb, and came out like a lion,' I wrote. 'Sarah Mottram said we'd done exactly the right thing by giving her absolute rest for forty-eight hours and then embarking on treatment. She gave her a massage and some ultrasound, and Anita came out transformed.' After that she had two more sessions, was pronounced cured and went back to college four days later.

In October Anita went to Lyon for the statutory third year in France that formed part of her European Studies degree. She went off with a friend from uni and stayed in a youth hostel for a couple of nights, then got rooms in halls at the University of

Lyon. Oby came with us to see her off at Gatwick and frequently went over to France to visit her at weekends. He too was at London University and attended Kings as a foreign student.

Anita came home for the holidays in December. Oby's father died a few days later and he flew to Nigeria for the funeral, missing Anita's twenty-first birthday. All her friends rallied round, and wafted her off with them in a group, returning about 4 am. Oby's return kept being postponed, and on New Year's Eve, which Anita had kept free for him, his Nigerian Airlines plane caught fire and had to make an emergency landing in Algeria. The plane wasn't allowed to leave again until some tax had been paid, and the passengers were locked overnight in a small room. It was a diplomatic incident and made all the news-papers, but Anita took Oby's non-appearance as a personal affront, though she was able to laugh about it eventually. Her friend Alex Norman from Frensham Heights kindly came over at the last minute to spend the evening with her.

Anita was really quite difficult during the Christmas holidays. At the time I put it down to Oby's absence, but I think now it probably had a lot to do with drugs. In the novel Anita wrote after the break-up of her marriage, she describes how, as students, she and Oby were constantly broke and spent their evenings eating pizza and smoking dope. At her age, I smoked hash for a year or so, but gave it up when I went to Italy, mainly because it was so difficult to get hold of. At the time, hash was considered harmless, but I was told afterwards that skunk, the kind of dope smoked by Anita and Oby, was much stronger and known to cause paranoia if smoked regularly.

At the end of December, we were sitting in the dining room having lunch when Anita reached across me to get something and I noticed with a shock how thin her arm was. Startled out of my complacency, I took her to the Hale Clinic to see Dr Ali. 'The moment we walked in,' I wrote, 'we knew we were in the hands of a genius. He seemed to intuit all her problems without us even telling him. He said her sebaceous gland was compressed because of her whiplash injuries, and suggested a course of massage and manipulation, a high-protein diet and yoga lessons for her neck. He then said she should teach the yoga exercises to me, as I had a neck problem too. This amazed me, because I *have*, but hadn't said a thing. He said she shouldn't go back to France for a month and should see him again before she went. At the end he clicked her neck, and magically I saw the colour return to her cheeks as a result of the improved circulation. It almost brought tears to my eyes! We went downstairs and got her vitamins and paid. Anita was stunned, after her National Health experiences, that a doctor could be so good.' A few days later, a beautiful Indian girl came to the house to teach Anita yoga. Anita later said that it was she who inspired her to train as a Pilates teacher.

As Anita got better – Dr Ali discharged her on 24 January 1995 and she went back to Lyon five days later – I got worse. That year's flu included a violent cough which it seemed impossible to shake off. I'd finished the first draft of my Marinella translation and was now researching the footnotes in the British Library. Something in the atmosphere of the North Library (where the more ancient books were kept) triggered the cough, and I had to reel out into the corridor and remain there, bent double till the paroxysms subsided. I'm sure it was at least partly psychosomatic.

Grosvenor Estates, our landlords, had finally fixed on a price of £498,000 for our freehold, so we knew that we would have to sell the house. We decided to borrow the money, roll up the interest for three years (until Juliet left Francis Holland) and then sell the house and pay it back. The house in France was let for the winter to some racing drivers, who only went there at weekends. Unfortunately the word had got round that the house was empty during the week with the result that it was burgled four times. These events, combined with the children's and my health problems, created a very stressful atmosphere, which I was only able to escape from at night, when I found myself sleeping ten hours at a stretch. Afterwards I wondered if I hadn't been aware subconsciously of the impending crisis, and gone into a state of semi-hibernation to strengthen me for the events to come.

In February I learnt that, to quote Princess Diana, there were three people in my marriage. Instantly I had one of my flashes of intuition. I saw with absolute clarity that I would cope with the situation, as my mother had coped with my father's death when she was my age, and that I would carry on exactly as I had before and continue to look after everyone. This vision appalled me. Like Jonah in the Bible, I wanted only to escape. I fled the house for forty-eight hours, asking a friend to let the family know I was all right.

The place I fled to was the Buddhist Centre in Richmond. I'd been introduced to the Buddhism of Nichiren Daishonin about ten years before, by a friend, Niké Williams. Nichiren Daishonin was a thirteenth-century priest from Kamakura, Japan, who declared that the way to achieve enlightenment was to chant *Nam myoho renge kyo*, 'I devote myself to the mystic law of the Lotus Sutra' – the Lotus Sutra being the masterwork of the original Buddha, Siddhartha Gautama.

I was told to try chanting *Nam myoho renge kyo* twice a day for ten minutes for a period of two months, focusing on something I wanted to achieve, and to see what happened. At the time I wanted three things – a new house near the children's school, a degree in English and to get a book published – and within a few years I'd achieved all three. The chanting seemed to show me how to unravel situations that had previously tied me in knots and I often gained powerful insights in the process.

Once I'd achieved everything I wanted, I stopped practising, only to be knocked back down by our money troubles. I started chanting again in 1992 and became a member of the Sokka Gakkai International, the lay organisation promoting Nichiren Daishonin's Buddhism.

Their headquarters are at Taplow Court, a former stately home in Buckinghamshire and, at that time, there was a centre in Richmond where members could go and chant, with a shop that sold books and incense. Members could volunteer for duty at the centre, and I loved working there and meeting Buddhists from other districts. One of these, Gary, told me about Dr Xu, a Chinese doctor who eventually cured Tabitha's ITP with his herbs.

On the day I left home, I took just a small rucksack and headed to Richmond by tube. My intention was to spend the day chanting for guidance. As the day wore on, I wondered increasingly where I should spend the night. There were no facilities at the centre for female Buddhists to stay, although male Buddhists, working to a rota, could stay overnight to guard the Butsudan or altar.

I knew a lot of Buddhists by this time, some of whom were there that day, and I dare say someone there would have put me up, but I wasn't yet prepared to discuss the difficulties in my marriage with anyone. I had a small amount of money with me, but I was thinking in terms of staying away until Anthony had come to a decision and didn't want to be traced by using my debit card.

As it started to get dark, I had a sudden intuition that I should go to church. I wandered out of the centre and, not really knowing where I was going, found myself at the pretty church of St Mary Magdalene nearby. It was halfway through evensong, and a woman priest was reading the parable of the Good Samaritan. At the end of the service, I waited till people had said their goodbyes and went up to her and said, 'Can I talk to you for a moment? I've left my home today, and I wondered if you could recommend a hotel somewhere near here where I could spend the night.'

The priest, Ruth, couldn't have been kinder. She took my arm and said I could stay the night with her and her husband – also a priest and a trained counsellor – if I wanted, and in the end I did just that. Ruth and her husband Chris said I could remain with them as long as I wanted, but two days later, through a combination of prayers and chanting, I realised I must go home again and look after my family and get well. My cough was so bad that I'd torn my chest wall, and in my hurry to leave home, I'd left my antibiotics behind. When I became Roman Catholic I felt in a strange way that Buddhism had led me to Catholicism through that experience of running away from home.

The following weekend Tabitha, Juliet and I went to Lyon to visit Anita, staying in a hotel opposite her halls. She was waiting for us when we arrived and took us across the road to her room, which she had tidied in our honour. Touchingly, she'd laid a table with wine and candles and cooked a delicious lentil dish for us. She listened sympathetically as I confided in her about our marriage problems, and our conversation was so engrossing that we stayed till 3 am. Anita was later to develop a talent as a supremely warm and welcoming hostess, and this was probably one of the first chances she had to demonstrate her ability.

A month later, Anthony and I separated. Unusually, none of the children were home at the time but, 'like four angels winging their way across the globe', as I put it somewhat dramatically in my diary, they started to return. Tabitha and Juliet came home the following day, Ingo, from Australia, four days later and Anita, from Lyon, after a week. My feelings at this time were very confused, but one thing I knew for certain was that I wanted to go on a long-planned trip to Japan with the Royal Ballet in May. I said at the time that I wanted to make a last attempt to save my marriage, but the real reason was because of Buddhism. The SGI Headquarters were in Tokyo, and I felt strongly that if I could go there I would somehow receive the wisdom and guidance I needed to make the right decision about my future.

When I confided in my friends, their opinions were divided. The older ones said I should be sweet and gentle with Anthony and treat him as if nursing him through an illness. The younger ones said I should throw him out. Although I felt neither young nor brave, the latter approach appealed to me more than the former. I hoped that if I acted bravely, my state of mind would eventually catch up and I would start to feel it.

Many people thought I was crazy to go to Tokyo, but my desire to visit the Buddhist HQ was the one certainty in the horrible new world I inhabited. I flew out alone on Japan Airlines. The Royal Ballet Company was arriving later that day from Korea. When I arrived at the Pacific Meridien Hotel, I was shown to a magnificent suite complete with overflowing fruit bowl and unlimited green tea. I was feeling absolutely panic stricken, but I said my Buddhist prayers and felt better. I booked myself on a tour of Tokyo the following morning and went to sleep, jet lagged, at about 9.30, missing Anthony's arrival altogether.

In the event there was very little communication between us. We were like polite strangers. I visited the Buddhist HQ the following afternoon, but it wasn't the great moment of enlightenment I had been hoping for. I was shown into a huge room, where I appeared to be the only European, and recited evening prayers with the other members. Later I asked about the possibility of guidance – the Buddhist equivalent of counselling. Unfortunately my request wasn't understood. It was assumed I was looking for a guide to Tokyo and I was directed to a nearby bookshop. I came home somewhat dispirited, wondering if my great pilgrimage was going to come to nothing after all.

Instead I concentrated on sightseeing. My last trip to Tokyo had been cut short by my mother's accident, and it seemed unlikely I would travel with the Royal Ballet again. If I couldn't get to the heart of Nichiren Daishonin's teachings spiritually, I could at least follow in his footsteps geographically. A member of the Royal Ballet Trust, Felicity Clarke, organised a trip to Kamakura, the Daishonin's birthplace, and the British Ambassadress, Julia Boyd, a Francis Holland mother, created a personalised itinerary for me to visit Kyoto and stay at her favourite Ryokan.

Going round the temples on my own, I was besieged by parties of schoolchildren, who produced questionnaires for me to answer and asked my permission to be photographed with me. They were sweet and polite and made me feel like a film star.

For nearly twenty years, my social life had centred round Anthony and the family, but now I was discovering that I could function on my own and often relate to people better as myself than as one half of a corporate couple. I was still desperately unhappy, but I did begin to recover a little bit of self-esteem.

I returned to Tokyo for the opening night of the Royal Ballet, and took my seat beside Anthony as I had so many times before. Afterwards there was a reception at the British Embassy. Anthony was leaving for San Francisco the following day, but I had one more day in Japan. Julia suggested I visit Nikko, a temple compound containing the shrines of the Shoguns. Felicity was returning to London next day, so couldn't come with me. 'Why don't you ask Jeremy?' she suggested.

Jeremy Isaacs had taken over as Anthony's boss in 1988. He wasn't particularly popular with the ballet company, most of who believed that he looked down on ballet and considered it inferior to opera. His wife, the music journalist Gillian Widdicombe, seldom appeared with him on ballet evenings. There was a juicy piece of gossip doing the rounds at the time about Jeremy and a member of Birmingham Royal Ballet staff. He had allegedly taken the lady out to dinner and said, 'I have a proposition for you, and whatever your answer is, we're going have a nice meal afterwards.' He then asked her to be his mistress. She declined – she already had a partner – and she and Jeremy went on to have a pleasant meal. Afterwards she confided in another member of staff, and the story did the rounds of both ballet companies.

I rather liked Jeremy for it. I thought it showed style. Gillian was known for her colourful past – a scurrilous version of the song Widdecombe Fair had been written about her, with the names of luminaries from the operatic world substituted for old Uncle Tom Cobley and all – and I assumed, wrongly I now think, that she must be having an affair. I had become quite fond of Jeremy during the seven years he had been General Director. He often put me next to him at official dinners and made an effort to talk on topics he thought would interest me. When *A Darker Shade of Love* came out, he asked me to give him a copy. At that time Gillian was Arts Editor of the *Observer*, where it was reviewed rather unfavourably as 'reading like a *Sunday Telegraph* editorial with *Sunday Sport* illustrations.'

I invited Jeremy to go to Nikko with me and he accepted. We arranged to meet the following day. After the reception, I had a last conversation with Anthony during which I realised that our marriage was truly over and that there was no point trying to save it. Seeing the effect the divorce had on our children, I questioned that decision many times but my final verdict on the matter, a sort of paraphrase of Madame Butterfly, was that if it's not possible to stay married with honour, it's better to divorce, and for that reason I think I made the right decision. My conviction that I would achieve clarity if I went to Tokyo had been right after all.

One good thing about the separation was that it healed my relationship with Bobo. When I told him my marriage was over, he gasped and said, 'My God, you're going to find it difficult at your age to find anyone else!' (Thanks Bobo!) 'You, at least, should be happy about it,' I said, trying to sound light-hearted, and he replied, rather sweetly, that other people's misfortunes never made him happy.

For my date with Jeremy, I dressed casually in jeans and a white shirt. I found him in the lobby looking very smart in a jacket and tie and, thus mismatched, we set off. He walked very fast, so I had to trot to keep up with him, but the hotel had given us good directions, and our journey to Nikko by train and bus went smoothly.

During the sixties, the last time I'd been single, I'd found that when a relationship ended, the quickest way to get over it was to start a new one as soon as possible. Obviously this was a very immature way of going about things, but it also happened to be extremely effective. Until now I'd held back because I wasn't sure if I wanted my marriage to be over or not. Now I saw no reason not to find out if the theory still worked.

The temples were spectacular. Because they were all together with no modern buildings around, it was easy to imagine that we'd been wafted back a thousand years. In one of them we were confronted by three enormous gilt statues – the largest Buddhas in Japan. To the right was the Goddess of Mercy with a basket in front of her to throw coins in and make a wish. I threw in my coin, bowed to the goddess and wished for Jeremy.

We were so drunk with the beauty of the temples that we forgot about the five o'clock closing time. Jeremy suggested we skip the bus and walk back to Nikko Station. Normally I'm not a great walker, but on this occasion I was perfectly happy to trot along beside him. We had time for a cup of hot saké at the station buffet. Nothing was said, but it was obvious we were in a state of infatuation, and I giggled inside, remembering one of Nichiren Daishonin's letters to his followers entitled, *On obtaining happiness*. 'Suffer what there is to suffer,' it read, 'enjoy what there is to enjoy, and when you drink saké, stay at home with your wife.'

Jeremy invited me to the ballet performance with him, but he was hosting a staff dinner afterwards and I couldn't face the speculation my presence would invite, so refused. Just as we were parting at Asakusa Station, he said, 'Shall I call you at midnight?' I said that would be lovely, and felt immense relief that we had sorted the whole thing out so easily.

In the four months that my marriage had been in crisis, I'd lost an awful lot of confidence in myself, but Jeremy restored it in bucketloads. I went down to breakfast early next morning and, to my amazement, the man at the next table started to chat me up. For the past four months I had been Siberia in the romance stakes, now, suddenly, I was the Promised Land. Whatever the aura was that Jeremy's lovemaking had bestowed on me, it held good when I got back to London. Suddenly every man I met made a pass at me, including many of my friends' husbands. It was like a gloriously funny joke that I couldn't share with anybody.

One thing that children of divorced parents told me repeatedly, was that the worst part was not knowing what was going on. Determined to avoid putting my children through that un-certainty, I told them about Jeremy immediately. Understand-ably, they weren't best pleased. Ingo summed the situation up in his usual pithy style: 'But Mum, you're just exchanging one unscrupulous man for another!' Looking back, I really don't think my affair with Jeremy did the children much harm. It certainly made me a lot more cheerful and didn't interfere with their daily lives at all.

I was fortunate to have two very good male friends who *didn't* try to make passes at me. The first was Alastair Langlands who taught English at Bedales. His marriage had broken up the year before mine, and we used to go to the theatre together and have long discussions afterwards in the dining room of the Travellers Club. I confided in him about Jeremy, indeed we once bumped into Gillian and Jeremy at the National Theatre, and amiable introductions were made in the interval. Next time I saw Jeremy he questioned me very closely indeed about my relationship with Alastair, which was all to the good! I found Alastair wonder-fully wise and soothing company and looked forward very much to our evenings together and to going to stay with him, often accompanied by my mother, at his lovely house in Selbourne.

My second male friend was a solicitor who I'll call Boris. I met him originally on a skiing trip with Julian Moulton in 1964. I'd never skied before, and when we got off the lift, Julian shot down the mountain, leaving me alone and petrified. If Boris hadn't helped me, I'd probably still be standing there now. He next turned up thirty years later at lunch with the Hill-Brookes. We stayed in touch, and he became my legal advisor.

The first summer after the separation, Anthony and I each took the house in France for a week. I went first, with Tabitha and Juliet and two of their friends, and he took over. Boris agreed to accompany me and the girls for my week, and was a great asset, escorting us to local fêtes, dancing with the girls, and generally putting on a much better show than I could have on my own. Both Anita and Tabitha expressed the hope that he and I might become an item. To be truthful I was a bit curious as to why he never appeared to be in any kind of relationship with anyone, and during a weekend with the Hill-Brookes, David told me that Boris only liked young girls. If I wanted him to make a pass at me, he said I should tie my hair in bunches and put on a school uniform. I thought this was such a good joke that I told Boris. To my surprise, he got very annoyed and, as far as I'm aware, never spoke to David again.

Later Boris moved out of London and invited me, my mother and the three girls to stay the weekend. He put my mother in one bedroom, Tabitha, Juliet and me in another, and Anita on the downstairs sofa, saying he'd sleep in the outhouse. In the middle of the night, I was woken by the sound of voices. I went downstairs to find Boris had come in and was sitting on Anita's bed. I didn't say much, but brought Anita upstairs to sleep with us, and left early next morning. Anita said he'd made a timid attempt to kiss her, so nothing much had actually happened, but I couldn't shake off the feeling that Boris had behaved extremely badly.

After a few months he invited me to lunch and said he wanted to apologise. He told me he was very fond of Anita and would like to take her out officially. I was privately convinced that she wasn't in the least bit interested in him. Oby was finally off the scene, but she had recently been introduced to Charles, her future husband. I told Boris that if she wanted to go out with him, I wouldn't do anything to stop them.

Alas poor Boris! Anita agreed to go out, persuaded him to take her to Annabel's where she knew Charles was going to be, dumped Boris there and took off with Charles at the end of the evening. Boris appeared to accept his rejection with equanimity, and over time our friendship resumed. He continued to give me legal advice, and I allowed him to stay in the spare room at Ebury Street once a week so he could attend a salsa workshop in Vauxhall.

The sorry ending to this tale was in December 1999. My divorce had come through, my mother had died and Debbie had kindly invited me to stay with her in the Cayman Islands prior to moving house in the New Year. Tabitha and Juliet were at university, but Ingo and Anita were at home. Anita had separated from Charles and was staying in my mother's flat.

Anita came in early after dinner and got undressed, only to be transfixed by the sight of a man sitting, crouched on the wrought-iron staircase outside the window, watching her fixedly. She screamed, whereupon he said, 'It's only me, Boris, I dropped my key.' This was hardly reassuring, since he'd made no noise coming down the staircase, as he certainly would have done if the story had been true. Anita was so spooked by the incident that she called Ingo, who came home to protect her. Boris departed and we never heard from him again.

I ran into him some years later at a birthday party given by Prince Mangal Kapoor. 'Oh bother,' I thought to myself. 'What on earth do I do now?' As I was dithering, he fled the party like a scared rabbit, so my problem was solved. What a sad and squalid ending to a long friendship.

Unfortunately many other friendships ended as a result of my divorce. Boris told me that the married couples would probably stay friends with Anthony and the singles with me, and this, illogical as it might seem, was more or less what happened, although we both kept the friends we'd had before marriage. On one occasion I was asked to give a recently widowed lady a lift to a party. She told me how good all her married friends had been to her since her husband died, but when I repeated this to Boris, he immediately asked if she was pretty.

'Not very,' I admitted.

'Well, there you are,' he said.

I got my decree nisi in December 1995, and shortly after that Jeremy was door-stepped by a news cameraman coming out of my house. He accused me of having sold him to the newspapers, and dropped me flat. Some time later, I managed to get a letter from the journalist who'd written the story saying that I had neither tipped her off nor been paid for the article. I sent it to Jeremy, who apologised, but by then it was all too late.

If 1995 was the year of the married man, 1996 was the year of the younger man. The married men lost interest once I got my decree nisi, but the Jeremy scandal seemed to make me fashionable. I was invited to an endless round of parties and my photo appeared in society magazines. I was also offered jobs, mostly unpaid, modelling for charity shows, appearing in bit parts in films and writing restaurant reviews. My next-door neighbour, Rupert Hambro, asked me to teach him Italian and it was this that eventually gave me the idea of becoming a Berlitz teacher. A dear friend and Francis Holland mother, Audrey Burns Ross, invited me on to the UNICEF Special Events Committee. The Jeremy incident had made me feel like a scarlet woman, so I relished this chance to redeem myself, and remained on the committee for several years. I had a couple of highly unsuitable flings, but ended them by the summer, so I could be around for the children's exams. Both Ingo and Anita took their finals that year, Tabitha took her A levels and Juliet her GCSEs. Happily they all acquitted themselves well. Tabitha took a gap year before university, while Juliet remained at Francis Holland for A levels.

After her finals, Anita went to New York for the summer vacation as part of the BUNAC (British Universities North America Club) programme for students and young people, sharing a flat in Greenwich Village with Alice. I saw her off at Heathrow on 17 June. For the past year, she and Oby had been having a series of spectacular break-ups, after which they always seemed to reconcile again. The first of these took place while I was in New York with Jeremy in 1995 for his birthday weekend, and he smiled indulgently as I attempted to console her over the telephone.

Although I became very fond of Oby, the idea of a mixed-race relationship was initially quite shocking to someone of my generation, while the difficulties in my own relationship with Bobo had made me wary of dating somebody from another culture. To be fair to Anita, I think she was totally unaware of these types of barriers and would have been very shocked if anyone had tried to point them out to her.

By 1996, my main objection to her relationship with Oby was not his nationality or colour, but the fact that he and Anita didn't seem able to be happy together. I remember taking her out to dinner when she was in her final year at Royal Holloway and listening as she told me she was convinced he was cheating on her. She asked me what I thought she should do, and all I could think of to say was that she should either make up her mind to trust him or, if she couldn't do that, hire a detective and find out the truth. Now, I think I should have said that without trust a relationship is pointless, but at that point I was hardly in a position to advise. She didn't listen to me, but continued to reiterate her doubts in a manner bordering on the obsessive. They also began to have physical fights. Rupert Hambro reported that he'd witnessed one in the street late at night, accompanied by some extremely colourful language.

Anita describes a similarly dysfunctional relationship in the novel she wrote in 1998:

She had not had a happy relationship with Oby who had lied to her and she had become very confused and turned to drink and drugs for solace. Now, in the aftermath of the break-up, she felt totally lost. She had been forced to finish the relationship by the fact she felt she was losing her mind. She had not wanted to. She had done everything in her power, too much, to try and make it work. She had even doubted her own instincts in order to accommodate the lies that he told her. In the end it was that which had made her mind unsettled because deep down inside everyone knows the truth however much they try to hide it from themselves.

Later she wrote:

Oby, her ex, was extremely good-looking, tall and black with short dreadlocks that she had twisted into place for him. Unfortunately he was also a compulsive liar. During the four years that they had been together he slept with other women and lied to her, shouting at her if she questioned him and telling her incessantly that she imagined things, so much so she had come to doubt her own mind.

'Look I told you where I was. This is ridiculous you are so paranoid. The reason I don't take you out with me is because you always make scenes, you are an embarrassment. It is not because I am picking up other women. God, you are mad.'

He had even started to hit her towards the end, when she had started to beg him to tell her the truth because she felt she was losing her mind.

That was when she left. She had had enough.'

Later in the book, she admits that she isn't attracted to nice men:

She finished with them immediately because they seemed dull to her and she needed drama in her life to feel normal even though it made her miserable.

The novel doesn't say why this was, but she once told me that her relationship problems stemmed from the two years when she was out of contact with Bobo and that she lost all her trust in men during that period.

I flew to New York in August to visit Anita with Miranda, her flatmate from Florence. Miranda was going to stay with Anita and Alice, and I was going to stay with my friend Fritz Wild-foerster and his partner Richard in their beautiful apartment on Broadway and 79th. When Anita came to meet us, we were startled to see that she'd had most of her hair chopped off and the rest dyed platinum blonde. With typical Anita luck, just as she'd run out of money, she'd been hired by Vidal Sassoon to model in a hair show in Washington for a fee of $3,500. I was delighted for her, even though it meant that she'd be in Washington for most of my visit. I also worried about her hair. It looked stunning fresh from the salon, but the colour would be difficult and expensive to maintain once she was back in London.

For the next few days I saw more of Miranda than I did of Anita. We went shopping and to a fascinating exhibition of Picasso's portraits with Brendan and James who were also in New York. Alice, with whom Anita was sharing a flat, was working and not around much. She and Anita weren't getting on well, and I didn't think it was Alice's fault. From what I learnt later, Anita's drug-taking was very heavy during that period and Miranda, who was staying at the flat, let slip that the squalor in Anita's room was unbelievable.

Anita travelled to Washington on a Thursday, and I followed her on Sunday, just for the day, to spend time with her and see the show. I entertained myself on the three-hour train journey by reading the latest depressing communication from my divorce lawyer. Anita and I met at the Renaissance Hotel at 2 pm for half an hour between shows. She seemed very spaced out, which worried me, though I tried to tell myself it could be just a hangover.

She gave me a pass for the convention centre, and I stood and watched the second show. Afterwards we met back at the Renaissance. When I showed her the lawyer's letter, she seemed to snap back into focus, as if emerging from a different element, and gave it her full attention, making intelligent and pertinent comments. She then accompanied me to the station where we had pizza together and she was very sweet to me, boosting my confidence and saying I should value myself more – all the things the family had been saying to her for the past year. We said sad goodbyes. I was leaving for London next day, but Miranda was staying on, and Anita would be back in London in less than a month.

On her return, I organised an interview for her with Azzy Asghar, the publisher of *Epicurean Life* magazine, which had its offices round the corner from us in Sloane Gardens. I met him at a party and he became a good friend to all the family. Juliet did work experience for him before her GCSEs, so successfully that he asked her to stay on in a professional role, Tabitha drove round with him on publication day, distributing magazines, and I was eventually offered a job as Arts Editor, which I did for five years and enjoyed enormously. Just before we left for Azzy's, Oby called Anita, and she arranged to see him that evening. She was extremely vague at the interview and non-committal about her plans. 'I wanted to shake her,' I wrote in my diary, 'but I do love her.' That night, to my dismay, Oby stayed over, and when I next saw Azzy, he looked very sad and told me he was convinced Anita was taking cocaine, as she'd kept sniffing when he talked to her. This terrified me, as I had no experience of cocaine at all and no idea how to deal with it. Soon afterwards, Anita flew to Venice for three weeks which at least gave me a breathing space as I knew she'd get no drugs there.

During the time she was away, I started a relationship with an army officer called Tim who, at thirty-six, was thirteen years younger than me. I met him at a party and he invited me to lunch at *La Poule au Pot*. Afterwards he came in for tea and fixed all the broken bulbs and fuses in the house, so we were suddenly overwhelmed with light. Experts say that we always know how a relationship's going to work out in the first ten minutes, but often ignore the signals. Tim told me that the longest he'd ever been out with anyone was six months, but I chose not to listen. In the meantime it was very pleasant to have him around. He painted the patio, opened a drawer that had been stuck for years, did the ironing and poured the champagne at my fiftieth birthday party.

Anita went to work for Azzy who was very good with her, taking her to parties and introducing her to new people. One of these was Marc Burca, divorced and living most of the year in Spain. He invited Anita, Tim and me on holiday there in March 1997. Anita became pregnant by Marc, who offered to marry her. They hadn't known each other long, but I felt he had her best interests at heart and that if she had the baby and went to live in Spain, she would escape the downward spiral of drugs and abuse with Oby. She may also have escaped cancer since it's probable she got it while living in Africa.

Instead she rounded on me in fury and took the morning-after pill. The problems with her periods restarted and she never conceived again. What I found most frightening about the episode was Anita's anger when a hand was extended to help her out of the abyss into which she was descending. In 2007 she had her horoscope done by Liz Greene, who pointed out her tendency to reject eligible men and said that eventually there would be none left. By that time Anita had gained enough self-knowledge to admit that this was probably true.

Tim and I parted in May, the statutory six months being up, and that autumn Anita was introduced to her future husband Charles by a mutual friend.

CHAPTER ELEVEN

29 – 30 June 2009

On the day of Anita's biopsy, I walked the dogs early and we left by taxi for University College Hospital at 9.30. She was brave and smiling, but as we got out of the cab and walked the few steps to the main entrance of the hospital, I was distressed to see that her complexion in the daylight looked very yellow. One of the symptoms of pancreatic cancer is to be jaundiced, and until that moment I had comforted myself with the fact that Anita showed no signs of this at all.

Anita was having two procedures that day – the ERCP which involved sticking a camera down her throat and inserting a stent to assist the drainage of her bile duct in the morning, and a liver biopsy in the afternoon. Just before the ERCP, a doctor appeared and told us everything that could go wrong with the procedure. I was absolutely furious at his tactlessness, but couldn't show it for fear of upsetting Anita. She hardly seemed to react – maybe she was putting on a good show for my benefit – and was extraordinarily calm and brave all day.

She came back about 1.15 and was put into a cubicle on the ward. The doctor told me the procedure had gone very well. She was sleepy, so I sat beside her in the cubicle while she rested. At 3.15 she had another ultrasound and then the biopsy, which was finished by 4.

The rest of the day was spent hanging around. We had been led to believe that Anita could come home at 10 pm, but the doctor who was supposed to give her permission to leave never showed up. Tabitha came to visit bringing snacks for Anita, and offered to lend us her car for the following day. Anita recovered well and was able to use the lavatory without any problems, but by about eleven, when the doctor still hadn't turned up, we agreed that she'd spend the night in the hospital and that I'd collect her at 9 am the following morning. She seemed peaceful and not in pain, so I kissed her good-night and took the tube to Knightsbridge where Tabitha's car was parked. At home there were no residents' spaces available, so after driving round and round, I eventually dumped it outside the house and got in at midnight. I said good-night to Juliet and went to bed with Petal and Snowy.

The next morning I woke at five and couldn't get back to sleep, so I did my work-out, had some breakfast and went to the hospital by tube, arriving just before nine. Anita was dressed and ready to go. She said she'd had a reasonable night. Dr Pereira appeared and discharged her. He told her she would get her results in a few days.

From the hospital we took a taxi to Harley Street to see Dr Jerome Poupel, a chiropractor and holistic practitioner recommended by some friends of Bobo. I was allowed to go into the consulting room with her, but was feeling too tired to take much in. I remember him taking some strange photo of Anita's bones and saying that her illness had been caused by exposure to herbicides, presumably in Africa. He treated her for an hour or so while I sat on his sofa in a daze of non-comprehension, then we came home by taxi. I settled Anita on the sofa with the dogs and went off to Sloane Square to get her two medicines which I found most effective and hoped she would too, Nytol sleeping pills and Weleda Massage Balm for her back.

It was very hot that day, and after lunch we both managed to sleep for an hour or so. Anthony visited at 4.30, the first time he had ever stepped inside the flat, and we hugged each other, much to the amazement of Anita and Juliet. We all had a cup of tea together in civilised fashion, then I left Anita with Anthony while Juliet and I walked the dogs, using Tabitha's car. When we returned, Ingo was there, and later Tabitha dropped by, as did Anita's friend Emma who she'd met in Sierra Leone. I went to the corner shop where I ran into Anthony and, stunningly, received the apology that I'd been waiting fourteen years for.

The evening wasn't so good. After dinner Anita started to get awful pains in her ribs. We called NHS Direct and explained her medical history. They said they'd send an ambulance, but warned us that it would take at least a couple of hours. I gave Anita two paracetamol and she called Dr Pereira, who calmed her fears. At midnight she said the pain was better, so I called and cancelled the ambulance, and we all went to bed. At 3 am the whole household was wakened by the insistent ringing of the phone and the sound of hammering on the door. The ambulance had arrived, and when we didn't respond to the doorbell because we were asleep, they called the police, who woke our neighbours as well as us, and made us feel like criminals. I'd always heard what a useless service NHS Direct provided, and now, in our hour of need, this was overwhelmingly confirmed.

*   *   *

I wasn't present at the meeting between Anita and Charles. She took her friend Abigayle with her and, at around 4 am, Charles and his friends convinced the girls to drive to Norfolk for the weekend with them in a hired limo. When they arrived, one of the men in the party had to be hospitalised because he'd taken so much cocaine. Fortunately common sense prevailed and the two girls returned to London by taxi the following morning. Abigayle's mother was dismayed when she heard of this crazy episode. I was less so. In the years I'd been single I'd become used to this sort of behaviour.

Anita was now working for *Good Life*, a free magazine distributed in Kensington, Chelsea and Belgravia. There were aspects of it she didn't like – selling advertising for example – but it gave her a chance to write and also to model. She even ended up on the cover, though the description in her book of her lack of confidence on the day of the photo shoot is heartbreaking.

In March 1998 Anita breezed in at lunch-time and told me she was thinking of giving up her job and going to live in Norfolk with Charles to decorate his house for him. I was horrified. Cracks had already started to appear in their relationship and I pointed out that if she went to live in the country with him she would be entirely at his mercy. She couldn't even drive a car. I said that if she was going to decorate his house, she must get some kind of contract from him otherwise it would all end in tears. She appeared to agree with me, and we arranged that I would have dinner with her and Charles two days later to discuss the matter.

I went to Charles's house in South Kensington on the evening of 2 April. Anita told me he'd passed out and that she couldn't wake him. Not an auspicious start. She and I walked round to a pizzeria in South Kensington, where I learnt to my dismay that she was still determined to give up her job and go to Norfolk and that she and Charles were thinking seriously about getting married. Nothing I could say would alter her determination, but I extracted a promise from her that at least she would remain in her job for the time being.

The following day she came home at five to say she'd been sacked from her job and was going to Norfolk that evening. Charles came round later to collect her. He tried his best to reassure me, promising that he'd organise driving lessons for Anita, and inviting the whole family to his house for Easter. I accepted. Only Ingo refused to come, preferring to go to Scotland with a friend from Bedales.

The rest of us, my mother, Tabitha, Juliet, me and our Bedlington, Tito, left for Norfolk on Easter Saturday at around four. The house in Ebury Street was looking very tidy because we'd had a viewing that morning. Although it had been agreed that we wouldn't sell until the summer, after Juliet's A levels, word had got round that it would shortly be on the market and suddenly every agent in London seemed to want to be in on the act. The morning's viewing had been with the composer Carl Davis and his wife, the actress Jean Boht. They were charming and said they loved the house, although I felt it was a bad omen when Tito bit Carl Davis's hand as he tried to stroke him. Tito was thirteen and getting very snappy. The vet said he had a heart murmur, but didn't seem unduly worried about him.

We arrived at Charles's house in Norfolk around seven in the evening. It was large and romantic, but in great need of the restoration that Anita was supposedly there to perform. She describes a similar house in her novel:

She could see that once the grounds had been beautifully landscaped but now they were sadly overgrown. Paths were blocked and old flower beds barely distinguishable as weeds mixed with thorns to produce a huge jungle.

The house was an extraordinary mess. One room had holes in the carpet and shattered glass and other debris. Charles had been clay pigeon shooting with the pigeons still in the box.

Another room was filled wall to wall with old-fashioned clothes.

'They were my mother's and my aunt's,' Charles explained and when Clara suggested giving them to charity he was horrified. 'I can't get rid of them,' he said.

Then there was what Charles referred to as 'the junk room' which was filled with the most bizarre selection of things from old lace, to broken chairs, to a huge first model mobile phone and camouflage netting, which Charles refused to get rid of.

Some of the other rooms were filled with dog shit as Tara had been left in the house for long periods of time and gone around using what had once clearly been beautiful rooms, as toilets.

Charles admitted shamefacedly that on occasions he had left

Tara alone for days at a time. Clara felt her gut wrench with pity at the thought of what Tara had suffered and she vowed to walk her every day and to feed her and look after her properly.

Anita was touchingly pleased to see us. She'd done a huge amount of clearing in preparation for our arrival, and put vases of wild flowers in our bedrooms. I felt the stirrings of hope. Her bedroom at Ebury Street may have been full of empty pizza boxes and overflowing ashtrays, with wine stains and candle wax on the carpet, but now she had her own place she was a changed girl. Tito took a great fancy to Tara, Charles's black Labrador, and followed her round lasciviously, while Charles was very kind and hospitable and cooked dinner for us all, washed down by copious quantities of wine.

The next day, Easter Sunday, Charles slept till lunch-time, so we were able to spend quality time with Anita, who cooked us a lovely breakfast of hot cross buns and gave us a tour of the house. In the afternoon we drove to Brancaster for a trip down memory lane. Marsh Barn appeared deserted, so we went down the drive where the children were transfixed to see the old gypsy caravan we had restored for them to sleep in with their friends, and the wooden climbing frame that Anthony and I had spent hours putting up for them on our honeymoon in 1975. Again Charles cooked dinner, which we ate at about 1 am. He had been wonderfully kind and hospitable and for the time being all my fears were allayed. 'Charles has been very kind,' I wrote, 'I've sensed no tension between him and Anita, the house has wonderful potential and I hope and pray that they'll live happily ever after.'

The next day, after an invigorating walk on the beach, during which Tito gambolled around like a spring lamb, we returned to London. Tito had been fine on the journey, but became unwell on arrival. At 4 am he collapsed, and died a few minutes later. We sat round him and prayed for the rest of the night. Anita was very sweet when I called to tell her, and we all agreed that at least he'd had a lovely last weekend.

On 3 May Anita called to tell us that she and Charles had got married four days before. Tabitha answered the phone and exclaimed, 'you idiot!' My mother and I were out to tea, and were greeted with the news when we got home. My first reaction was an ignoble sense of relief that I hadn't been asked to fork out for an expensive wedding, since I felt fairly certain the marriage wouldn't last. I called Anita immediately, but got the answerphone, so left a message of congratulations, which I tried to make sincere. Anita told me afterwards that she'd been certain the whole thing was a joke and that she'd just gone along with it to humour Charles. Even when they drove to the Registry Office, she was sure he was going to say 'April fool!' or the equivalent at the last moment. Her fictional account of the wedding day is particularly vivid:

She was wearing a blue cardigan that some girl had left at Charles's house, a pair of grey baggy trousers and a pair of black stiletto boots. Her hair was a greasy mess, matted at the back, and her eyes were bloodshot.

Charles wore a blue jacket that matched her cardigan.

They both looked sickly and had white faces tinged with green.

As Charles was driving to the registry office a voice resonated inside Clara, warning 'This is a mistake . . . this is a mistake'. It was very loud and very disconcerting, rather as if someone were shouting in her ear. Clara did not know where it was coming from.

She looked at Charles and she smiled. She simply didn't know what else to do or that she had a choice.

She dismissed the voice as insanity instead of welcoming her intuition and realising that it was getting married that was insane.

When they arrived at the registry office the others were already there.

'Drunk', they laughed when they saw the bride and groom.

Clara made a grimace, which was meant to be a smile. She felt her face twitch.

The others looked much happier than she felt. She felt sick not euphoric as she had always supposed she would feel on her wedding day.

She looked at Charles and grimaced. He grimaced back. They were trying to smile.

They went into the office and said their vows. They had rehearsed a couple of times before with a piece of paper that they had been given to read through.

It was over before Clara really even registered that it was happening.

Was that it?

She was married.

Oh my God she was married. She thought she might throw up or pass out.'

Anita came to visit us in London a few days later, on an errand for Charles. She must have put up a good show of being happy, because my diary entry is upbeat, 'then darling little Anita, Sadie, Sadie married lady arrived, and it was all one long cup of tea and gossip!'

Around this time I made a new friend who was to become a rock in my life for the next seven years until his death in 2005. Two modelling friends, Patsy and Decima, who lived in Chiswick gave a party where I noticed 'an attractive craggy faced man called John who lives in the grounds of Chiswick Park'. John had lived in Africa for a long time, and had the permanently tanned skin and far-sighted blue eyes of one used to gazing into infinite distances. We just hit it off. It was never a romantic relationship, just a very great friendship. We spoke every day, met each other's families and friends and he accompanied me to UNICEF events and *Epicurean Life* freebies and, bless him, claimed to enjoy everything equally.

I was with John when Anita called me on 17 June to tell me her marriage had broken up. Probably my diary entry expresses it best:

At 6.30 I was starting to dress for my date with John Knight when I was electrified by a call from Anita. Charles had beaten her up, so she'd left him and was going to stay with David Goodman [her lawyer and friend]. She'd also taken £7000 from Charles's safe. I was then rung by Charles, who seemed more concerned about the money than about Anita. I said I'd heard he'd been violent and he said he'd had to "restrain" her. While I was speaking to Charles, Michael, (the friend who had intro-duced Anita to Charles) rang him on the other line, and I was then rung by Michael offering to mediate. By now I was about forty minutes late for John. I'd offered to cancel him, but Anita said no, she was having dinner with David. Off I went to Chiswick and was just enjoying a gin and tonic when Juliet rang in tears. Charles had rung home again and my mother had said he could come and stay the night. Kicked myself for not having warned them, but thought I'd sorted the situation. I had to tell John, who kindly left the room while I rang Charles. The £7,000 had become £11,000 and he said Anita was probably going to spend it on cocaine. He agreed that we mustn't upset Juliet before her last A level (which was next day) and said he'd stay with Michael. Tried to ring Juliet back to reassure her, but the line had gone dead. Decided I must leave. John was very sweet and understanding. David rang to say he and Anita were at San Martino in Walton Street, so I went home first and checked that my mother and Juliet were OK, then went on to San Martino, where we quite enjoyed ourselves in a melancholy way. Anita's done just the right thing consulting David. She's going to the doctor for a medical report and pregnancy test tomorrow, and the money's being put in his safe. We all went back to Ebury Street and Anita listened to various messages from Charles. Ingo then unplugged the phone. Anita and David left and we all went to bed.

The next day, after seeing Juliet off for her final A level exam, I met Anita and David at Dr Rose's surgery in Sloane Avenue. Dr Rose examined Anita and did a medical report on her bruises. 'I just wish I'd had this sort of service when I was married to Ken,' I wrote. Anita came home with me afterwards, and we had lunch and greeted Juliet, who'd finished her exams. In the evening David came round and I dropped him and Anita at Chelsea Police Station, to register a second report on Anita's injuries.

It was agreed that for the time being Anita would stay with David and that none of her family should be given his home address, so we wouldn't be able to pass it on. She came round most days to see us.

Eventually Anita paid back most of the money she had taken from Charles and decided she must get a job. One day, walking through Chelsea, she saw an advertisement for a cocktail waitress in a bar, describing a similar episode in her book:

She went for an interview and she got the job.

A whole new world opened up to her and yet the old one still clogged up her mind. She was walking through the present and yet living in the past. She felt that she was still the abused wife. That she was still bound to Charles.

The bar was filled with prostitutes and one of the barmen was a cocaine dealer.

She became involved with the cocaine dealer, Scott.

He lied to her about his age and turned out to be only twenty-one. Clara was older than him.

The first night they had sex, she phoned Charles when Scott

was in the bathroom. 'I just fucked someone else,' she said, and hung up.

She wanted to hurt Charles, like he had hurt her. It still made her sick to think of this other girl with him . . . and she hoped that the thought of her with someone else would make him feel sick too.

Two days later she discovered that Scott had slept with one of the other waitresses the night after he'd slept with her and dumped him.

He continued to chase after her, saying what a dreadful mistake he'd made and eventually she got back with him.

She was finding new dramas to occupy herself with, new things to destroy herself with and all the while she still had Charles in her mind and her head was filled with pain.

One of the other waitresses became involved with their boss's son who became a good friend of hers and they started to hang out together, keeping the bar open after hours for a select few.

The nights stretched on into the mornings as the bar was licensed until 3am even before the lock-ins, when the girls stayed back with the other staff and some of the regulars, drinking themselves into oblivion.

The bosses encouraged the girls to drink as much as possible as they wanted the punters to spend their money. Clara obliged wholeheartedly. She drank only champagne or Baileys, which were among the most expensive drinks there, so the bosses were pleased and soon began to order bigger bottles of Baileys as Clara consumed such a large amount.

It was in this way that Clara managed to function; by trying to ignore her problems, by trying to obliterate them, she hoped they would simply vanish.

Her daily routine was to arrive at the bar at four in the afternoon and tidy the place up from the night before, mopping floors, washing glasses and laying the tables.

Clara soon got moved from the bar to reception because her

mind was so weighed down with thoughts, drugs and alcohol, that she never remembered how to make any of the cocktails. The bosses didn't want to get rid of her as she was getting bought so many drinks and was pulling in punters.

The other two girls, Natasha and Rachel, who were New Zealanders, would start to make cocktails as soon as they arrived and as Natasha was sleeping with one of the bosses, no one objected to the amount the girls got through.

Customers started to arrive at about 6pm, although it didn't get busy until 10.

There was a kitchen and the chef made the girls a revolting dinner before the customers arrived.

Drinking continued through the night until last orders at 3am.

The pay was low but life was fun as Clara needed to divert her mind from its morbid thoughts and eventually she moved out of Chris's and in with the two New Zealand girls.

Chris had started charging her rent because she had been there for some time and she was working. He thought that she wasn't desperate anymore. Rent was cheaper with the girls.

She made friends with some of the clients and she slept with a couple of them. Many more tried to buy her services.

She was horrified when she discovered that one of the boys she had slept with was a male gigolo. Still she joked at least he had paid for everything!

She and Scott kept splitting up and getting back together, as was her pattern.

Then one day he had a fight with one of the clients and started to threaten him.

The police were called and Scott was fired.

She continued to see him and he offered to get a flat for them both, saying that she wouldn't have to work, that he would support her with his cocaine money.

She was not interested in being kept by him, nor by any

man. She said she wanted to look after herself and yet she was so lonely that she was unable to stay without a man for any length of time.

Although she liked Scott she was by no means in love with him. She felt sorry for him, as she always did for her boyfriends.

He was a traumatised kid who had been born into a good family. His father had beat him so ferociously when he was young that he still had huge lash marks across his back. Scarred for life.

He was always in trouble with the police and he had nowhere to live for a short while and so it materialised that in spite of his good intentions it was her that ended up supporting him by sharing her room with him. Her flat mates were extremely pissed off about it.

She had cut right down on the amount of drugs she took because she didn't want to end up like Charles. She had made the connection between his insanity and the drugs he took.

She still hadn't registered the full extent of her own insanity or linked it with the way she abused her body.

Meanwhile she continued to drink huge amounts and started to socialise with the prostitutes that hung out at the bar. Then it dawned on her how much more money they made than her.

Charles had always said that if she left him, the only way she would be able to support herself would be to become a prostitute and she began to play with that idea.

She still spoke to Charles and one day she gave him her mobile number. When he came to London he would phone her and she would go and meet him and sleep with him.

Then he would go back to the other girl in the country and ignore Clara's calls.

He would not finish with the other girl and Clara was in hell every time he left.

She decided that she would book a holiday to Venice, she needed to get away from the vice that was surrounding her and go and purify herself, otherwise she realised that she would sink further into the shadows.

Reading this account, I realise that I must have been relying on the 'see no evil' technique again. I simply wasn't aware of the half of it. John and I would often go to the bar where Anita worked for late-night drinks after the cinema, as would Tabitha and Juliet, and she always seemed happy and pleased to see us. The customers also seemed friendly and charming and used to congratulate me on my three beautiful daughters. Oh dear! One story Anita told me pleased me a lot. Her boss, who was plump, middle-aged and pony-tailed, eyed her up one day and said, 'You should get a boob job,' whereupon she retorted, 'And you should get liposuction,' after which he left her in peace.

In September Anita and Juliet went to Greece. When she left Charles, Anita reminded me that when my first marriage to Ken had broken up, my mother had paid for me to go to Greece with Aunt Dorothy. This was perfectly true, and I wished I could do the same for her, but I simply didn't have the money. Amazingly Juliet then won a competition – two weeks holiday for two in Greece. She originally invited a school friend to go with her, but the friend let her down at the last minute because she had to resit her A levels. This coincided with the break-up of Anita's marriage, so, with great serendipity, the two sisters went together instead. Less than a week later, Ingo, who had been doing a TEFL course, was offered a job teaching English, also in Greece, and went off on 21 September. Tabitha went back to university soon after, so from having had a house that was full to bursting point, I suddenly found myself suffering from empty-nest syndrome.

Anita moved back home in October, helped in the move by Oby who had now become a devoted friend. She left her job in the bar a week later, and soon afterwards went to Venice to stay with Bobo for what was originally intended to be a month, but which stretched into two. She writes about this period in her novel:

In Venice, safe at last, she had a nervous breakdown.

She gave up smoking and drinking, so she had no way to escape her feelings and they overwhelmed her. Here, she was finally able to release some of the anguish that she had sought to obliterate for so long.

The agony was almost too much for her to withstand. Her pain came to the forefront. She couldn't look anyone in the eye. She couldn't hold a conversation with anyone.

All the darkness that was in her, she saw in others and she was terrified of people, thinking always that they were laughing at her, mocking her, trying to drag her down. She thought she had to smile, not to show anyone how she was suffering and she tried to hide the pain that she felt and all of the shame that went with it.

She was having Italian lessons at a school near her house and she felt excruciating pain as she sat in the classes.

She became aware that her face was twitching, badly, and when she knew that other people had noticed, it got worse. She could not hide her disease and all of her attempts to, and each time she berated herself, she made it worse.

She felt so ashamed of herself, of her past. Of her marriage, the drugs she had taken and the abuse that she had suffered. She saw clean-living people all around her and she felt so dirty. So heavy, dark and ashamed.

She found she was unable to interact with others during this time. Only her father managed to penetrate into her world as a figure of kindness. Everyone else she was terrified of and saw only their shadows and none of their light. She felt that she was mad and that everyone could see she was and was convinced that no matter how hard she tried to behave like a normal person, everyone could see that she was not.

Charles was right. So were her mother and grandmother. Somehow she was deficient. Not good enough.

Everyone could see that she had taken drugs and slept with

224

pigs and been fired. That she was useless and despised. That she was a slut and a drug user.

Her father was very kind to her during this time and she clung to him, he was the calm in the storm to which she was able to anchor herself. And yet she was scared that if he knew what she was really like he would hate her.

For the first time in her life she was close to him and a part of herself that had always been missing, fell into place with the establishment of this relationship.

She knew that he felt her pain and yet she could do nothing to spare him. She could not stop her face from twitching and she knew that it was worse than it had ever been before.

She was afraid. She thought it would always be this dark for her. She felt as if it always had been and she knew nothing else.

Then her father became ill while she was there.

He'd had problems with his back for some time and now they came to a peak. He couldn't get out of his bed and she would hear him scream in agony although he tried to spare her and hold his screams in.

She, her stepmother and her sister were worried that he might be crippled. There was talk of him having an operation to staple together three of his vertebrae, which would take away the pain but would seriously reduce his mobility.

The idea of her father being crippled made Clara feel physically sick; he was such an active man. He never liked to sit still. To be imprisoned inside a body that couldn't move would be a living hell for him. More so perhaps than for anyone else she knew.

He went to Austria for the operation. It was decided that first they would staple two of the vertebrae and see if that was enough. He would still be able to move if it worked.

Clara found it very hard to be in Venice without him. She missed him. She had spent her whole life missing him in England and now to be in Venice without him she missed him more that she had thought possible. He was her rock during this time and now it seemed to her that even he was not solid.

Was anything permanent?

She felt like a feather in a storm and longed for sunshine.

Yet even in the depths of his illness her father spoke to her about her suffering and he would do his best never to mention his own. She felt his love so much during this time and she loved him passionately in return.

Clara had found her father and their relationship was intense.

As her mind reeled from all the events that were striking her she began to understand that her insanity was a form of protection for her. Her reality had been too hard to face so her mind had adjusted, it had bent and allowed her to see things in a different way, a way that was not true but that was in some ways less painful than the truth.

Clara was so pleased to be able to love her father and be loved by him in return that the idea of anything happening to him, now that she had found him, was too much for her to bear.

She did her best not to think about it. She could not face it, yet the fear was with her.

Even though her father was with her most of the time, she remained lonely.

She was always lonely; she did not trust other people enough to let them get close to her. Nor did she trust herself.

She had a handful of friends but they were not like her, they had nothing in common with her. They were quiet people that had lived peaceful lives and she felt apart from them. They could not understand her and she could not understand them, they could not have understood the turmoil that she wrestled with, that tormented her from the depths of her soul. All of the men that she had slept with and all of the drugs that she had taken and all of the opportunities that she had messed up.

She was yearning for something so desperately, but she did

not know what it was. She could not imagine that anything could satiate her.

She thought about Charles a lot and she meditated for him all the time. She was glad that she was not in the same country as him. Here at least she did not want to call him. She had her father. Still, the terrible fear she had that Charles was going to die did not leave her and she meditated feverishly as the only way she knew to protect him without exposing herself to any danger by speaking to him.

One night she had a peculiar vision. She was not sure if she was asleep or awake, when a shadowy figure drifted into her room.

It was Charles and he got into bed with her and they lay together as she fell into a deep slumber, her arms protectively around him.

When she woke he was gone and she was not sure if it had been a ghost or a dream, or indeed if there was much difference between the two.

She felt more peaceful that day than she had done for some time and she knew that Charles would be okay.

Meanwhile, she was not okay.

Her mind knew no peace and she wondered if she might be schizophrenic. She heard voices in her head.

She was utterly fragmented, it even occurred to her that she might have numerous personalities, more than two.

She thought she might have to go into a lunatic asylum.

She knew she was not sane and felt that she was incapable of functioning normally. She could not possibly hold down a job. She was not even capable of holding a conversation with anyone without hearing voices in her head and twitching chronically.

So many thoughts overwhelmed her and weighed her down and she did not know where they came from, why she felt them. She did not understand why they plagued her.

She was terrified at the thought of what life might hold for her.

It was all too much for her.

She was totally unaware that the fact she was detoxing was in itself enough reason for her to be feeling like this. She had abused drugs and alcohol and smoked cigarettes since she was fifteen. They had helped her escape her life.

Now she was facing crises of no small proportions having fled a violent marriage and with her father being seriously ill, and she was facing them without any crutches.

It was normal that she should feel so completely insane, so completely overwhelmed.

That was all it was.

Reading this, I see so many parallels between the way Bobo protected Anita and nursed her back to health after her broken marriage and the way he did the same for me in 1969. In times of crisis, as I said before, he was absolutely wonderful. The problems started to occur when I got well and strong again and wanted to reassert my independence.

While Anita was away, my divorce settlement was finally agreed. In the end, with the high court looming, Anthony and I sorted it ourselves in just two mornings at the house of an accountant friend of mine, John Tuohy, and I got my decree absolute. It actually made very little difference to my life, as everything hinged on the sale of Ebury Street, which hadn't happened yet, in spite of great interest and numerous viewings. By now I'd acquired a certain Buddhist serenity, and was sure the right purchaser would come in time, as indeed he did.

Anita came home from Venice for Christmas and went back at the beginning of January. Ingo, who had decided English teaching wasn't for him, joined her there at the end of the month. Tabitha went to Southampton University, and Juliet, who had got into Leeds and was now in her gap year, took off for Thailand with her friend Arethusa, supposedly for three months, which she eventually extended to six. We were all extremely sad to see her go, but my mother felt it particularly. I remember saying to her, rather patronisingly I now realise, 'Well I suppose we just have to let go.' I wish now that I'd been more sympathetic. My mother never saw Juliet again.

Ingo and Anita came back from Venice together on 10 February, looking very well and beautiful. 'Anita is coming back,' I wrote in my diary a few days earlier, 'so fasten your seat belts everyone!' In fact she was on her best behaviour. She found temporary work almost immediately, as did Ingo, and all went well for several weeks, although there was a quarrel about money in March, after which I wrote, 'Anita received a couple of mysterious calls about midnight which disturbed me greatly, as I feared they were drug dealers.'

In April my mother's oldest friend, Gwen McKellar Thompson, had a brain haemorrhage and was rushed into hospital. My mother and Gwen had been at school together and kept in touch ever since. Gwen's husband died in 1984 and she had no children, so would call my mother almost every day for support. I don't think I'd realised until then how important the need to be needed is in keeping someone alive. Not that we didn't need my mother, of course. We did, but perhaps not in an obvious way. We drove to Ashford to see Gwen in hospital, but by then she was in a coma, and we had no idea whether she registered our visit or not.

On 15 April we received a visit from Charles, Anita's husband. 'Bombshell of the day,' I wrote, 'Charles turned up. He's detoxing at the Priory and is allowed out one weekend a month. He was a changed character, admitting all his offences and apologising, reconciled with his family etc. I pray it's sincere and that it lasts.' Charles ended up staying the night, and the next day Anita went to Norfolk with him for the weekend.

Gwen died in April, and was buried next to her husband at Hampstead Cemetery with drinks afterwards at Ebury Street.

My mother and I went to the funeral with Ingo, Anita and Tabitha. Gwen's nephew Mac gave the eulogy, which inspired Ingo so much that, to our astonishment, he insisted on giving an equally moving one for my mother, just two months later. Anita was asked to read the Henry Holland piece, 'Death is nothing at all,' which she did beautifully and I, to my amazement, found myself weeping inconsolably. When we got back to Ebury Street for the drinks, a new washing machine was being delivered and installed by Peter Jones.

To my horror it flooded at the first wash, and water poured down my mother's walls. One of the estate agents recommended an end-of-tenancy cleaning firm and 'a big fat man with a big fat dehumidifier arrived,' I wrote, 'and set that to dry her carpet.' The dehumidifier left a great burn, and the fumes, even though she slept in a different room, triggered a respiratory complaint that led to my mother's death.

The doctor thought it might be some kind of allergy and prescribed steroids and a chest X-ray, but three days later, when I went to say good-night to her, she said, 'Darling, I think I'm dying.' Since my mother had always maintained stoutly that there was nothing the matter with her and that she intended to live to a hundred, I didn't waste time protesting. I took her hand and sat on the sofa beside her, and in half an hour we arranged everything from her will to her funeral. After that she left her flat for ever and came up to sleep in my room where, with the aid of my wedge pillow, she had quite a good night.

The next day Tony Greenburgh came to see her. He said her heartbeat was irregular and fast, but could be cured by the right drugs. As she didn't have medical insurance he suggested we call in our National Health GP, who confirmed his diagnosis and arranged for my mother to go to the Chelsea and Westminster Hospital next day for tests.

We were picked up at three by hospital transport – my mother walking bravely and unassisted. She was seen by a doctor, given an ECG and told she must be admitted as her heart rate was so high. How I wish I had refused. Once she was in hospital my mother went downhill very rapidly. The nurses were quite kind to her because she was so sweet and polite, but she lost her appetite, and picked up a hospital infection which killed her within two weeks. The children were wonderful, visiting every day so that she was never alone during visiting hours, and I was suddenly very grateful to be single, since I probably wouldn't have been able to devote so much time to her if I'd still been a corporate wife.

On her last day, she was very sleepy, but smiled when I told her an anecdote about one of the children's friends. At one stage I said, 'Love you, 'and she mouthed 'love you' back. Those were our last words to each other. She was moved into a private room by the nursing desk in the afternoon and we went home about 8.30 in the evening. As usual we left strict instructions to call us if there was any change in her condition and they promised to but didn't. We were called at 5.20 the following morning and told that she'd died in her sleep ten minutes before.

Some acts of kindness from that time stand out. Ingo's friend Tim Tetlow came round and cooked for us all, Azzy sent us a beautiful bouquet with a card saying, 'the world will be a sadder place without Granny,' and the estate agents gave us a week off from the relentless round of viewings. Juliet was at a dive station in Australia with her friend Sara and sobbed and sobbed down the phone, as did Dicky when I called him in the evening. Looking back, I think I made a mistake in trying to carry on as usual. The Victorian period of mourning, so derided in novels, was, I now think, an admirable institution. To see someone dressed in mourning was to know instantly that they must be treated with a certain sensitivity, but because it was what I thought people did, I just carried on with my little round of UNICEF and *Epicurean Life* events and summer parties which I attended with a rictus grin on my face and a knife in my heart.

Anita came to the funeral with Charles, and a few days later asked if they could move into my mother's flat together. I said yes. My mother had been all in favour of young love, and I was impressed by the way the two of them were turning their lives around. Anita had started to go to AA and Al-Anon meetings and fallen in love with the twelve steps philosophy.

At the beginning of July, I had a letter from the Chelsea and Westminster Hospital, saying that tests had shown my mother had lung cancer, which had spread everywhere. I felt unreasonably upset by this, but Tabitha pointed out that at least my mother had never known about it, and we no longer needed to feel as if the hospital infection had robbed her of some more good years with us.

Later that month I spent the morning with Letizia going over the proofs of my Marinella translation and her introduction to it for the umpteenth and final time. We posted them to Chicago together from Islington Post Office, and that was it. The end of the most tumultuous six years of my life. As my New York editor put it, we had finally brought the beast down.

In August there were two major eclipses, lunar and solar, that astrologers predicted would bring about major change – perhaps even the end of the world. They certainly brought about the end of my world, and played havoc with Anita's too, since she and Charles parted again during that period. In September we finally exchanged contracts on Ebury Street. We agreed a three-month delayed completion period, and moved just after the millennium, on 6 January 2000.

I decided to rent for a year or two until we all knew more what we were doing and found a house in Pimlico, just a ten-minute walk away. Since there was a two-week gap between us leaving Ebury Street and the house being vacant, it was agreed that I would rent the one-bedroom basement flat for that period. Tabitha and Juliet would be back at university, and Ingo was invited to stay with his friend Bill, so Anita and I moved into the flat together. We weren't getting on particularly well at the time, and I worried about the enforced intimacy, but told myself it was only for two weeks. I wonder what I would have thought if I'd known that we would end up staying in the tiny flat with all our possessions in store for the next five months.

CHAPTER TWELVE

1 July 2009

I was woken at 7.30 by a team of gardeners vaulting the railings outside my bedroom window to water my window boxes. My window-box service is one of my extravagances that I suppose I ought to do without, since I often hardly notice when they've been replanted. They do, however, give me the occasional stab of acute pleasure when I look at them, which perhaps is the most one can hope for in life. My neighbours love my window-box team. John and Mario call them the flower fairies.

At eleven o'clock Anita received a text from Dr Pereira saying her results were through and that she had an appointment with a Dr Bridgewater at the Rosenheim building at University College Hospital at 1.30. A colleague of Anita's at the RAC had cancer, and Anita knew from her that the Rosenheim building was the cancer wing, so realised that the results of her biopsy must have been positive (ironic that word).

At first our shock protected us. Anita thought of her colleague, one of the few people she'd confided in, who appeared to be recovering well after treatment. I went into a spin because I had a three o'clock appointment with my clairvoyant Owen Potts in Vauxhall. I generally saw him once a year, and had booked this appointment before I had any idea Anita was seriously ill, but after her scan I'd been clinging desperately to the thought of seeing him. I got Anita to ask if she could see Dr Bridgewater at one instead. This was agreed, but I still worried about time. I could get to Vauxhall quickly from Warren Street, but I couldn't let Anita go home alone if the appointment overran. At this point Anthony called, so we asked him if he could meet us at the hospital and bring Anita home in a taxi afterwards, which he kindly agreed to.

'We duly went along at one,' I wrote, 'and found Anthony already there. It was a filthy old building with loads of people there, and we were kept waiting for an hour and a quarter because, as we later discovered, Anita's notes hadn't been sent over.' It was a very hot day, and Anita was in considerable discomfort, rocking to and fro on the hard bench, trying to get comfortable. I felt a slow burn of fury building up inside at the inefficiency and general squalor.

When we finally got in to see Dr Bridgewater at 2.15, he was pleasant and apologetic. It was obvious he knew nothing about Anita's case, and was improvising as he went along. He told us that Anita had stage four cancer, and, when pressed (not by me since I already had a good idea of the answer from my internet research), said she had about three months to live if she decided not to have chemotherapy, or six months if she did.

At this point I had to go to my appointment. I was still feeling quite confident, 'What do you know?' I was thinking. 'We're going to China and Anita's going to have cryosurgery and brachytherapy and immunotherapy, which are a lot better than your piddling chemotherapy, so there!' and I kissed Anita, swept out and ran to the tube.

I got to Owen Potts on the dot of three. I had been going to him for thirteen years by now, and he'd never been wrong. When my marriage broke up, I freely admit that I overdid the clairvoyant bit. Tom Corbett had died, so I sought his replacement in the highways and byways. I didn't just see clairvoyants, I saw tarot readers, astrologers, white witches, mediums, healers, numerologists and feng shui experts. The problem was that all of them, apart from a few who were absolutely hopeless, saw my present situation with remarkable accuracy, so can I be blamed for trusting them when they assured me that my future would be rosy, that my prince would come and/or that Jeremy and I would end up together?

Owen Potts was different. I saw him for the first time just after Jeremy had been door-stepped outside my house. He told me Jeremy had feelings for me, but wanted to do the 'right' thing and wasn't going to leave his wife. I left feeling upset and angry, convinced Owen Potts didn't know what he was talking about.

It wasn't until several years later that I remembered him and realised that everything he'd told me had come true. I visited him again, and eventually gave up all the other clairvoyants. He was a medium as well, and one of the things he told me that moved me enormously was about my mother. After the hospital called us to say she'd died, we all, Ingo, Anita, Tabitha and I, rushed over to sit with her and say goodbye. She was wearing her wedding ring, which she never took off, and we debated whether or not to remove it, and eventually decided we should. On my next visit to Owen Potts he said, 'Your mother's here. She's so pleased you've got her ring. It makes it much easier for her to communicate with you.'

On this visit, he saw at once that Anita was ill, and said I should take her to China right away and he was sure her situation would improve. He then said, which I didn't pay much attention to at the time, 'It's a good thing she's agreed to go with you.' After that we talked practicalities. Should I resign from my job? Should I take my pension now, instead of deferring until I was sixty-five as I had hoped to do? Would I be able to manage financially? All of which he answered in the affirmative. Finally I asked him if he could see and predict death, and he replied that he had specifically asked his spirit guides not to be able to predict it because of the danger it would bring of playing God.

I left feeling immensely cheered and got home about 4.15. The family was congregated in the garden, with Anita reclining on a sun bed. Once again the atmosphere was good. Everyone was full of support and love, and determined to help Anita get well.

The next morning I wrote a brief e-mail to Berlitz, explaining the situation and resigning from my job.

*   *   *

On the day of the house move, I dropped Anita off early in the basement flat in Pimlico and drove back to Ebury Street to attend to last-minute matters. Bill came to collect Ingo and I lent Tabitha and Juliet my car to drive to Anthony's for the few days before they went back to university. The new owner and I read the meters together, then I left the house alone, on foot, with only my least favourite of the estate agents to say goodbye to. She was actually quite decent, and asked if I'd like to have a last look round the house, but I declined. I'd done it earlier, and it was now just an empty shell.

Anita had moved the furniture round in the flat so we had a room each. She was in the former sitting room, facing the street, and I in the bedroom at the back with a tiny patio. She had unpacked as far as she could, but numerous cardboard boxes lay stacked in the corners. That evening I collapsed into bed among the packing cases feeling strangely relieved that the whole thing was over.

Next day the owner called me from Brussels to welcome me to the flat and explain the situation with the upstairs tenant, Mr Smith. He had moved in after his marriage ended and was a perfect tenant for the first year. After that his payments became erratic and he hadn't paid any rent for the last two months. This was the first I knew about the situation. A few days later I heard that Mr Smith was refusing to move, so the owners were going to have to take him to court and would have him out in six weeks maximum.

I felt curiously unmoved. My feelings at the time were that I'd survived some cataclysmic disaster, a shipwreck or an earthquake and been washed up safe but exhausted on the beach. For the time being I simply couldn't be bothered to strike out in search of civilisation. All I wanted to do was lie with my face in the sand and the sun on my back till I felt stronger. My divorce settlement had been paid into my bank account and I was richer than I had ever been, but the same time felt more anxious about money than at any other time in my life. I decided I'd give myself a year off work – a breathing space in which to decide what I really wanted to do with the rest of my life.

Anita was much more energetic than me. She was attending regular AA and NA meetings and had taken a temporary job. In order to get to work on time, she set her alarm at 6 am every morning, which woke me too, since the flat was so small. She also decided to give up smoking, which was of course admirable, and got very cross if I smoked in the flat. Since we hadn't agreed in advance that it was to be a non-smoking flat, I felt distinctly aggrieved, but somehow lacked the spirit to assert myself. All I wanted was to be left in peace, and perhaps this was what worried Anita.

I wasn't completely idle. I'd enrolled on a counselling skills course at the Westminster Pastoral Foundation, which I went to once a week, with the idea of eventually qualifying as a counsellor. I also did work experience at a day centre for adults with physical disabilities, which turned out to be both rewarding and extremely moving, and had my own counselling sessions with a psycho-therapist recommended by the foundation. Fascinating as these activities were, the length and cost of the training eventually put me off. The course wasn't wasted however, since I found the counselling skills I'd learnt very useful when I became a Berlitz teacher.

In March Anita started a new job as receptionist for a shipping firm in Berkeley Square. She looked on it as a recovery job – something mindless that would keep her occupied while she eradicated all traces of drugs from her body. The boss's wife was having her apartment feng shui'd, and Anita and I arranged to have her team, Kenny and Christian, visit us in the flat at the end of April. According to them, everything was wrong, from the position of my bed to the three wastepaper baskets stacked in my relationship corner. Things certainly started moving after I implemented their changes. Mr Smith was finally dispatched, and Anita and I were able to move up into the main house just in time for Tabitha and Juliet's summer vacation, Ingo having bought a flat with Bill just round the corner.

Anita had now been 'clean' for five months but relations between us were still fairly tricky. I opened up to my group at one of the final sessions of my counselling course, saying how Anita's hostility towards me reminded me of Balbina's when I was the only one of her four daughters in law to offer her a home after her illness. One of the group asked me if the way I dealt with Anita's hostility was the same way I'd dealt with Balbina's, and I realised with a shock that it was, ie skulking in my room to avoid a confrontation, a prisoner in my own home! The difference between the two situations was that Anita was basically warm hearted, and if left alone to think things over, did often see she'd been in the wrong and offer an apology. She also got over her outbursts quickly, and seldom held a grudge.

Kenny and Christian paid a second visit to the house at the end of June and spent three hours in my bedroom. They told me their first aim was to stop me from being treated as a scapegoat/doormat by my daughters. I filled the house with crystals, semi-precious stones and tinkling water fountains and I have to say it seemed to work and relations between us all started to improve. They also determined to help me find a boyfriend, and in this they succeeded, if anything too well.

Just three days after Kenny and Christian's visit, I went to a party where I met an artist called Martin whose looks reminded me of my father's at the age I'd known him best. After the party he came back to the house with me for a drink on the roof terrace. Extraordinarily Anita also met someone that night at an AA meeting. She also brought him back to the house, although neither of them stayed, and was soon involved in a tempestuous on–off relationship with him. This was actually against AA rules, which recommend that there should be no relationships until members have been clean for one year. People who break these rules and come on to newcomers are said to be thirteen-stepping them. A lot of members tried to thirteen-step Anita.

After a few dates Martin told me that he was involved with a married woman who was a talentless artist, using him for his connections within the art world. Instead of being horrified by his disloyalty to his mistress, I foolishly felt sorry for him and determined to rescue him. We embarked on a passionate affair, conducted mainly at his studio, where I came to understand and appreciate his art. His work was very different from Bobo's and was autobiographical in style, focusing on his relationships. I was flattered to recognise myself in some of the more tortured compositions! When his mistress came to London and he told me he couldn't end it with her because it would hurt her too much, I broke things off in a fury, and then missed him terribly.

A few days later I went to another party where I was introduced to Sir Clement Freud. I found him extremely interesting to talk to and was flattered when he called a few days later and invited me to lunch. To my dismay, as he was giving me the tour of his flat, he said casually, 'and this is my wife's office.' I had imagined, naively, that he was divorced. He took me to his local deli to buy some food, then fixed me a gourmet meal in about two minutes, which was extremely impressive. I told him about Martin and he told me a funny story about one of his daughters who, when her relationship ended, wrote the words, 'No penis' in her ex's passport under the heading Any Distinguishing Features.

On a second date, he took me racing to Lingfield. It was an extraordinary sensation to be out with someone so very famous. The crowd of race-goers parted to make way for us as if we were royalty. The first person I saw there was my divorce lawyer Raymond Tooth. We hadn't parted on the best of terms after he tried to get me to sign a document saying I'd pay the difference if Anthony taxed his bill and got it reduced. I said I wasn't prepared to do so unless I saw an itemised account, which he was strangely reluctant to give me. On this occasion I felt very glad to be, as it were, under Clement Freud's protection, but after my experience with Jeremy I had zero interest in dating a married man, and our meetings soon fizzled out.

Another new friend was the biographer and critic David Fingleton. He'd written a book about Kiri Te Kanawa, and I met him at a biographer's club event. There was no physical attraction, but I found him extremely amusing. He once asked me if I'd really loved Jeremy, and I replied dramatically, 'I thought he was God!' 'Oh well he did too, so no wonder you got on,' he said deadpan. David seemed to take a genuine interest in my work and gave me several good suggestions for *Epicurean Life* articles as well as inviting me to some wonderful operatic events.

In August I went on a week-long beginners' astrology course run by the Faculty of Astrological Studies at Jesus College, Oxford. It was one of the most enjoyable weeks of my life. I'd always been interested in astrology, but never really progressed beyond the sun signs. Now I felt, like the apostle John, that I saw a new heaven and a new earth! During that week I read a book called *Relating* by Liz Greene and decided that at all costs I must see her for an astrological consultation. She lived in Switzerland, so it wasn't easy, but I finally managed to get an appointment with her in November, and flew over to Zurich for the day. I also had my chart drawn up and discovered that, since my ascendant was in Taurus, the ruler of my chart was Venus, which explained a lot.

After returning from Oxford I went off again almost immediately to the Buddhist HQ at Taplow Court to work as a volunteer for a week. There were eight volunteers at any one time, and our schedule was extremely well organised and included prayers twice a day and an hour's chanting. I also had guidance from the head of the organisation in the UK, Ricky Baynes. I told him I had no idea what to do with the rest of my life and he suggested taking any sort of job and trying to create something of value from it. This tied in well with what Owen Potts had said on my last visit to him some months previously. 'All these courses are all very well,' he said, 'but you need to make some money.'

On my return to London I enrolled with a temping agency and took on such diverse jobs as writing visitors' names on badges at the Guildhall and handing people certificates to say they'd climbed the three hundred odd steps to the top of the Monument. Later I took on a permanent part-time job for a charity awarding grants to PhD students. When the idea of becoming a Berlitz teacher came to me, I filled out an application form, and sent it to them with my CV, but heard nothing back for months. About this time Ingo, who had been looking for work in computing, managed to get his first job as a programmer, since when he's never looked back.

I had learnt by now that, contrary to what people told me, there *were* single men of the right age for me in London, but the problem was that many of them had a deep-rooted fear of monogamy. At the beginning of the year I'd broken off a short-lived relationship with a journalist called Richard for much the same reasons as I had the relationship with Martin. I kept bumping into him at events, however, and he was always very friendly. I still found him attractive, as I did Martin, so was eventually struck by a bold idea on the 'if you can't beat them, join them' principle, and decided to date both of them, telling each about the other.

Looking back at my diaries I see that a few days after I reconciled with Martin, Anita got back with Charles. I hope and trust it wasn't my example, but rather some supremely unstable astrological transit that was influencing us both as Sagittarians, or perhaps the over-zealous efforts of our feng shui experts! She went to stay with him in Norfolk, but the relationship ended again a month later. On 25 November she celebrated her one year clean (of drink and drugs) anniversary, by buying her first packet of cigarettes in months. The following day she went off to Venice for a week, where fortunately Bobo's stabilising influence was sufficient for her to give up smoking again.

I flew to Zurich to see Liz Greene on 28 November. We spent two hours together, during which she explained to me that my childhood – my parents' inability to marry, a twin dying in the womb, my cousin Rosalind dying when I was two – had left me with deep feelings of vulnerability which I sought to reaffirm through my relationships with men. I was attracted only to the ones who compounded my feelings of insecurity. I told her about Martin and Richard and that I'd 'switched jealousy off', but she said it wasn't possible to switch it off, only to drive it underground where it causes internal damage. She recommended that I go into therapy – I'd stopped when I finished the counselling course – and said she saw a great renaissance of creativity provided I sought help. There was no need to break off my relationships immediately, since they would change anyway when I started therapy. She also said that the aspects to my chart at the beginning of the year, Pluto square Sun, had been so hard that if she hadn't known my age and state of health, she might well have imagined that I would have died under them. I left feeling shocked but comforted. Liz Greene had explained my marriage break-up to me and also my shadow side, 'which wasn't a raging minotaur,' I wrote, 'but only a poor whipped cur.'

On my return to London, I started to implement the changes she had recommended. My first step was to find a counsellor. Suzy was recommended by a friend who'd had an even more tragic childhood than me. Both her father and her brother had committed suicide, her first husband was a heroin addict and her second husband was an alcoholic who robbed her and beat her up. She was now happily engaged to Michael, who I'd known for years. I reckoned that if Suzy could sort her problems out, she must be well worth knowing. Incidentally Michael, when told I was seeing Martin and Richard, apparently exclaimed, 'Oh God, the two biggest misogynists in London!'

I found my flat in October, and it was arranged that we'd move out of the house on 15 January, after Tabitha and Juliet went back to university. Tabitha had graduated in the summer and started a one-year post-graduate diploma in London, but spent a good proportion of her time at John's. For Christmas there were eight of us, me, the four children, the two Johns and a surprise guest, Anita's former boyfriend from AA, Ricky, who had a car crash early on Christmas morning, turned up at our house in a state of shock and ended up staying for lunch. Soon he and Anita were together again and ended up getting engaged.

I moved my furniture and books into the new flat on 9 January, four new beds were delivered the following day, and – luxury of luxuries – a professional picture hanger came on the thirteenth and spent the whole day at the flat arranging my paintings so beautifully that I fear I'll never be able to do without one again.

Juliet went back to Leeds on 14 January, and Tabitha's term started on the 15th. Anita (who had kindly taken two days off work) and I were left to do the final clear up at the house with the help of Mirjana, my wonderful cleaning lady who's been with me since Josie retired in 1998. The house agent came over at three, and we went through the inventory together and read the meters. Suddenly we remembered that the single mattress in Tabitha's room had been lent to us by John Knight. For some reason we found this terribly funny. Anita and I managed to stuff it in the back of my VW Golf and we drove off to the new flat (about two minutes away) in gales of giggles.

Six days after the move, Anita developed a high temperature, which lasted about a week. Her room and Juliet's room were situated in the back extension, which was less well insulated than the rest of the flat, and matters weren't helped by the fact that the central heating packed up the following day. Shortly after she got better, I ended my relationships with both Martin and Richard. I like to feel that it was something in the atmosphere of the new flat protecting me from any more destructive behaviour. For once my daughters were absolutely delighted with me, which helped me to stay strong through the withdrawal period.

On 13 February Anita was sacked from her job with the shipping company. Her bosses told her there had been complaints from other female staff about her 'attitude problem'. They were very nice about it and paid her until the end of March and said she could write her own reference. Shortly afterwards one of her boss's sons asked her out on a date, which I can't help feeling was rather shabby behaviour.

I decided it was time for more feng shui. Kenny and Christian had vanished, but I found an expert called Paul, who took the assignment very seriously and got me, or rather Tabitha, to draw a detailed plan of the flat in order to assist him. I remember that he was worried by the position of Anita's bed, which he said could be made safe for her if I ordered a pine headboard and hung a Chinese coin sword above it. Naturally I did so, and from that time until she moved into her own flat about fourteen months later, she never suffered another day's illness.

Two days after Paul's visit, Anita was offered a part-time job working for the Prince's Trust, where she was to remain happily for the next year. On the days she didn't work there, she wrote her novel. She later told me that her time at the Prince's Trust had proved valuable in setting up her Pilates business, because she'd learnt how to do PR and create a business plan. In the meantime I had been called by Berlitz, several months after my application, and told there was a training course starting in April. To be a Berlitz teacher in those days, the only qualification necessary was to have a degree in any subject and to have completed the one-week Berlitz training course. Now a Berlitz teacher also has to have a CELTA (Certificate in English Language Teaching for Adults). Berlitz paid for me to get this qualification in April 2008. If I had wanted to teach large groups of students, the course would have been very useful, but it had very little relevance to my job at Berlitz where the teaching is mostly one to one.

At the beginning of April, Juliet went off to Pau University as part of her French and Italian degree. I saw her off at Stansted and wrote, 'Strange that we're all about to make new beginnings, she in Pau, Tab doing a six-month work placement [as part of her diploma], Anita at the Prince's Trust and me at Berlitz.'

On 10 April I heard noises in the night, and in the morning Anita told me that she and Ricky had quarrelled. He sent her a rude text so she dumped all his belongings, including his passport, in the big black bin at the end of our road. I told her she should go and get them back, but she said the bins had been emptied. Frankly I felt that her reaction was way over the top, but by evening, as I learnt the full facts, I changed my mind. What she did was awful, but what he did, ending their relationship with a spiteful text message at 3 am on the day she started a new job, was, to my mind, worse. Ricky himself took it quite well. A pair of shoes had been overlooked in the purge, and he came round to collect them a couple of weeks later. Anita was out, and I had to hand them over to him, cringing with embarrassment. I suppose mothers have their uses occasionally.

I started the Berlitz training course at the end of the month. All went well, and I taught my first pupil, a Japanese lady, on 30 April 2001. David Fingleton wickedly advised me to go into the classroom and say, 'There's a nasty nip in the air,' but of course I didn't. The training kicked in, the student was polite and attentive as, with very few exceptions, all my students were, and apart from my nerves, the whole experience was really quite pleasant.

In those days Berlitz had two London schools, Grosvenor

Street, where I trained, and Oxford Circus. In June the Grosvenor Street School closed down, moving, in July, to its present quarters in High Holborn. A year or so later the Oxford Street School was amalgamated with the High Holborn School, but in the meantime, after a slow start, I found myself frantically busy, teaching up to eleven lessons a day until things quietened down again at the beginning of October. Although I had been told I would never teach more than one person at a time, I frequently found myself walking into a room and being confronted by a group of up to eight students of all ages and nationalities. I just had to get on with it.

One of the perks of the job was lunch with a student, and my most embarrassing moment as a teacher happened after one such lunch during my first summer. I'd had lunch with a middle-aged Turkish businessman and we got back to the school about two. As we passed the ladies' room on the landing, I said, 'I'm just going in here for a moment.' He bowed politely and said, 'Please do. Go and play with yourself!' Our instructions were always to correct students if they made mistakes, but on this occasion I simply couldn't bring myself to do it.

Towards the end of June I was stunned when Anita told me at about midnight that she was going out for a drink with Charles. She didn't return for four days. Their reunion followed the usual pattern of breaking up and making up until September, when it finished again. This time they decided to divorce, which they managed by themselves without the help of lawyers.

Letizia called me that summer and told me about a new MA course at Royal Holloway called 'Representations of Italy'. I'd been toying with the idea of doing an MA ever since leaving college, and this seemed to fit the bill perfectly, filling the gaps in my knowledge and covering many of my interests. Berlitz agreed to give me two days off a week, starting in October, and I enrolled.

Anita was doing well at work and seemed happy. She was going to be twenty-eight in December and had started house-hunting. She took advantage of a shared ownership scheme for first-time buyers run by the Westminster Housing Association, and found a lovely flat in a new development in Carlton Gate off the Harrow Road. It had a large sitting room with a balcony overlooking the canal, a small but attractive kitchen and bathroom and a good size bedroom. I loved it the moment I saw it, but was afraid she'd feel lonely living there all on her own, miles from the rest of us. Through my therapy, however, I realised that I was, in fact, projecting and that it was I who would feel lonely when she moved out, since Juliet was abroad and Tabitha spent half her time at John's.

On the relationship front there'd been nobody since I ended the disastrous Martin / Richard duo, but in December I suddenly met three really attractive men, all of whom were eager to take me out. Not wanting to miss this opportunity, I made a too hasty decision to date the one who seemed the keenest and most available. He was also, almost certainly, the worst of the three.

Nick was a football journalist, six months younger than me and long separated from his wife though not divorced. He was charming and easy to talk to. His parents, both in their nineties, were still together and lived in a lovely house in Sussex that reminded me a bit of Chandos Lodge. I went there for lunch and found them both delightful and welcoming. Nick spent his weekends travelling around the country to watch and review football matches. Sometimes I was invited, but at other times he would stay with his ex-girlfriends, of whom he seemed to have an inordinate number. At first I thought naively what a nice person he must be to remain on such good terms with all his exes. Alas, I quickly discovered that almost everything he said was untrue. It wasn't so much that he led a double life, more a sextuple one, with the accent on the first syllable. Dicky roared with laughter when I told him about it, but I found the whole thing so horrible that I renounced men completely for several years. At least my daughters were pleased. They all commented on how much nicer I was when I wasn't in a relationship.

Anita moved out on 13 April 2002. I'd given her a bed, and a dining table and six chairs that had belonged to my parents. Bobo gave paintings and antiques, Hélène a beautiful velvet bed-cover from her shop, and Anthony a dishwasher and fridge that he'd been storing from Ebury Street. She herself had put down a new kitchen floor and white carpet. 'So – the terrible morning of Anita's departure,' I wrote. 'We both got up early and the removal men came about nine. Helped her pack a little – she had done most of it – and she was off in the van about ten. Charles was meeting her there at twelve so I didn't go with her, but we're all going to have dinner there on Thursday. Nearly cried as I said goodbye to her, but I *know* it's good for her. It's a lovely flat and now that her first Saturn return is upon her, it's going to be the place where she grows up.'

Anita and Charles were now divorced but, true to form, they got back together again. Anita quit her job at the Prince's Trust and began to spend a lot of time with him in Norfolk.

CHAPTER THIRTEEN

2 – 11 July 2009

Thursday 2 July

I accompanied Anita to the chiropractor at 12 and she came out much energised and full of hope. Later Anthony came over and stayed most of the afternoon and we were visited by Anita's boyfriend, Jeff, who she met through her work, and who was very charming and seems supportive. Tab came over later and Anthony took Jules and Tab to dinner at Goya. We could have gone too, but Anita wanted to stay here, so I stayed with her. Finally David Goodman came over to do a healing treatment on Anita.

Friday 3 July

A visa letter of invitation arrived from China. Anita's pupil Antonio came to see her at 9 and arranged two treatments for her today, one with an acupuncturist and one with an oncologist. Philip from the Fuda Cancer Hospital called on Skype while he was here and Anita spoke to him at length, then seemed cast down when he didn't offer a complete cure (although he said some patients had survived five years). She became a bit weepy and Jules and I comforted her. Anthony came at two and was very good at soothing the girls. He then went off back to Denmark and Anita went to see the acupuncturist. She came in briefly, then went off again to see an oncologist in Harrow (driven by Antonio). When she came back, she was thoroughly over-stimulated – maybe she'd do chemo, maybe she'd go to the Marsden, maybe she wouldn't go to China. Jules cooked her some pasta that really bloated her stomach and we went to bed. Anita came into my room crying with pain and fear at 1 am. I rubbed her back with Weleda balm and got her a hot bottle and eventually the pain went and she went to sleep.

Saturday 4 July

All the family – Ingo, Victoria, Max, Tab, John – came to see Anita with everyone giving advice and saying that even if China was the right choice, it had to be Anita's decision and all the usual psychobabble. I went off to collect Anita's vitamins from the PO in Howick Street (theories are good, but the practical stuff has to be done as well). It wasn't a good visit. Everyone was arguing and I cried in front of Max. Tab and John dropped Anita at the Hale Clinic to see Dr Etienne Caillebout, whose father died of pancreatic cancer and who has spent his life researching it. I was left with Mirjana, who comforted me. She is a cancer survivor (leukaemia). She told me about a programme on Patrick Swayze who also has pancreatic and liver cancer and I trotted downstairs to watch it on the computer. Anita came in about 4 and told me about Caillebout, who is going to work out a programme for her. She then said she might transfer from UCH to the Marsden. I've always felt a sense of dread and horror when driving past the Marsden and said so. (Yes I think I was right to. Mothers' instincts are usually good.) This led to a God-awful row. She accused me of being a control freak and said I'd prevented her modelling at 18 (although at other times she admits that if she'd really wanted to model she would have taken up some of the many offers she had instead of letting them all drop) and made her go to university. What a crime! I realised she was holding a great deal of resentment, which Louise Hay (author of *You Can Heal your Life*) says is the first thing that has to go if you can cure yourself of cancer. She said she wasn't. At this point I went to church. I'd previously decided not to but I'm so glad I did. It made me feel much better. When I came back,

Anita was resting. She came up and we ignored the quarrel and watched some mindless TV to cheer ourselves up.

Sunday 5 July

Today we all got on better. Jules stayed the night with her friends, so only Anita and I were here. Tab and John came at 1.30 followed by Ingo, Victoria and Max. Max was adorable and is getting very polite. Jules came back at some point during the afternoon and was quiet and pleasant. At five the father of a friend of Jules's came to talk to Anita. He'd been diagnosed with cancer of the throat ten years ago and refused chemo, mainly because he disliked his specialist, gone to see the Dalai Lama's doctor in New York and been cured. He seemed very serene and relaxed and we enjoyed talking to him. I think Anita will follow up that link. (Anita was eventually offered an appointment with Dr Dhonden, the Dalai Lama's former doctor, in San Francisco, but by then she felt too unwell to travel.)

Monday 6 July

I didn't keep my appointment at the Chinese Embassy. Tried to call to cancel, but the number was permanently engaged. Anita had an appointment at the Victoria Medical Centre to see the Vietnamese acupuncturist/GP who works there and who Antonio had introduced her to. He was pleasant enough and admitted that he had no answers to what would be Anita's best course of treatment. He said acupuncture without chemo wouldn't help, so goodbye acupuncture (Anita has decided not to have chemo, and we all agree with her since nobody claims it will cure her). He said that rather than refer Anita to the Marsden, where she's determined to go, she should make a private appointment to see her specialist there and then, if she likes him, be referred. Good idea. I got her some beetroot juice on the way home and we had lunch. Anita is interested in seeing Dr Gonzales who's had good results with cancer patients in New York. She has to write to him describing her case. She started to look on his website and found some of his results which were frankly pretty poor. Naturally she was frightened and depressed (so was I) and cried and said, 'Mum, do you think I can get better?' I said, 'Yes, but I think it's up to you,' which she resented furiously. She then tricked me into saying I thought Fuda was the best option (I do) and screamed that I was pushing her to go there. More bile came out about me being a control freak and how if I didn't change my attitude, I'd kill her. She called Ingo in hysterics and he came over and was a calming influence. We managed to agree that 1) we wouldn't talk about Fuda. 2) I wouldn't accompany Anita to appointments. 3) my only duty was to make her morning porridge. Tab came over and agreed to walk the dogs with me in Battersea. We worked out a way I could do it alone, (by putting them in the boot), so in future I'll take that on too. I've asked Tab to name days that she can definitely lend me her car to walk the dogs and she said, 'Take it all the time.' I accepted it gratefully for this week.

Tuesday 7 July

Anita had an 8 am appointment with the chiropractor, so I dropped her there. Came straight home and actually slept till 10.30 when Anita came back. We tried to sleep some more, but two parcels arrived and the phone kept ringing and poor Petal did bloody poos on the carpet. Anita's back hurt a lot and I massaged it for her which seems to help. Father Pat called and invited me round for a chat at 3.15. I went and told him what was going on and he told me that his youngest sister had been his mother's closest carer when she was dying of cancer and taken the brunt of her moods, then contracted cancer herself after her mother died. Went to the health shop to get rye bread and olive oil spread for Anita and made her scrambled eggs and rye toast. Her sponsor, Renicke, came round and did healing with her and helped her complete her application for Dr Gonzales.

Wednesday 8 July

I walked the dogs alone, putting them in Tab's boot. Did various local errands for Anita, sending a fax to Dr Gonzales and posting a sample to the lab. Met Tab, Anita and Jules at Goya, where we all had supper at an outside table. Anita had dealt with her post, with Tab's help, and was feeling pretty good. Dr Caillebout had suggested a substitute for Omneprazole, which can have horrific side effects and is making her ill.

Thursday 9 July

Slept till nine, which was extraordinary. Started reading *A Time to Heal* by Beata Bishop (who cured herself of cancer through the Gerson diet and is, amazingly, a friend of Serge's). Drove Anita to Harley Street, posted some samples for her at the PO and walked the dogs. At 5.30 I drove Anita back to Harley Street for a last appointment with the chiropractor before he gets married. (Sadly, because I think he helped Anita, he then disappeared off the scene.) When we got back, Anita called Beata Bishop (Serge had arranged it) and also Dr Gonzalez's clinic. They wanted copies of Anita's CT scan and blood test. Jules printed them out and we were able to fax them from a hotel in Belgrave Road.

Monday 10 July

Jules went off on a camping trip for three days. Anita didn't have any medical appointments, but went off to meet her colleague from the RAC, who also has cancer. Later I managed to lie in the sun, where I was joined by Anita. We had late lunch, then I did some shopping for her at Revital and walked the dogs at 5. Ingo came round and I tried to talk to him about a Plan B if Dr Gonzales rejects Anita (he only accepts two out of forty patients), but Ingo told me I was being negative. I knew I'd have to take the brunt of Anita's disappointment if it was no. Ing left at 7.15 and Tab arrived about the same time. I cooked rice and beans very badly (beans were too hard) for

Anita's and my dinner. At 8 she rang Gonzales and the answer was no because 'her stomach was bloating and he didn't think she'd be able to swallow the necessary 175 supplements per day.' She then immediately called the Gerson Clinic in Mexico. The doctor Anita spoke to said the same as Gonzales – they could probably take her, but need more info.

Saturday 11 July

At 12 Anita's ex-fiancé Alan came round to see her, fresh off the plane from Sierra Leone. They sat in the garden so Mirjana could work. Later Tab and John came round, and Tab, John, Alan and Anita had lunch together, then went off to drop Anita at an appointment in Belsize Park with a nutritionist who didn't show. I was alone! I finished *A Time to Heal* by Beata Bishop, which was very moving and later went to church. Jo had loyally arranged to meet me there. We had a drink after, then came back. Anita was here, and dear Jo was her lovely, sweet self and told a Gerson success story which cheered Anita (and me) up no end. Anita told us that she'd asked to go to Alan's house (to use the loo or something) and he pretended he didn't have the key and that he must have left it here, so she came back and looked for it and, lo and behold, there it wasn't. She thinks he has a woman installed. No change there then.

*   *   *

Anita met Alan in September 2003 at a party given by a friend from Frensham Heights. Before that, she had shown commendable willpower by not having a relationship for a year. Her last reunion with Charles had continued longer than most, nearly five months. They'd spent a lot of time in Norfolk, so it must have been hard for Anita to come back to London, alone and jobless, to start a new life in her new flat.

To her credit, she coped with it very well. After considering various courses, she decided to train as a Pilates teacher and told me, shortly after starting her training, that she'd found her vocation. Bobo sold his studio at about the same time and gave Ingo and Anita a share of the proceeds. Ingo was able to pay off his mortgage and Anita to buy another chunk of her flat, so that she now owned fifty per cent. Anita started to do bits of journalism and also some modelling for an agency called Lee's People that she'd been introduced to by our neighbour, Anton. They specialised in commercials and film work and Anita said it wasn't really modelling at all, but I think she quite enjoyed it. Astonishingly, I then met Lee at a dinner party given by a UNICEF friend, Chris Sandland, and promptly signed up myself. Anita and I even found ourselves working on a couple of commercials together.

To keep her company during her relationship-free year, she bought a Chihuahua called Petal. I was horrified when she told me, because as far as I could see, it meant she'd never be able to work again. She'd already told me after leaving the Prince's Trust that she'd kill herself rather than do another office job. She bought Petal at Crufts, and I met her for the first time in a pub near Berlitz, where Anita was having an Italian lesson with my colleague Elena. I have to say that one glimpse of her little pointed face peering out of Anita's shoulder bag was enough to make me totally besotted.

Anita brought Alan to meet us at the beginning of October. He had been born in Sierra Leone, and his parents, Scottish father and African Lebanese mother, still lived in Freetown. Alan had been educated in England and lived and worked in London, but made frequent trips home. Anita told me he was very kind to her and had a very soothing personality, so I was disposed to like him and indeed did, very much. One thing she told me worried me, however, which was that Alan had a one-year-old son who he never saw. Anita was now nearly thirty, and thinking about having children herself, but somehow couldn't see that with this track record, Alan might not be ideal father material. She took him to Venice to meet Bobo – the first boyfriend to be so honoured – in December 2003, he moved into her flat the following summer, and she began to talk about going to live with him in Sierra Leone, which she first visited in May 2004.

In the meantime Ingo had not been idle. In July 2002 Juliet, who had completed her year abroad and was back in London for the vacation, told me that she had just paid an unexpected visit to Ingo's flat. While she was there, a pretty, blonde girl let herself in with a key and looked very surprised to find Juliet there. This was the first any of us were permitted to know about Victoria who, when she had recovered from her surprise, said how glad she was to have met a member of Ingo's family at last. I wasn't allowed to meet her until October, but when I did, I liked her very much. 'They were here for an hour or so,' I wrote. 'I found them very touching and had to restrain myself from asking about their wedding plans. I feel it might work out.'

Two days after meeting Victoria, I had another fateful meeting with Father Pat Browne who was to convert me to Catholicism. Some years earlier, Alastair had introduced me to Monsignor Alfred Gilbey at the Travellers Club. He looked at me searchingly and asked if I was a Papist. I mumbled that I wasn't, and as we parted, he shook my hand, and said, 'God bless you.'

My first thought was that God certainly wouldn't bless *me*. I was far too great a sinner. But I felt I had somehow been branded. I started attending services with my Portuguese friend Tona Page, and we agreed that I should find out more about the Catholic faith. My nearest Catholic church was the Holy Apostles in Winchester Street and I signed up for their RCIA (Rite of Christian Initiation of Adults) course starting later in the month. Before that, I went round to the Presbytery to meet Father Pat.

This was an enormous stroke of beginner's luck. Later, when I told Bronwen Astor, a fellow parishioner, that Father Pat had converted me, she replied, 'Oh well, he could convert anyone!'

I'm sure she was right. I came away from that first meeting really looking forward to the course, and delighted to have discovered that in the eyes of the Catholic Church I was a single woman. Since both Ken and Anthony had been married before they married me, neither of my marriages counted in the eyes of the Church and I was free.

Ken had, in fact, died earlier in the year of cancer that spread to his bones and brain and caused him to suffer terribly. 'It's strange how there's no satisfaction in hearing of old enemies suffering,' I wrote. 'I'd so much rather he'd been kinder and died a peaceful death. My "revenge" was to write *A Darker Shade of Love*, after which I was completely purged.' I heard of his death in a roundabout way, so it was too late to go to the funeral. Instead I lit a candle for him in Westminster Cathedral, and said a prayer.

Studying Catholicism brought about the end of my psychotherapy. I'd been seeing Suzy for nearly two years, and she appeared pleased with me. In June 2002 she remarked that when I was single, as now, I was at ease with myself, full of confidence and had the ability to make plans, whereas when I was with a man, I forgot about my life and concentrated on his. She said that this should be *my* time of pleasing myself and deciding what *I* wanted to do.

In December I tried to talk to her about my feelings over some residual complications to do with my divorce. To my surprise she refused to listen to me, and said my feelings stemmed from rage and bitterness. 'Well, according to the Catholic Church, it's a sin for a man to abandon his family,' I remarked. To my astonishment, Suzy then shouted, 'You're just like my mother!' and terminated our treatment, saying I should ask the Church to find someone to counsel me, who shared my 'fundamentalist' principles.

I came home deeply shocked and confided in Anita and Tabitha. Anita was blisteringly unsympathetic. She said that if

Suzy got so angry with me I should maybe consider that she was right. I agreed that she might be right over the issue, but that as a psychotherapist, she definitely wasn't right to shout at me. Anita then said I was probably exaggerating. Tabitha, by contrast, was appalled. She said that regardless of whether I was wrong or right, I should have been able to air my views in front of my therapist and she should have listened to me calmly and helped me work through my feelings without interrupting and imposing her views on me. Tabitha thought I should make a formal complaint, but of course, being me, I didn't.

I didn't have any more counselling after that, but I took to religion in a big way. I was still going to Buddhist meetings, but I'd changed groups when I moved house, and found myself with a lot of young foreigners, whose grasp of English wasn't that good and who sometimes lectured me on matters that I felt I knew more about than they did. I began to long for a more formal structure, to be taught by a trained priest who'd been to a seminary and really knew his subject. I also loved worshipping in church, rather than at home, and dropping in to London's beautiful Catholic churches, lighting a candle and saying a prayer when I felt low. At the same time as my RCIA classes, I did an Alpha Course at Holy Trinity Brompton, a pretty church that I knew from Ingo's days at Sussex House. I found this extremely interesting and well structured, and the services at HTB were very inspiring, but the sense of coldness and sadness I felt in most Anglican churches meant that I never really considered being confirmed in the Church of England. The final straw was when I visited St Paul's Cathedral with a friend from Alderney, Robin Whicker, and we were told it would cost us £6 each to look round. (I believe it's now £13.) 'That's it,' I told Robin. 'I'm going to be a Catholic. Catholic churches are free.'

My three daughters came to watch me being received into the church on 19 April. I'd been nervous beforehand, but in the end enjoyed the experience and found it very moving. Ingo and

Victoria were now engaged, and couldn't come because Victoria was being a bridesmaid in Cambridge. They joined us the following day for Easter lunch at Tabitha and John's. I'd sold my car by now, and John Knight, my rock, came to collect me and Juliet to drive us there, picking up Anita and Petal on the way.

John started to get ill the following summer. He'd retired in 2002, but been allowed to stay on in his pretty cottage. At first he was too delicate to talk about his symptoms, but when he did, it was obvious to me that they were the classic ones of prostate cancer that anyone who had ever read a book or newspaper would have picked up on immediately. Anyone but his NHS GP.

His illness meant he couldn't accompany me to Ingo and Victoria's wedding that August. They were married on the last glorious day of summer in the exquisitely pretty Poynings Church near Brighton, with a reception at Cuckfield. It was an extremely happy occasion, where I was delighted to see all Ingo's old school friends at the ceremony and again in the morning, since we were staying in the same hotel. Bobo didn't make it. He was now seventy-six and had decided not to travel abroad any more, but Anthony was there, and we even managed a semi-detached dance at the end of the evening.

John collapsed at the end of August and was taken by ambulance to Charing Cross Hospital and placed in intensive care. Tabitha and John accompanied me there the following day. John was unconscious and on a ventilator, but looked very peaceful. I was only allowed in for a few minutes, but I told him that he'd been the most wonderful friend to me, and that I'd never have another like him. A couple of days later I was told that he had prostate cancer, which had spread.

John was to live for another five months. As soon as he moved out of the emergency ward, his care degenerated horribly, and he caught the Clostridium Difficile bug. After his death in January 2005, I wrote a letter of complaint over the neglect he had suffered, but since the correct procedure was to send it to the Director of Nursing at the Charing Cross Hospital, I realised from the outset that I was unlikely to receive a balanced response. I showed it to a solicitor, who said I had a good case for suing for medical negligence, but unfortunately, as I wasn't a member of the family, the hospital was able to refuse to answer any of my questions and withhold John's medical notes. The nursing staff also managed to stir up dissent between his friends and family, so that whenever his friends expressed concern about his poor treatment, the hospital called his daughter and implied we were criticising her.

After this unhappiest of experiences, I found myself unable to concentrate on work. My dear friend Jill Lockwood came to my rescue, as she had once before, the year my marriage broke up. Jill and I met as teenagers. Her family lived in Buenos Aires and she was a weekly boarder at Queen's Gate School, and often used to stay weekends with me and my mother. At sixteen I travelled to Buenos Aires with her by ship, and was present on the night she met her altogether delightful husband, Geoffrey Pratt, at a dance at the Hurlingham Club. There were years when we were looking after small children that we didn't see each other, but we never completely lost touch, and when we were able to meet, our friendship was just as it had always been. I followed the news agog when her father, Charles Lockwood, was kidnapped by terrorists in 1975 and held prisoner for two months until rescued during a shoot-out in which all his captors died. Fortunately he didn't suffer any lasting ill effects. On my next visit to Buenos Aires twenty years later, I watched in admiration as he danced with Jill's mother Mabel till 4 am at a family wedding.

After the kidnapping, Jill's parents moved to Punta del Este in Uruguay, which was more stable politically than Argentina. Jill and Geoffrey also bought an apartment there, where I visited them for the first time in February 2005 after John's death. It was the ideal holiday. Jill and I spent mornings on the beach, went to the local multiplex cinema in the afternoons and, on the rare occasions when the weather was bad, explored the peninsula by car. Jill and Geoffrey were kindness and generosity personified, and I left feeling very much healed. On my way home I stopped at the Iguassu Falls. I happened to be alone there on Valentine's night, and sat on my balcony at the Sheraton, overlooking the falls. I toasted John in Argentinian champagne and hoped he was in a better place.

Shortly after my return, Anita and Alan went to Sierra Leone for a three-week visit. Alan had bought Anita a second Chihuahua, Snowy, to keep Petal company when they were away, but the idea was that they would eventually move to Sierra Leone together, taking the dogs with them. Alan's mother owned land out there and was planning to build a hotel with a spa, which Anita would manage. Of course I worried terribly about the dangers of Sierra Leone, where the civil war had only recently ended, but Anita and Alan seemed so happy and enthusiastic about the project, that I tried not to voice my fears too much.

Anita and I had our last terrible quarrel before her illness in May 2005. She and Alan had gone to Sierra Leone in April for five weeks, leaving Petal and Snowy with me. Their presence changed my life. For a start, since all the experts said dogs shouldn't be left alone for more than six hours a day, I had to give limited availability at Berlitz, which represented a con-siderable drop in income. Added to this, I got into the habit of staying home most evenings because I felt guilty about leaving the dogs. I accept that this may have been my own neuroticism, but I felt it just the same.

The reason I agreed to take the dogs for such a long period was that Anita had told me she and Alan would be in London throughout June, July and August, after which they would be taking Petal and Snowy to Africa with them, so I understood it was a one off. At a family dinner in May, however, Anita told me she wanted me to look after them again for six weeks (May to July) and again in August. I was going away in June and said I couldn't do it. Juliet, who was still living at home, said she couldn't help out, and the whole thing escalated into a ghastly family row, which resulted in Juliet moving out into Anita's flat and neither of them speaking to me for nearly two months until Ingo reunited us all in the Garden of Remembrance at the beginning of July.

Anita and Alan gave a farewell party at the Cobden Club on 23 July and departed for Sierra Leone with the dogs on 13 August. All my children were going away on holiday, but I was stuck in London because it was the busiest time of the year at Berlitz and my only chance to make serious money. I would have felt a lot more cast down if it hadn't been for a phone call I received at the end of July from an old friend, Nigel Wooll. He told me that he'd recently been in touch with my childhood sweetheart, Mike Gross, who lived in Devon and whose marriage had just broken up. He said Mike was too shy to call me after a gap of thirty-four years, so he, Nigel, was calling to ask if I'd like to hear from him.

Naturally I was delighted. We had a long chat, and Mike came to London to see me. This was the start of a wonderful year, during which we met each other's families and went on some exciting trips together, both in England and abroad.

In March 2006, Tabitha and I went to visit Anita in Sierra Leone where, after a slightly rocky start, she had settled well. Work hadn't started on the hotel that Alan's mother was proposing to build, but by advertising her services as a Pilates teacher at the British High Commission, Anita had quickly built up a large clientele and was earning good money. Alan was also doing well – he had bought a fleet of speedboats which he hired out for fishing trips and other excursions, and the two of them had a joint commission to write about Sierra Leone for the *Rough Guide*.

Tabitha and I travelled on Astraeus Airlines who flew direct from Gatwick to Freetown.

The scene at the airport was utterly chaotic, but Alan had organised for us to be met by an airline employee, who whisked us through passport control and immigration. We changed £200 at the airport and were handed a vast bundle of extremely dirty notes, which was much too big to fit inside my purse, but soon got rid of about £50, buying helicopter tickets to the mainland. There were only two modes of public transport, the helicopter (known as De Ellie) and the hovercraft, which had currently broken down. I'd been quite nervous about taking my first helicopter ride, but by the time we arrived, I was so tired, hot and bewildered, that all I cared about was getting to our destination.

There was a British Army presence in Sierra Leone – Tony Blair had sent out a peacekeeping force to bring an end to the civil war – and two British officers were on the flight with us, which I found immensely reassuring. A sign told us to fasten our seat belts, but a quick look round showed us that the helicopter wasn't equipped with any. No matter. Once we got going, it was so dark we couldn't see a thing and might as well have been on a bus.

Anita and Alan met us at the helicopter port. They were living in a chalet at the Solar Hotel, which they had kindly given up to us, and were renting a room in the main building for the duration of our stay. Tabitha and I were sharing the chalet with Petal and Snowy, who gave us a rapturous welcome, and with Morris, a wild deer who had been spared by some hunters and sold to Alan. Anita and Alan had also rescued a litter of street puppies, several of whom had died. The survivors were now residing in luxury with Alan's mother.

Travel agents were saying that Sierra Leone was the up and coming place. Certainly it was unsurpassed for natural beauty, but the appalling condition of the roads made sightseeing, for me at least, something of an ordeal. On our first day, Alan drove us to the River Number Two beach which, with its white sand and blue water, was one of the most beautiful I'd ever seen. You could lie in the creek and float round on the current into the river, but next day I woke up aching in every limb because of the bumpy roads. There was actually a perfectly good beach near the Solar Hotel. I would have loved to lie there every day reading Graham Greene's *The Heart of the Matter*, set in a fictionalised Sierra Leone, but I was told it was too dangerous, as drug addicts frequented the beach at night and buried their syringes in the sand.

Anita and I used some of our time together to teach each other work-outs. She taught me the rudiments of Pilates and, thanks to her, I was able to exercise my aches and pains away. I taught her the preliminary exercises to the facial work-out, which I learnt from a lady called Eva Fraser in 1990, and perform religiously four times a week. Done properly, it definitely makes a difference. When I first met Eva, I thought she looked about thirty, and was stunned and delighted when she told me she was sixty-two. When, at fifty-nine, I asked at the post office what I had to do to get a freedom pass, I was told to come back in twenty years.

Beauty treatments in Sierra Leone were ridiculously cheap, I had an excellent massage for £7, and my legs were sugared (in Freetown they use sugar instead of wax) for £10. We also bought materials in the local market and had them made into skirts by Anita's tailor, Kex.

Alan owned a football team, the Giants, and took Tabitha to watch some of their matches, while I went to Mass at the Cathedral of the Sacred Heart in Freetown. I was the only white person present and, although the service was in English, I couldn't understand a word of it, though I was able to follow on the sheet. The local language was Krio, a form of Pidgin English that sounded to me a bit like baby talk. When you met someone, the conventional greeting was, 'How de body?' to which the correct reply was, 'De body fine, tankee.'

Everywhere we went, we saw hordes of bright-faced school-children in uniforms that reminded me of England in the 1950s. Apparently the standard of primary education was very high, so if Alan and Anita had children, they planned to send them to the local schools. Many of the names of both people and places hinted at the country's colonial past: Darlington, Smokey, Mama Balfour, Lumley Beach, the Country Lodge.

There were some excellent restaurants, and we were also treated to wonderful Lebanese vegetarian home cooking from Alan's mother's chef, Mohammed. When Alan's mother visited us, I was pleased to see that she and Anita got on well and that Anita had a sweet, playful manner with her. ('Wish she did with me,' I wrote). Anita and Alan bickered a bit, but on the whole I was reassured by our visit. Anita obviously loved Sierra Leone and had carved out her own niche very successfully. After we left, the manager of the Solar Hotel offered her a studio there, rent free, on condition that she decorated and equipped it herself. She did, and it turned out to be another resounding success.

On the day of our departure, Alan drove us to the airport in one of his new boats. It was quite rough, and we got soaked, but we appreciated the gesture. When we arrived, to our amazement and horror, Alan moored the boat off shore, and he, Anita, Tabitha and I, our luggage and two carved elephants Tabitha had bought, were carried ashore by native porters standing up to their chests in water. It was wonderfully funny and chaotic ending to a unique and unforgettable holiday.

I was sixty that December. Mike and I were having a blip, so the children organised a surprise party for me. Victoria found the venue, Tabitha and Juliet called my friends and Anita flew over especially from Sierra Leone to be with me. Because of the number of guests, we couldn't all fit on the same table, and the children sat separately. Much as I was enjoying myself with my friends, my eyes kept straying to the children's table and my thoughts were full of maternal pride and affection. Three months later it was Tabitha's thirtieth birthday party, and once again Anita flew over from Sierra Leone to join the festivities.

Alan rarely accompanied Anita on these visits. According to Anita, their arrangement had been that she would try living in Sierra Leone for two years, and if it didn't work out, she and Alan would return to London together. Since the hotel still hadn't been started, Anita felt, with some justification, that it was time to return home. Added to this, Petal had become ill, and Anita was convinced she would die if left to the tender mercies of the African vets.

In April 2007 Anita called me from Venice. She was there with the dogs and I gathered that she and Alan had separated. Shortly afterwards I was deeply distressed to get another call from her saying that she had been made to feel unwelcome by Bobo and Hélène, and had moved out and was staying in a pensione near Piazzale Roma . Petal had been diagnosed with a form of Crohn's disease, and was having a colonoscopy in Padua in two days time. Anita was determined to come back to London as soon as possible so she could start work again, and had given notice to Juliet to leave her flat. As the quarantine laws stood, pets returning from Africa could either go into quarantine for six months in England, or spend six months in Europe, after which they were deemed safe to return. Bobo's unwelcoming attitude towards them seemed to have put paid to the latter option, and I was deputed to inspect the two sets of quarantine kennels serving London. Frankly, I found them pretty horrific. I also found out that DEFRA (Department for Environment, Food and Rural Affairs) didn't recognise the anti-rabies vaccine the dogs had been given in Africa, and that they would have to be re-vaccinated in Italy, thereby losing the time that Anita had already spent there with them. It didn't help that the Italian vet Anita was seeing, rightly incensed by the hypocritical and cynical quarantine laws in Britain, kept assuring Anita that the dogs were fit to return to England straight away and that she should smuggle them if necessary.

Anita's call upset me so much that I booked a flight to Venice that weekend. Anita met me off the airport bus in Piazzale Roma. We were sharing her room in the Pensione Arlecchino. It had a pull-out bed and a balcony for the dogs. Petal had come through her colonoscopy, but was far from well. She had lost her appetite and was pooing small drops of blood.

We spent the next day wandering round Venice. Alan had given Anita a diamond engagement ring which she was trying to sell to fund the new life that she was going to have to begin all over again from scratch. Lovely as it was to see her, I found her situation heart rending. If, as some people maintain, the root of cancer is emotional, I believe that this was the moment it probably started. For years she had put Bobo on a pedestal and now he had let her down badly whereas I, the bad parent in her eyes, had come through for her. For the first time in years Anita thanked me for my unselfishness in coming to help her. Of course I was gratified by this, but I'd so much rather that Bobo had helped her, even if it had meant him keeping the moral ascendancy forever. I'm not suggesting, by the way, that it was Bobo's unwelcoming attitude that caused her cancer, but rather the chain of disappointments of which it was the culmination: Sierra Leone, her relationship with Alan, the worry over the dogs, leaving her successful business for an unknown future, all of the above.

On the surface, however, things were civilised. When Bobo heard I was in Venice, he invited us both to dinner. I found it ridiculous that we had to leave the dogs alone in the Pensione, but knew Bobo well enough to realise that I would achieve nothing by criticising him. Anita and I took the boat across to the Giudecca on my last evening and I visited Bobo's new house for the first time. 'The house is enormous and beautiful,' I wrote, 'and Bobo and Hélène were very kind and welcoming and had cooked us both a delicious meal. I guess they just have a blind spot about dogs.'

I packed Anita's winter clothes in my empty suitcase and brought them back to London with me. At least we had made some sort of plan. She and the dogs were taking the train to Nice at the weekend, to spend a few days with her sisters and Anthony at our French house and then going on to stay with her friends Brendan and Lucy in Monaco. I'm sure Anthony would have let her stay in the house indefinitely, but as she didn't drive, the idea wasn't practical.

In the end, Bobo came up trumps after all. Two of his close friends, Bernard and Dominique, who lived in an enchantingly pretty mews house in Paris, kindly offered to look after Petal and Snowy for six months so they could avoid quarantine. This was the happiest of solutions. Bernard worked from home, so the dogs had company all day, and was a professional healer, which I'm certain had a beneficial effect on them after all the traumas they had suffered. Paris was near enough for Anita to visit frequently, indeed she and I made several short trips to see them there. I was totally reassured about their wellbeing, and quite envied their luxurious lifestyle. We also spent a happy week with them in Alastair's enchantingly romantic house in Burgundy at the beginning of July.

Anita returned to London in May and stayed with me for a few days before returning to her flat. Shortly after her return, she had a tremendous stroke of professional luck. A friend of hers, Christian Testorf, a successful Pilates teacher, had decided to spend a year travelling, and offered to pass on his pupils to Anita. Naturally she was delighted. I think nearly all of them stayed with her, and she also acquired new ones of her own.

Busy as she was, Anita missed Petal and Snowy very much. As soon as the six months were over, we brought them home in triumph in Tabitha's car. As we arrived at Anita's flat, Petal suddenly realised where she was and bolted as fast as her tiny legs would carry her to the front door. She might have been away for more than two years, but she hadn't forgotten her home.

Anita's career went from strength to strength in 2008. She organised a Pilates retreat in Estepona, Spain at the beginning of September, taking Juliet with her as a helper. I went along too as a client, and Anita and I went to Spain together for a weekend in May to do a recce beforehand. Because we were both single for most of her last year, we spent a lot of time together and became closer than we had probably ever been before. Attending her classes on the retreat, I realised what an excellent teacher she was and what a sweet and patient manner she had with her pupils. It made me truly proud to be her mother. One of the reasons I had booked on the retreat was out of loyalty, in case she made a financial loss. I needn't have bothered. The retreat was over subscribed and everyone who went said they wanted to go back again the following year.

My birthday fell on a Friday that year, so we planned a family celebration for the Saturday. On the day itself, all the kids were working, but Anita took the afternoon off and we met at the Wolseley for high tea, then went to the cinema together. After Anita died, one of her pupils wrote to us:

> She always spoke about you all in terms of such fondness, especially her Mama. One day I saw her when I was suffering from a minor hangover, the day before having been my birthday. She told me that she had had a very special time with her mother too, whose birthday it had been as well. And that seems so very Anita . . . she had a wonderful ability to share people's experiences, good and bad.

For her own last birthday, a week later, we met for lunch at Carluccio's in Westbourne Grove, and were joined for coffee by Helen Knox Johnston, whose birthday was the following day. She and Anita went off afterwards to be pampered at the Porchester Spa.

That Christmas only Anita and Tabitha were in London, so we were just four, with John, for Christmas lunch. John was going to his family for dinner so, to my great relief, I didn't have to compromise my principles by cooking a turkey. Tabitha left next day, but Anita and the dogs stayed with me until 4 January. What did we do? Very little. We went to the theatre and watched old movies together on television. I had some guest passes for Dolphin Square, so we went there, I to swim and she to do yoga. Her siblings dropped round fairly frequently, and on New Year's Eve Jo came to dinner and she, Anita and I went to midnight Mass. Anita told me about her new boyfriend, Jeff Atmajian, an American composer, who spent half his year in London and half in Los Angeles, where he was at the moment. Anita's holiday was greatly enlivened by a series of e-mails from him that she wouldn't let me see. When I heard that he was forty-eight and single, I decided that he was probably a commitment phobe or else secretly married. Finally she showed me a photo of him that he'd sent by e-mail. Over the years Anita had introduced me to several boyfriends and always, much as I'd liked or wanted to like them, a voice inside me had said, completely involuntarily and somewhat to my annoyance, 'Oh no, you're not the one.' I wasn't expecting much of Jeff, for the reasons I've mentioned, but to my great surprise, the moment I saw his photo, the voice said, '*You're* the one!'

I decided to say nothing to Anita for fear of putting her off him. After family lunch on 4 January, she went home with Petal and Snowy in order to get ready for work the following day. 'Gosh I'll miss her,' I wrote. We'd been extraordinarily close during the Christmas break. Not a single cross word had been exchanged, and it seemed that Anita and I had finally healed our relationship and that all was peace and harmony between us at last.

CHAPTER FOURTEEN

July – August 2009

After Anita decided not to go to China, things between us were never the same again because I knew she was going to die and that there was nothing I could do to save her. At the same time I couldn't reveal this knowledge to her, but had to watch, silent and impotent, as her health declined each day. We weren't in conflict about a boyfriend or a job any more, but about her very life.

Why did I want Anita to go to China so much? Because the Fuda Cancer Hospital was the only place that offered any hope of curing her condition through orthodox, medical treatment. It seems entirely logical to me that if your own country can offer you nothing, and if you're lucky enough to have the money, as Anita did from the sale of her flat, that you should go to a country that can offer something. Anita had published articles about health issues, and an account of her cancer treatment in China would have proved an invaluable contribution to the field. I could have assisted her by keeping a daily record in my diary and by communicating with her medical team, using my Berlitz training which, for eight years, had enabled me to coax people who thought they couldn't speak English into doing so. Do I think she would still be alive if she had gone there? I have no idea. But I do believe one hundred per cent that it was her only chance.

I watched the documentary about the Danish woman who went to China with the same cancers as Anita. It showed her sitting up in bed, cheerful and fully conscious, receiving Brachytherapy through long, acupuncture-type needles. She returned from China cured. Is she still alive? Again, I have no idea. But a year after Anita died, there was a front-page article in the *Daily Mail* describing Brachytherapy or, as they called it, Selective Internal Radiation Therapy, as a breakthrough treatment for liver cancer that could prolong life for up to twenty years. How did I feel? I wanted to scream.

Why did Anita change her mind about going? The only thing she said that made any sense was that she didn't want to be used as a guinea pig. She had watched the documentary with me and perhaps been upset by the sight of the long Brachytherapy needles, or perhaps by her conversation with Philip in which he told her he couldn't guarantee a cure. Obviously a tried and tested form of treatment would have been preferable to an experimental one. But there wasn't one available.

And so the days wore on. The nutritionist who didn't show up on 11 July came to visit Anita at home the next day. He had an organic food shop in High Street Kensington and worked out diets for cancer patients. Anita and I went to his shop a few days later and stocked up on ingredients. Tabitha worked out menus for her and I cooked. At first Anita was enthusiastic about my creations, but eventually found them too bland and barely touched them. The nutritionist also told Anita that the 'flow of energy' in Tabitha's room, where she was sleeping, wasn't good for her, so we swapped rooms. At first she said she thought it made a difference and slept better, but that didn't last either, and soon her nights in my room were as painful and interrupted as they had been in Tabitha's.

Her friend Emma was with us on 14 July when we called the Gerson Clinic in Mexico. They said they were very concerned about her condition and that she would have to follow a modified regime. This upset her and made her cry. 'Emma and I, but mostly Emma, comforted her,' I wrote. 'She was adorable. Thank God she was there.'

Meanwhile Dr Caillebout had come up with a programme for Anita that was so complicated it took her siblings days to work it out. It involved swallowing 120 tablets a day. Her stomach started to get very bloated and a week later the doctor from the Victoria Medical Centre said she should stop taking them as her liver couldn't cope. He also said he didn't think she should fly to Mexico. Privately I agreed with him. The cancer had progressed very fast, and whereas I'm certain Anita could have coped with the journey to China when she was first diagnosed, I no longer felt at all sure she was up to a long flight. I had learnt by now, however, to keep my opinions to myself, unless tricked into giving one inadvertently.

Bad days were generally followed by good days. Screaming at me actually seemed to make Anita feel a little bit better, and I read somewhere that it's an acknowledged therapy for cancer. Both Louise Hay and Beata Bishop used it, but in controlled circumstances. Not in the faces of their ancient, terrified mothers.

We had good moments too. Jeff was a great help. The first time he came round, shortly after Anita was diagnosed, he said we reminded him of a family in a Noel Coward comedy. He couldn't understand why we weren't all sunk in gloom (that was in the days when I still thought we were going to China). One therapy we all agreed on, was the importance of laughter. We started a campaign to make Anita laugh every night. She was still well enough to go to the cinema, so the whole family went to see *Bruno*, which made us shriek with laughter, and Jeff took her to see *The Hangover*, which had a similar effect. He also invited her to the premiere of *Harry Potter and the Half Blood Prince*, which he'd arranged the music for, but unfortunately it clashed with one of her medical appointments, so she couldn't go. Victoria recommended *Curb Your Enthusiasm*, and lent us the first series on DVD. This worked a treat, and Anita and I watched an episode together every night. Ironically we were watching the last episode of Series One the night before she went into hospital. Alice and James arrived to visit her, so I switched off the DVD and retired to the study. We never saw the end. Some weeks after Anita died, I finally found the courage to watch it. It was absolutely hilarious and made me burst into floods of tears.

The next set of people to enter our lives was the pain nurses. They came on a Wednesday morning and were polite, attractive and firmly versed in the prescription- drugs-as-God tradition. If I were choreographing a ballet I would turn them into robots, dancing dolls of death, advancing with high kicks and flexed feet, strewing pills in the air instead of rose petals. They admitted that the bloating in Anita's stomach that was causing her such distress was probably caused by the painkillers she was taking, but said that the way to combat it was to take more. When Anita said she was taking one and a half Cocodamol tablets every four hours, they said, 'Why not take two?' and contradicted her kindly but firmly when she told them she believed she was going to get better. I think what I found scary about them was that they appeared to be totally without compassion. But then how could they afford compassion in their line of work?

In the afternoon Anita went to the Marsden for an ultrasound to try to get to the bottom of the bloating. Tabitha accompanied her there, and I dropped them both off and walked the dogs. The ultrasound proved inconclusive. There was some fluid in Anita's stomach, but not enough to drain, and they thought the rest of the bloating was caused by constipation, for which she had started to take coffee enemas. That evening she saw Dr Caillebout, who changed her regime again to just soups. Ingo met her at the surgery and brought her home. When she started to complain about her new diet, he told her quite sternly that that was what she would have to follow if she wanted to get better. Anita took it well from him. 'If I'd said that, I'd have been told I was abusive and controlling,' I wrote, somewhat enviously. Fortunately Jeff then telephoned which cheered her up considerably. I massaged her back with Weleda balm and for once she had quite a good night.

Checking my e-mails a few days later, I found one from the healer Matthew Manning offering Anita an appointment the following week. This cheered me up and gave me renewed hope. Anita was pleased too. She went swimming and I met Audrey at the organic supermarket in the Chelsea Farmers' Market. She'd told me about Dr Red's Blueberry Punch, which had been shown to shrink tumours in mice, and I bought a bottle for Anita. Audrey and I had coffee afterwards, and she was deeply sympathetic over the fact that nobody in the family was willing to take my advice on medical matters. Anita loved the punch, which I made for her every morning, and took to her in bed. Thanks to that, her last days at home always began with a smile.

My diary entry of 31 July reads: 'Anita'd had a bad night and stayed in bed all morning while I ran around fetching stuff for her. She was actually very grateful and appreciative. Tab came at 12.30 and I drove her to work, then used her car to buy stuff for Anita at Revital. Anita had a 3 pm appointment at the Marsden for visualisation (followed by two more appointments at the pain clinic and with her consultant). At first she felt too tired and full of pain to attend, but I made her some lentil soup and persuaded her to get dressed and into the car, and by the time we got there, the painkillers had kicked in and she was OK. Left her with the nice therapist and came home to eat my lunch and put the finishing touches to the soup. Later I walked the dogs. Got a call about 6.45 to collect Anita and Tab (who'd joined her for the consultant's appointment). Anita was in tears because the consultant, in trying to bully her into having chemo, had related an anecdote about a man "with about a month to live like you", who was still alive eight months later thanks to chemo. Drove them home and Tab and I comforted her and plied her with food and painkillers and eventually she cheered up. (Tabitha and

I complained to the hospital and Anita later got a letter of apology from the consultant.) We all watched two episodes of *Curb Your Enthusiasm* together. Tucked Anita into bed about 10.30, then Tab went home. She'd been a saint.'

On 1 August Tabitha and John drove Anita to Kew to see a homeopath. When Anita came back, she was feeling sick and ill, but we managed to get her to eat some rye bread and home-made hummus. Unfortunately she had a very bad night. She had been told to take vast quantities of laxatives, and was awake all night. I stayed with her most of the night, 'in a state of pity and terror'.

The next day Anita was very sleepy, but I got her out in the garden for an hour or two and she dozed in the sun. Her siblings came to visit at tea time, and she got into a terrible state, lying in bed crying about her swollen belly. This time little Max defused the situation, by saying firmly, 'Get dressed now!' whereupon she actually did and came upstairs. It's worth noting that the laxative the homeopath had recommended, Normacol, which she took that evening, worked much better for her than the Movicol the doctors had prescribed, which had given her diarrhoea and insomnia the night before. 'She had three normalish bowel movements and slept six to eight hours,' I wrote.

On the Monday Juliet helped Anita with internet shopping. We finally managed to find her a water filter that was medically approved and sounded excellent. Anita and Juliet went swimming and, at Anita's request, I got three will forms from the post office for her, Ingo and Tabitha, the last two so that Anita wouldn't feel singled out. She asked me, touchingly, if I wanted her to leave me any money, and of course I said no, but one thing we never discussed, and now I can hardly believe I was so foolish as not to think of it, was what provisions she wanted made for Petal and Snowy.

We were due to visit Matthew Manning in Suffolk on 5

August, so I bought our train tickets the evening before. We agreed that it would be easier to travel by train so Anita could move around, rather than sitting cramped in Tabitha's mini. The 4 August was quite a good day. Anita had a massage at the Marsden – one thing I did like and approve of was their complementary therapies – and received various visitors in the afternoon. In the evening she felt well enough to accompany me and Tabitha to Battersea Park to walk the dogs.

Every time I go to Battersea now, I remember that last day. Anita made it as far as the Buddhist Pagoda, but she was very feeble and kept repeating how much she'd deteriorated. We sat down on one of the benches before attempting the journey back to the car. Most of the benches by the Pagoda have dedicatory plaques on them, including the one we sat on. If it hadn't, I would have liked to dedicate it to her, as it is and always will be in my heart.

That evening James came round. When he heard we were going to Suffolk, he offered to drive Anita there, but I told him we already had our tickets. Now I wish I'd accepted. The train journeys weren't too bad. They were fairly empty and Anita was able to lie across two seats and stretch her legs across the gangway and rest her feet on the seats the other side, but for some reason the seats in the black cab we took home from Liverpool Street were terribly uncomfortable for her, especially as we got stuck in a traffic jam on the Embankment.

We arrived at Matthew Manning's house at about 3 and waited on the large, squashy sofa in the waiting room. He called her in for the treatment at 3.30, and I accompanied her. We both liked him very much. He was sympathetic and knowledgeable about her condition. For the treatment, he put on a CD of crashing waves with background music. Tears started to pour down my cheeks, although Anita appeared peaceful and serene. Afterwards we had some time before our taxi came, and Anita lay down on the sofa in the waiting room and slept like a baby for half an hour and woke, as she told me, feeling quite different and restored to her old self.

Unfortunately the journey home knocked her right back again. As we arrived at Liverpool Street Station, Anita turned to me with relief and said, 'At least I'll never have to go on a train again.' What did she mean? It certainly sounded as if she knew she had only a short time to live. If she had once broached the subject of death, or given me a hint that she was prepared to admit the possibility of it, I would have tried to adjust and accommodate her in a way that would bring her comfort. But in case I was wrong and she hadn't meant that at all (although I have no idea what else she could have meant) there was no way in the world I was going to be the first one to concede the fact that she might not get better.

The taxi ride from the station was very bad. I gave up my seat so she could lie down, but that wasn't comfortable either. Eventually we got home and I gave her supper and got her settled on the sofa. Alice and James came round, and I left them alone together. 'Alice and James tucked Anita up in bed,' I wrote. 'I slept with the dogs and Snowy peed in my shoe.' It was Anita's last night at home.

The next day Anita woke earlier than usual, and got into a terrible state about her swollen stomach. Tabitha and John came to spend the day with her. Anita had a 3 pm visualisation appointment at the Marsden, so she and Tabitha arranged for her to go there early to have her stomach looked at. In the meantime Tabitha and I sent off an e-mail, attaching Anita's CT scan, to the Hammersmith Hospital, recommended by Matthew Manning, where some kind of ground-breaking treatment for liver cancer was being tried out (they never got back to me), and I went to the post office to get a parcel of vitamins for Anita, which she never took.

When the others left for the Marsden, I went to see Victoria and Max. 'The three of us went to the common. Max has a new double buggy (in preparation for the arrival of his baby brother), which he climbed into unasked. When we got there, he just ran and ran and ran – to the road, to the lake – fortunately I can still keep up with him!' At 5.30 Tabitha called to say Anita was being admitted to the Marsden to have her stomach drained.

I stayed with Victoria and Max till Ingo got home, and then he and I went to the hospital together. Anita was in a side room opposite the nursing station in Ellis Ward. She was nil by mouth, and hooked up to a drip in order to hydrate her. She'd had an X-ray, that showed nothing out of order, and I was able to speak to the nurses and say that if any subsequent tests showed a deterioration in her condition, I didn't want her to be told. I believe I was right in this. Bobo was never told he had cancer at all, and survived much longer than expected (a year). Hélène also told me that she'd been shown how to increase his dosage of pain killers infinitesimally when needed, so as to avoid as many side effects as possible. I regret very much that Anita wasn't treated with the same protectiveness and consideration by her medical team.

I think it was the draining that did for Anita. I wasn't there when the drain was inserted on the Friday afternoon. I'd borrowed Tabitha's car to walk the dogs. When I got back, two litres of fluid had been drained – the maximum amount considered safe over a twenty-four hour period. Anita was high on morphine – she mistook a ventilator in the courtyard outside her window for a man climbing the wall – and also very happy that her stomach was flat again. Alice and James came to visit her in the evening, so I left around eight and came home exhausted.

When I arrived at the hospital next day, the fluid had built up in her stomach again and it was as big as it had been before. I'd brought her some gazpacho and tahini from Daylesford Organic, and she was touchingly sweet and grateful. All the family visited in shifts. I left again at 5 to walk Petal and Snowy and go to church, returning to the hospital soon after 7. In my absence I was told that a weekend agency nurse had performed a liver flush and drained seven litres of fluid from Anita in under an hour. Tabitha was concerned at the speed with which the procedure was carried out, but the nurse assured her that while Anita's blood pressure remained stable, it was safe for her to continue. In fact the procedure caused her blood protein levels to drop, which created distressing swellings, and destabilised her cardiovascular system, thereby, as we believe, hastening her death.

I was offered free counselling during this period, and my burning question was, of course, why Anita was being so hostile towards me and so nice to everyone else. I was told it was very common. People know that their mothers will love them whatever they do, so they feel it's safe to remove the mask when they're with them.

Jeff called several times from LA during her last days and arranged to fly back earlier than intended, in order to see her. During one of their conversations he told her that he loved her, and her little face glowed with happiness afterwards and she said it was like a fairy tale. On another occasion, talking to Tabitha and a young female doctor called Amy, she said how wonderfully supportive and affectionate Jeff had been since her diagnosis.

'He's going to get an awful shock when I get better,' she joked.

Amy said nothing, but Tabitha told me that she looked suddenly very sad.

*   *   *

Shortly before going into hospital, Anita asked me, almost playfully, what I'd do if she died. Taken aback, I allowed myself for once to be spontaneous. 'Oh it'd be the end of me,' I said.

At this she got very distressed and made me promise I'd keep going after her death, so of course I did, feeling both touched by her concern and bewildered by the fact that for once we were being allowed to mention the unmentionable. Since she died, I've sometimes asked myself what on earth the point is of me remaining here once my child has gone, but my thoughts always come back to this conversation, and I feel I should stick around as promised, even if I don't know why.

One of the things I thought I could never do was organise Anita's funeral. Thankfully we were all fully united over the arrangements. Father Pat officiated, Ingo did the eulogy, Clare Arden's fiancé, the actor Peter Hinton, read Sonnet 18, John read Corinthians 13 and Anthony read the Bidding Prayers. One of these, at Catholic funerals is, traditionally, 'Forgive Anita her faults and failings.' Some of the family felt this was too harsh, but Jeff defused the situation brilliantly by suggesting we alter the word 'her' to 'any'. The man is a born diplomat, as well as being the ideal son-in-law I never had. He also arranged for a grand piano to be moved into the chapel for the day, so he could play a lovely and moving piece he'd composed especially for Anita.

For Anita's thirty-fourth birthday, shortly after she came back from Sierra Leone, she shared a party with two Frenshamian friends, Helen and Sam. It was just before Christmas, and a lot of people were going to be away. I remember she got quite dramatic about it and cried and said she didn't have any friends, but the West Chapel at Golders Green, which holds 150 people, was jam packed, standing room only, for her funeral, and the hundred Orders of Service we had printed were woefully inadequate.

Afterwards we stood in the garden and looked at the flowers, and a long line of her friends, many of whom I hadn't seen for years, came up to greet me and offer their condolences. I felt so happy to see them all and so proud of Anita for inspiring so much devotion and love. I think I completely forgot it was her funeral and felt as if we were all assembling in order to pay her tribute and that she, the guest of honour, would make her appearance at the end, and be greeted by wild applause. After-wards we had drinks at the RAC Club, where she had been so proud to work, and I met many of her former pupils, all of whom told me what an inspirational teacher she had been.

All this time Bobo hadn't even been told Anita was ill. He and Hélène were at their house in the mountains, with no medical facilities, and Hélène wanted to keep the news from him until they were back in Venice with his doctor at hand. I remember Ingo and I discussing the matter when Anita was in the Marsden and agreeing that Bobo really ought to be told, but events then moved so rapidly that it became too late. He was finally told on 27 August, and he and I had a long conversation the following day. He decided to hold a memorial service for Anita at the Church of St Eufemia on the Giudecca on 5 September. Sadly Ingo couldn't go. Freddie was due on 18 September, and Victoria's mother Estrid had arranged to go away on the weekend of the 5th so that she'd be back in good time for the birth. I flew out alone and stayed at the flat of some friends of Bobo's. I'd never been to the church before, but apparently Anita had liked and visited it often. It held about 250 people and once again was jam packed, with all Bobo's family – my family – who I hadn't seen for years and who were wonderful to me, and many of my English friends from the days when the children were little. I found the experience overwhelmingly moving, and was so very, very glad I went.

After Anita came back from Sierra Leone, when we were both single, she sometimes used to say that she was sure that if I found love, she would too. Now, thanks to her, I have. Mike heard of her death and wrote me a beautiful letter, which led to us meeting again. The pleasure his letter gave me was a lesson to me always to write to people, even if one feels shy or reluctant, because of the comfort it bestows. And of course his presence in my life offers greater comfort still. Anita liked him, and I'm absolutely certain she sent him back to me. I'm equally certain that in leaving Petal and Snowy to me without asking me if I'd have them, she knew the benefits they'd bring me in terms of being needed and loved and, in the early days, forced to get up and dress and go out into the world to walk them.

When Anita was on drugs, she had a near-death experience that she told me about some years later. She was advancing towards the light when suddenly a door slammed in her face and a voice said, 'No. It's not your time!' I hope so much that this time the door opened easily for her and that the light surrounded her and that she's found the love she was so sure she'd receive once I found mine.